I Was a
Trophy Wife

And other essays

Books by Shannon Page

Novels

Eel River
Our Lady of the Islands (with Jay Lake), The Butchered God, book 1
The Butchered God, book 2 (forthcoming)

The Nightcraft Quartet:
The Queen and The Tower
A Sword in The Sun
The Lovers Three (forthcoming)
The Empress and The Moon (forthcoming)

The Chameleon Chronicles
    (with Karen G. Berry, writing as Laura Gayle)
Orcas Intrigue
Orcas Intruder
Orcas Investigation
Orcas Illusion (forthcoming)

Collections

Eastlick and Other Stories
I Was a Trophy Wife and Other Essays

Edited Books

Witches, Bitches & Stitches (anthology)
The Usual Path to Publication (collection)

I Was a Trophy Wife

And other essays

Shannon Page

I Was a Trophy Wife, and Other Essays

The events and conversations in this book have been set down to the best of the author's ability, although some names and details have been changed to protect the privacy of individuals.

The essays in this book are adapted from pieces written between December 2018 and July 2020 and published on Medium.com. They have been edited, sometimes substantially, for inclusion here.

Cover art and design by Mark J. Ferrari
Interior design by Shannon Page

ISBN: 978-1-61138-929-6

www.bookviewcafe.com
Book View Café Publishing Cooperative

In loving memory of Keith Salonen
Who so enjoyed reading my essays

(But he was, of course, so very generous that way)
(He even read Grandpa Larry's *Reprieve from Chaos* all the way through)

I miss you, Keith.

Contents

MONEY

AFTERWORD

Introduction by Karen G. Berry

There is something special about Shannon Page. As a friend of mine said after meeting her, "She has a *beauty* to her." And no, that's not just physical beauty, which Shannon has in abundance—after all, she was a trophy wife, and she did pose for *Playboy* magazine, as you'll soon read in this collection of essays. There's a deeper beauty to Shannon, composed of intelligence, wit, and the self-awareness that illuminates every word she writes. She has such a *voice*.

I understand that claiming this voice, both spoken and written, has been a process for Shannon. The world holds rewards for those who are quiet and pretty, but those rewards come at a cost. Finding her way to her present self was a journey that stretches from her early years as a quiet hippie child on a commune, through her enviable but confining time as a trophy wife, through her adventures in polyamory, to her current life as a writer in a storybook cottage on a remote island in the Pacific Northwest. And yes, I've been there, in fact I'm the friend who got engaged in her living room.

I first met Shannon through written words, way back in her blogging days. As I've said before, introverts invented blogging. Extroverts ruined it. Shannon is an introvert's introvert; circumspect in person, fearless on paper. She talks about all of it here—love, death, sex, yoga, travel, cooking, and that most taboo subject of all, money. It's an entertaining ride and a fascinating read. These essays will make you laugh, cry, wince, and wonder.

So settle in, pour yourself a glass of your favorite red, and enjoy.

Life Stories

I Was a Trophy Wife

It was a joke. The kind of joke that's actually true, but you laugh about it in the hopes of deflecting that truth. A thing you bring up first, before anyone else can. "Haha, she's my trophy wife! Aren't we funny!"

I was in my early twenties when we met; he was already over forty, seventeen years older than me. And seventeen gazillion times wealthier. He had a nice house and a lucrative business partnership and a 401(k) and an Audi. I had student loans and a toaster oven and two cats.

Well, I soon had just one cat. It was decided that I would give away one of mine before we married. He already had two, and four cats would be just too many. One of mine had to go. I got to make a "Sophie's choice" about it, though. I chose Grub even though I'd raised him from a newborn kitten.

(That wasn't the first time I yielded, though it was an early one. How clear all these signposts are in the rearview mirror.)

"You're going to miss your thirties if you marry him," my therapist warned me. "You're going to start being his age, hanging out with his friends, living his life."

I protested. Wasn't it just as likely that I would bring vibrant, young energy into his life? My creative interests and my hip friends? (Well, semi-hip, I guess. I mean, we were all young; that's hip by definition, right? Right?)

The fact was, his life looked pretty good to me. My own life was a panicked, disorganized mess when I met him. I was in a miserable relationship, had an abusive job, and was broke and freaked out. I had no idea who I was and what I wanted or what to do about any of that. It's why I was in therapy in the first place. And then, suddenly, here was this man with his life all figured out. He was smart and attractive and stable—such an adult.

I wanted a grown-up. I wanted to *be* a grown-up.

So I married him.

❊ ❊ ❊

I'M NOT GONNA LIE: Having money makes so many things easier. If I miss anything from my trophy wife years, it's that. The first time I walked down a grocery aisle and realized I could just put things in my cart without having to keep a running tally in my head—it was amazing.

I didn't stop at groceries. I began to haunt malls. I loved how familiar and comfortable they felt, so bright and clean and safe—all the nice stores with all the nice clothes in them, clothes I could take home and wear and feel pretty and rich. I collected far too many pairs of boots. I started getting my hair cut at a fancy salon downtown and then frosted too. I developed a craving for jewelry. Was I filling the vast emptiness inside? No, of course not. I was just indulging in things I'd never been able to have when I was poor and lost.

My life got better in so many ways. I left the horrible, abusive job for a much gentler one. It wasn't the job I'd really wanted, the one I'd interviewed for and was offered. That one would have had me working long hours and sometimes even weekends; it would have been challenging and paid well. But my husband wanted me around and didn't want to lose me to work, so my gentle job was also part-time. My salary didn't matter to us anyway; he still made many times what I did. And I was able to take care of the laundry and the grocery shopping and going to the cleaners and keeping the social calendar and always being home when he got home.

It was easy to give in to what my husband wanted. He was kind and reasonable; he told me that his first wife had made so many non-negotiable demands, and then she'd left him anyway. He'd been badly hurt, and he'd grown from it and learned how to assert his needs. Anyway, the things he wanted? They all seemed like good ideas. Didn't they?

Like travel. My gentle, part-time job was also very flexible, and god, how we traveled. All over the U.S. and abroad as well: Paris (many times), London, Cyprus, Sydney, Geneva—it would take me half a page to list all the places we went. His job sparked a lot of the travel, and then we'd add on a week or two if the place was interesting. "You are, like, so totally loving it," said the young woman I hired to house-sit for us during these many trips. She wasn't wrong: I enjoyed it. Who wouldn't? I met other pampered wives at my husband's work meetings. We toured Buckingham Palace and met rock stars and dined in world-famous restaurants. We stayed at a resort where the swimming pool came right up to our patio and all the women swam topless. We took helicopters and river barges and safari jeeps to amazing places.

We lived plenty well when we stayed home too. The wine was always first-rate, and we were both accomplished cooks. We dined out a lot, too, in our city's fine restaurants. All that bounty could make a person fat, so we joined the city's premier gym and hired personal trainers to help us keep slender for our fancy clothes.

I was good at my gentle part-time job, and though I turned down one offer to move up the ranks, I accepted the next one. My husband was proud of me. The job still wasn't high-powered or demanding; it was at a university in an interesting academic department. That's what a trophy wife is, after all: It's not enough that she be young and attractive; she must also be smart and accomplished.

We were living the dream. Our home was beautiful, our cars were shiny, our cats were fluffy, and our passports were up to date and full of stamps. Friends would open conversations with "So, what's your next trip?" We were, like, so totally loving it.

And then.

❀ ❀ ❀

AND THEN I APPROACHED my thirties. Then I entered my thirties. My new position at work got a little bigger, crept closer to being full-time, with more responsibility. Email became a thing, so I could think about work stuff even when I was at home. I was good at what I did, and I enjoyed it. It made me feel, well, smart and accomplished at something that wasn't about my husband and our life together. Something that was mine.

Not only that, but I remembered how much I'd always wanted to write. I mean, I hadn't forgotten that, exactly; there had just not been any time to devote to it, what with all the traveling and the chores and errands and our busy social life and the increasingly full-time work and our cocktails together after work and—oh, yes—the gym and the yoga and the haircut-and-color appointments and and and…

My husband encouraged me to write. After all, writers are intellectual and successful! What better trophy could there be than a young and lovely wife who managed to pen an elegant bestseller in her spare time?

Now, I'm not saying that my choice to write about witches and magic was what killed our marriage—but it didn't help. "I thought you were going to write literary books," he complained mildly. "Isn't that what you read?" And then, after I'd pressed him to read a draft of my first novel, "I'm sure it's very good, but it isn't my thing."

A gentle rebuke like that would have put me back on my heels in my twenties. That's about as hard as he had to push to get me to give Grub away, to turn down that first job offer, to pass on the first promotion at the university, and to wear more Brooks Brothers and less Express (not to mention less eccentric vintage).

But then, I found myself pushing back. The witches and warlocks and magic and fairies and darkness wanted to be written about. It was the story I had in me, the thing that felt right.

❁ ❁ ❁

I was beginning to find my voice. I'm not there yet. I don't know if I will ever be there. I think it's a practice—something that, if you work at it, you are forever becoming. I'm growing into myself. My self.

There, in my thirties, began a long, painful process of becoming the sort of person who could even write that last paragraph. It was awkward and unhappy, and I'm not proud of a lot of parts of it. I became super aware that something huge was missing in my life, something that boots and jewelry and travel and gin weren't beginning to fill. I looked in all the classic wrong places for that something: I had affairs, I doubled down on the acquisitions, I even bought a little red sports car. (I still have it. It's a great car—but at the time, it only solved my specific transportation-and-parking problem.)

Did I miss my thirties? Was my long-ago therapist right? Well, I did important work then (if ungracefully), and I learned a lot, and I even had fun amid all the chaos and uncertainty and distress. Does anyone do their thirties right? What's that supposed to look like, anyway?

I just knew that I wasn't happy. I didn't have any friends that weren't his friends—and often they were even older than he was. We didn't travel to any places that I had dreamed of going. I didn't wear any clothes that he didn't like. If I wanted to see a movie or go to a reading he wasn't interested in, it was basically not worth all the soothing and apologizing I'd have to do afterward (whether he ended up accompanying me or not). My job was engaging me intellectually and demanding more and more of my time while my husband felt neglected and resentful. He was nearing retirement, looking forward to a life of leisure and even more travel. I was trying to grow up. Trying to be the adult I had never managed to become.

❈ ❈ ❈

AFTER SLOWLY UNDERMINING MY marriage for years, I blew it up spectacularly not long after I turned forty. There would be no going back. I didn't do this consciously, but somehow, I must have known that I was never going to be who I wanted to be—who I could be—if I stayed. I had to jump off the cliff, over the edge, into the fire.

It was scary. Terrifying. Because I'd done it behind my own back, I was completely unprepared. I didn't have a plan, a place to go, any savings or separate assets or anything. I just went.

I didn't just leave my husband either. I left my job, with its retirement plan and excellent health benefits. I left the entire state, where I was born and where all my family were.

I started over.

❈ ❈ ❈

I'M GOOD NOW, so good. There was, of course, a divorce settlement, so I didn't have to go back to baking water-and-Bisquick paste in my toaster oven to make it to the next payday.

I built a new life in that new state. I made new friends, and I later even broke up with a few of them when I realized the friendships weren't healthy for me. I began gardening and remembered how much I loved thrift store clothes. I took myself out to concerts and movies and talks that sounded interesting. I tried different relationship styles. I found a different kind of job altogether: I'm now a freelance editor and proofreader. I write and publish books about witches and magic, and I actually get paid for all those things.

I married a man who is my partner and not my boss. In fact, since we're both freelancers, I am, more often than not, our major breadwinner. This feels better than I can possibly explain, even in this era of uncertainty.

I'm my own trophy now.

Heading to Shit Hill with My Trowel

When I was five, my parents sold everything they owned and bought a piece of property in northern California.

Just raw land—we first lived in an old army surplus tent (with my baby brother in a crib at one end of it) while they built a shed; then we spent the winter in the shed while Dad and a friend worked on a one-room A-frame house.

The house had a loft where we all slept. And windows, which were a great improvement over the shed, as was the insulation. I don't remember a lot about the winter in the shed, except that it was *cold*. And the floor wasn't quite level.

The house also had cold running water (eventually, when Dad ran black PVC pipe down the hill from a spring), and a wood heat stove, and a wood cook stove. It had a big braided rug in the center of the room, and a cold-cabinet on the north wall for perishable food. At mealtimes we sat on the floor around a low octagonal table—only about a foot and a half high—that Dad made, which folded up when not in use.

The house did not have: Electricity. A phone. Hot running water. Or a bathroom.

❉ ❉ ❉

THE BASIC ARRANGEMENT WAS: you could pee anywhere you wanted to—outside of course (and don't be a jerk and do it on the path, people walk barefoot here, come *on*); for more serious business, you went to "Shit Hill," a low, heavily wooded rise just beyond the edge of the front meadow. When you needed to go, you took some toilet paper and a little trowel, and tried to find a place where no one had dug before.

This got harder as time went on.

The first time my Grandma Cleta came to visit, she was horrified by this, as you might imagine. "It just breaks my heart, seeing that sweet little girl heading into the woods with her trowel!" Grandma Cleta was a highly civilized lady, with coordinated pastel polyester pantsuits and perfectly permed hair and a dusty-floral-smelling perfume and makeup that would rub off on your face when she gave you one of those side-swiping kisses, so of course our rough and rustic lifestyle freaked her out.

What I didn't put together till much later, though, was what this all must have meant to her. She'd grown up dirt-poor on a farm in rural Texas, with far too many siblings; as quick as she could, she escaped to the big city (Dallas) and got a job in a department store, before meeting my grandpa and moving with him to suburban southern California. Her whole life had been a journey *away* from small dark shacks and an utter lack of creature comforts. And now her daughter—my mom—was deliberately *choosing* such deprivation?

She never did understand it, even when we eventually built a compost privy just off the front porch. (Fancy!)

❊ ❊ ❊

IT WAS A GRAND experiment. It was the early seventies, and my parents were very young, and very idealistic.

At first it was just the four of us, but that was never the ultimate intention. My folks searched hard for "like-minded people" to come join them on The Land, to create a community, and little by little some came. Also, my dad liked to pick up hitchhikers and bring them home. At its peak, there were maybe a dozen of us living in various places on the property—sheds, camper vans, makeshift houses abandoned halfway through their construction, the gaping holes covered in plastic.

I tell people I grew up on a commune, and that's *technically* true, but it was never a very functional one. It was the *idea* of a commune…and the reality of a bunch of hippies coming and going, some helping, some freeloading; everyone getting stoned and swimming in the river; lots of dogs running around, and chickens and goats and turkeys and, for a while, a great big asshole of a red horse who loved to kick and bite people and a great small asshole of a Shetland pony who—well, she kicked and bit too, and ran under low tree branches when you tried to ride her.

❈ ❈ ❈

THERE WERE OCCASIONALLY OTHER kids, too, though not many of them, and none my age; I spent a lot of time alone. That's when I developed my love for reading, and my ability to entertain myself.

My parents were very busy managing the complex personal interactions of all those people, and their own eventually faltering marriage, and the difficulties of our frontier-style rural life. I was fed and clothed, and I was sent to school, though in the good-weather months I walked a mile and a half to and from the bus stop—the bus wouldn't drive through the ford, so the end of the line was Houndtown, a terrifying (and probably illegal) kennel operation on the other side of the Eel River.

I also made my own lunches, usually cheese or peanut-butter-and-honey sandwiches. Because of course we were vegetarians. I couldn't eat the cafeteria meals, with their brightly colored lunch meats and tantalizing pork products.

God, all I ever wanted was pigs in a blanket.

❈ ❈ ❈

I'M TRYING TO TELL you about strength, about independence. About all the things I learned how to do for myself, and how this is something I'm happy about, grateful for.

Even if I did yearn for TV and lights you could turn on with a switch and tasty pork products.

I'm glad that I learned how to do so many things for myself. I'm glad that I learned how to be alone, and how to cook, and how to solve problems—how to light a fire and milk a goat and bandage a bad cut. This self-reliance has stood me in good stead countless times over the years. I'm also really grateful that I had the opportunity to be different from my peers growing up—even though, like any self-respecting child, I just hated it at the time. It's given me a flexibility and adaptability that, again, has served me so well. It's enabled me not to be knocked over by change, by the unexpected; to regroup when things don't go as planned. It's made me such a stronger person.

If you're reading this and you actually know me, you're probably starting to wonder right about now. *Hey, wait a minute, Ms. Planner, She Who*

Hates Surprises. What gives?

Well, okay. What is *also* true is that, like Grandma Cleta, I took a hard turn against the frontier lifestyle, as soon as I got to be in charge of myself. I *love* my creature comforts, and I'm *not* actually very flexible. In fact, I embrace routine, and planning, and order. My first reaction to anything unexpected is *NO*.

But then…I find I'm able to get past that, and "do what's actually happening," as my husband and I are fond of saying. Because all the planning in the world only gets you so far. Then reality intrudes, and you have to be able to deal with it.

Yes, I just love being able to flip a switch and have the room light up. But when the power goes out (as it does with some frequency out here on our island), I also know how to light a kerosene lantern; heck, I spent my formative years reading by them. I'm attached to my smartphone as obsessively as anyone, but I can also put it down when I need or choose to—I'm never tempted to pay for airplane wifi even on long flights, and I've enjoyed any number of off-the-grid writing retreats. I'm a princess who loves her feather pillows and down comforters and high-thread-count percale sheets, but I can…hmm, okay, well I *used* to be able to sleep anywhere under any conditions. Now, not so much.

(As long as we're telling the truth here.)

The point is: I think my weirdo, off-the-grid hippie upbringing prepared me for life in this modern, chaotic world in a lot more ways than are immediately obvious.

And I am truly grateful for that.

On Hunger

I've been poor, and I've been hungry, but I've never been *chronically not enough to eat for months or years on end* poor. My poorest and hungriest was during college, when I supported myself. I lived in a co-op—which provided three meals a day, except during winter break and spring break, when residents were supposed to go "home." Well, the co-op *was* my home.

The kitchen was closed, and winter break was five weeks long. I had, in my room, a toaster oven, and a box of Bisquick. I mixed the Bisquick with water from my bathroom sink and baked it in the toaster oven. It was gross, but it was food. I also worked in a restaurant, very part-time; on the couple days a week when I had a shift, I got a free meal. I ate well on those days. A few of the cooks liked me. More than once, I went home with bananas and bran muffins in my pockets, for later.

❋ ❋ ❋

Weirdly, or maybe not so weirdly, the other time in my life when I was the hungriest was when I was the wealthiest. When I was a trophy wife, I worked very hard to be as thin as I could be.

Well—that's a slight overstatement. There was a point at which my efforts succeeded so well, I actually got *too* thin. I was cold all the time, and I bought all new clothes in really tiny sizes (that part was fun), and my bones jutted out, and there was a big gap between my thighs. It wasn't anorexia; I didn't think I looked good, and I actually wasn't trying to lose weight, at least not after I'd reached my "goal." I just…had a momentum problem. I had worked so hard to get there, and then I couldn't stop the process.

Eventually, you'll be glad to know, I did manage to turn it back around. It required liberal application of ice cream, plus wine and butter and all other good things. I've never had that problem since.

I saw a doctor when I was at my thinnest. I told him I thought I was too thin, and asked what I could do about it. He said I was perfectly healthy, and that there was nothing to worry about.

I was both reassured and dismayed by that.

❄ ❄ ❄

I WAS HUNGRY ALL the time when my mother was dying, last summer. The days were so hot, and she was so *not* hungry…though she still wanted to eat. She wanted to be served a full meal on her plate, just like the rest of us, when she still had the strength to come to the table. She could only eat a few bites. Swallowing was so hard for her.

When she no longer came to the table, we brought her sorbet, pudding, popsicles, ice cream. She would manage a bit, and then cough and cough. But she kept wanting to try.

I would eat the rest of the sorbet and the pudding and the popsicles and the ice cream. It was *so hot* and I was *so hungry*.

❄ ❄ ❄

How DO I KNOW what I'm really hungry for? What else in me is asking to be fed? Because I am not literally in anything like hunger now: I could live for weeks on just what I have stored around my middle. But I feel hungry every day, again and again.

And I eat.

As if the next bite might be the one that provides the answer.

On Beauty

You know what beauty is. As soon as I utter the word, you get an instant picture in your mind. So do I.

Our pictures are, of course, different.

"Beauty," like "love," is way too big to define, to nail down. The flowers and butterflies in my yard are beautiful. The women in all those magazines are beautiful. My breakfast this morning of farm-fresh eggs and our first homegrown zucchini of the year was beautiful. The experience of reading a well-written turn of phrase is beautiful.

Am I beautiful?

❀ ❀ ❀

I NEVER FELT BEAUTIFUL, or even pretty, growing up. I was shy and skinny, and my nose was too big, and my hair was too thin and too straight. The pretty girls were obvious even then, when we were single-digit kids: strong and tanned and lushly blonde, outgoing and popular. They mimicked the older cheerleaders, learning and performing dance routines on the playground. I watched them with mingled envy and disdain, then went back to reading books starring skinny shy outcasts.

I've still never really felt beautiful. Over the years, I have felt sexy, desirable, attractive, even sometimes pretty (and also plain, overweight, underweight, big-nosed). But all those things just describe appearance. Beauty is…I can't even think of the word without sayings and clichés leaping to mind: "in the eye of the beholder," "only skin deep."

My husband thinks I'm beautiful. Because of course he does. And I believe him, because of course I do. That's why we're married. Well, that and a million other reasons.

❋ ❋ ❋

My LIFE IS FILLED with beauty. Visual beauty (the flowers, the butterflies, the blue-eyed man across the breakfast table who finds me beautiful), and deeper beauty: the freedom to be me. Having a marvelous roof over my head and enough really excellent food to eat, even if I do worry about the finances a lot. Being able to challenge my creative brain in new ways all the time. All the people I love, and who nourish and challenge and support me: my parents and the rest of my family, my friends near and far, and that blue-eyed man.

Beauty is there in the music I blast in my car when I'm driving alone. And the fact that I *can* drive alone. Beauty is making a kill shot in racquetball—all the more beautiful for how rare it is.

People are beautiful when they are full of life, of experience and satisfaction and mistakes and wounds and lessons and joy.

Old is beautiful. New is beautiful. Young and fresh and shiny is beautiful. Weathered and seamed and scarred and tough is beautiful.

❋ ❋ ❋

I THINK WHAT IT comes down to is that beauty is energy: that sparkle, that *je ne sais quoi* that shows that something, someone, has juice in them. "Though I may be tired, I am not done."

Beauty is showing up, again and again and again. Trying, for just another day.

And then another.

And another.

The Last Time I Quit Therapy

I don't go to therapy anymore.

Therapy is great, don't get me wrong. Life-saving, even. I first found my way to a psychotherapist when I was trying to figure out whether I should leave my first husband (surprise: the answer was *yes*). She taught me so much—about myself, about the marriage, about the job I had at the time. She encouraged my writing, and challenged me about my desire to never have children. I saw her for several years, off and on, quitting and then starting up again whenever a new crisis erupted.

I had good insurance at the time, which paid for much of the cost of the sessions. Even so, there came a point when I knew I'd learned all I was going to absorb, and I was ready to try life on my own.

It went well. Years passed.

Eventually, my new marriage, my new job, my stalled-out writing—my whole life—felt painfully out of balance once again. Confusing and overwhelming. I was drinking too much, crying unexpectedly, feeling attracted to other men.

I needed to go back to psychotherapy.

❀ ❀ ❀

I CHOSE A DIFFERENT therapist this time. I don't even remember exactly why—my first therapist had done well by me, and I know she was still practicing. Perhaps I just wanted a different perspective. Perhaps I didn't want to have that same old argument about not wanting children.

My new therapist was utterly different from the first one. She was very clear about boundaries, right from the start: she was *not* my friend, or my mother; I was not allowed to know anything about her personally—not even whether she was married or had children, or what city she lived in. She was my *therapist*, and our work was entirely about me and my issues.

My previous therapist had been a bit more casual about such things, though she was still perfectly professional.

But my new therapist—we'll call her N.—was crisp and classy and sharp. She didn't talk much, just kept looking at me until I said more about whatever it was I was trying to sneak past her. Her office was lovely and sophisticated. It even had a couch to lie on, with her chair set behind it, just like in a cartoon about Freudian psychoanalysis; we actually tried that for a while, but eventually I found my way back to the comfy chair with the *de rigueur* box of Kleenex beside it.

She was very, very good. Despite not saying much, she challenged me like crazy. She didn't seem to care about whether I wanted children or not—*hallelujah!*—she just took me at my word, and we went from there. We unpacked what was wrong with my job, and worked on what to do about it. We spent a huge amount of time figuring out what was wrong with my marriage, and brainstormed ways to work on that (including couples therapy, with a different therapist, which…I know it works for lots of people, but it was a big old fail for us).

The biggest thing she did for me was to champion my writing. She picked that out from the sea of issues I brought up with her on the very first day, immediately challenging me to explain to her why I wasn't de-voting more time and energy to it, since it was clearly the thing I most wanted to do in life. The thing that was most deeply entwined with my personality, my aspirations, my creative expression.

"I'm just so busy," I told her. "I've got a full-time job and a huge com-mute and a marriage and…"

N. gave me *that look*—the one I would see so many times in the com-ing years. "You find time to shop and travel and socialize, and to do an hour and a half of yoga every day, but you can't find *any* time to write?"

❋ ❋ ❋

I DID START WRITING—AGAIN. I took it very seriously this time, pushing aside some of those other activities to make room for it. I figured out how to write on my commute (which turned out to be easy, since I took public transit). I eventually joined a community of writers, which led to a critique group, and—at last!—completing a novel.

It was a dreadful novel, though that didn't stop me from querying a bunch of New York agents and publishers for it; or from writing a second, slightly less dreadful novel. (That one, much revised, eventually did get published, though it killed two publishing houses in the process; the first novel, even more heavily revised, has seen the light of day as well.)

And taking my writing seriously led to other good, even seemingly unrelated things. I stood up for myself at my job, and was able to escape a long-entrenched pattern of saying yes to everything and getting nothing in return; I actually did some scholarly research and writing related to the job, and as a result got sent to two international conferences—in Rome and South Africa—where I presented papers.

I stood up for myself in my marriage, which did lead to some progress (plus that afore mentioned unhelpful couples therapy, alas). But things did get noticeably better, for a while.

I got my first short story published during that time, and got *paid* for it.

N. was a great therapist.

❊　❊　❊

I'D BEEN SEEING HER for three or four years when the break came.

Despite all the improvement, I was still unhappy. Restless, feeling misfiled, unfulfilled. I was lonely in my marriage, and frustrated at how hard it was to break through in publishing. I'd reached the apparent limits of improvement in my job, and had finally quit and found a different job at the same university, one that was supposed to be part-time (to give me time to focus on my writing!) but was already mission-creeping into the same territory as my last job.

It was at this pivotal moment that I went to a writers' conference and... well, met someone.

He was a catalyst, and I was primed and ready to fall—the results were predictable.

I told N. about all of this, of course. She was dismayed at my marital dishonesty, that was clear; but she remained professional, and "on my team," working to help me through this. We had some hard sessions then. I was deeply divided. N. maintained that affairs are rarely about the love-object; they are reactions to the unsatisfying situation in the marriage. (Well, yes. That was obvious enough, even before the affair.)

My lover wanted me to leave my husband and move to Oregon to join his polyamorous community. That was crazy, on so many levels…leaving my comfortable home, my family, my established career, my marriage. Not to mention—polyamory!

But oh, the longer this went on, the more I wanted to. My heart and mind were on fire—my *pants* were on fire.

That was when N. basically shut down. I told her I wanted to talk seriously about moving to Oregon.

"You can't just move to Oregon. We haven't even talked about it."

"That's what I'm trying to do: to talk about it," I protested.

"This is just so precipitous. It just came out of nowhere."

I suspected her chief objection was the polyamory; I found articles—written by therapists—for her to read about it, and even considered switching to a more poly-friendly therapist.

But N. wouldn't talk about it. She just kept stonewalling.

❀ ❀ ❀

Weeks of this went by. Expensive weeks—my insurance no longer covered therapy, and my husband and I were wealthy enough that a discount was out of the question. I felt like N. and I were arguing in circles. I felt that she wasn't listening to me.

I finally realized, *I can stay home and be not-listened-to for free.*

In what turned out to be our last session, N. admitted that she felt maternal toward me. "You could be my daughter," she said. "I want to save you from making a terrible mistake."

I was stunned. She had never revealed anything so personal to me, in all our years of work. I didn't know what to do with the information. If she felt so dang maternal toward me, why wouldn't she *listen* to me?

I left her a voicemail after the session saying I wouldn't be back. And that I was going to Oregon.

She called several times, and I—coward that I was—never answered or returned her calls.

❀ ❀ ❀

I left my husband and I moved to Oregon and I joined my lover's big polyamorous community. It wasn't a terrible mistake—it was life-changing and astonishing and I don't regret it in the least—and now I am no longer in Oregon, no longer with that man, no longer polyamorous.

I regret nothing.

❉ ❉ ❉

I WAS HURT AND confused about the ending of my therapy. I felt ashamed of my cowardice, about not working this part out with her. About just running away—which had been my response to uncomfortable situations all my life, and was something that I had been working hard to overcome in our therapy together. And I also felt resentful toward her, at her stubbornness, at her continuing to not listen to me, at her trying to manipulate me with that whole "maternal" line of bull.

What I finally, much later, realized about N., though, grew out of her unprecedented admission. She *did* feel maternal toward me. She probably had for some time, but her strict professionalism had prevented her from ever saying anything, or showing it.

That didn't matter, though, as long as I kept coming back. Everything that had been going on in my life while I was in therapy with her—the jobs, the writing, the marriage—were things we dealt with together. She saw me week after week, year after year. But if I moved to Oregon? I'd be leaving her.

It wasn't the polyamory she was objecting to. She didn't want me to move away.

And yet she couldn't say so. She could only hint at it, by speaking of her maternal feelings. She was so professional, she could not say *I have grown attached to you; it will hurt me and make me sad if you leave.*

Would that have made a difference? Probably not, in the larger sense; my life trajectory was heading to Oregon pretty much no matter what, at that point.

But it might have made our ending easier, or at least more honest. Instead of feeling unheard, I might have had to face her actual human feelings toward me.

I might have been able to leave therapy without such a feeling of failure.

❉ ❉ ❉

I AM NOT, IN theory, opposed to ever going back into therapy—but I have not yet felt tempted to, all these years later. Therapy is great, and it got me through some really dark, really confusing times in my life.

But now I think I can fly on my own.

Why I Never Wanted Children

I never wanted to have children. Even when I was a child myself, I played with Matchbox cars, not dolls, though I wasn't otherwise particularly tomboyish. (I didn't play with a lot of other kids either, but that's another story.)

I did always imagine getting married, and I have certainly done so sufficiently; I'm on my third marriage now. "Always a bride, never a bridesmaid."

I *like* kids, though I confess I don't know very many of them, and not very well. I don't really know how to talk to kids.

When I was a teenager, I babysat a lot. Perhaps that's a factor. My favorite of the kids I took care of was a newborn. She mostly slept.

I do love being an auntie, to the World's Most Adorable Nephew, but I think most of the credit has to go to him on that one—he's just charming and happy and, well, adorable. He also lives two states away, so I don't get to spend a lot of time with him. I've never, for example, babysat him. We did have a lot of fun playing with little cars together last Christmas.

❀ ❀ ❀

I FEEL LUCKY THAT I passed through my potential childbearing years in a time and place where it was possible to choose to be childfree. (Though just a few short years ago, I would have phrased that sentence differently, more absolutely… Sadly, many parts of the U.S. today are working hard to take that choice away from women.) (More on that in a minute.)

I feel lucky that I haven't gotten a lot of pushback for my choice, as so many other women have.

If acquaintances or employers have looked at me with disgust about this, they kept it to themselves. Certainly people ask—"Do you have kids?" is just another one of those standard getting-to-know-you questions—but I've never experienced any negativity about it when I've said "Nope."

I've been lucky in my marriages, where there was no pressure to procreate. My first husband, who I married right out of college, did not want children. He'd had a difficult childhood and did not see himself as having the potential to be a good father. (Amusingly, he's a father now, and very happy about it—and, as far as I can tell from this distance, wonderful at it.)

My second husband did not want children. He had too much else he wanted to do with his life. I was his second wife; he also felt lucky, to have found two women to marry who didn't want children. "The only two women on the planet who feel this way," he often said.

My now-husband *did* want children. He loves young people; he's been a teacher and has run various youth groups, and has mentored and coached many youngsters. He always wanted to be a father, but he never found a life partner (until me), and did not consider single parenthood. When we met, he was over fifty, and I had already had my hysterectomy. Not to mention: *I never wanted kids.*

I feel sad that he did not get to be a father—he would have been great at it—but also sort of secretly relieved not to be a stepmother.

Okay, maybe not so secretly.

❀ ❀ ❀

MY MOTHER WANTED ME to have children. She didn't give me a bad time about it, much; she just expressed her wish to be a grandmother.

Fortunately, my brother took care of that for her.

Seriously, nothing I produced was going to come close to being as magnificent as that little nephew-dude.

❀ ❀ ❀

SO, WELL, *WHY* DID I never want to be a mother?

That's the hard part—hard to explain, hard to understand. I just *didn't.* The active, overt desire was just…not there.

I like to be alone. (Despite all this getting-married I seem to be so fond of doing.) From my perspective out here, it looks as though once a woman has a child, she is basically never again alone until they grow up and move away. I just don't know if I could enjoy *anyone's* company that thoroughly, that unceasingly.

My husband had the flu last week, and holed himself up in the guest room to sleep it off and to keep his germs from me. After four or five days, I really started missing him. I'm pretty sure you can't do that with kids, sick or otherwise—can't just leave soup at their door and check on them a couple times a day.

Of course there's all the practical considerations too: child-rearing is expensive; you have to think about their schools, and their clothes, and pay attention to their friends and what they do online; you have to guide and shape them and turn them into decent human beings. But those are just reasons to pile on to support a decision that came from somewhere far deeper, far less accessible to me.

It seems to me that people who want children are just fundamentally different from me. In the past I've said that there's a piece missing from me, the wanting-children piece; but I no longer really resonate with the negative connotation of that. Just as I don't like the word *childless*, and am happy that others like me have settled on *childfree*, even *childfree by choice*. I'm free of having had children. I got to choose that.

I'm really, really happy about that.

I don't actually feel like something's missing in me. I feel complete, in fact almost *too* full of things I want to do, things that drive me, things that interest me. I work and I write and I read and I cook and I love and I sleep and I hike and I garden and I swim and and and...

I feel you should really *want* to be a parent, if you're going to be one. It should be an active, conscious, rational *and* emotional choice.

It would be desperately unfair to a child to oblige them to have me as a mother.

❋ ❋ ❋

AND THEN THERE'S THE studies showing that women, in general, are happier without children *or* a spouse. It would be interesting to quantify that, to know how much of that happiness is from being child-free versus being spouse-free, though I imagine it would vary from situation to situation. Because my husband was single till past the age of fifty, he developed a high degree of independence, and also mighty homemaking skills. Our marriage doesn't look very (stereo)typical: though I do laundry, vacuum, and manage the household finances, he does the shopping and cooking, most of the gardening, and he handles more of our social calendar.

These unburdened women who are happier: an article I read about this didn't specifically say so, but the implication was that taking care of other people is *freaking exhausting*. I know some people really do love to caretake—and almost everyone enjoys doing nice things for those they care about (even me, I'm not a *monster*)—but there's a vast difference between choosing to take care of others and being required to. Adults can negotiate a huge variety of ways to organize their shared home, as my husband and I have; but you can't very well expect young children to cook and shop and run errands and use the weed-whacker.

❊   ❊   ❊

THE FORCED-BIRTH MOVEMENT THAT'S sweeping a growing portion of our society horrifies and sickens me. Because that's what this whole anti-abortion thing is, really: denying bodily autonomy to women and other people with uteruses. Taking away the choice that I feel so fortunate to have had.

Though even phrasing it that way starts to stick in my craw. Is it right that I feel *grateful* and *lucky* to have enjoyed a simple human right? No, actually; that's pretty wrong. Because, as we are seeing, these simple human rights are being snatched away by those in power. As if they were temporary, conditional, the fashion of a political moment. As if they were privileges, not rights.

I'm furious that whole generations of people growing up behind me are having to fight all over again to reclaim basic human rights that my generation—I won't say "took for granted," because we didn't. Birth control, access to abortion, the freedom to divorce—heck, even the freedom to keep my own name when I married, to own property, and to have a credit card—were recent enough "victories" for women that I knew I was lucky to be born when I had been, and not two hundred or even twenty years earlier.

Sadly, this all gives me one more reason to be glad I'm not raising children. It's sad because I *do* care about the World's Most Adorable Nephew and all his generation, even if I didn't want children of my own. Children are our future. Even a childfree-by-choice woman can see that. And I want the world to be getting better and better for them, not worse. I care what happens to the human race, even after I'm gone.

❊ ❊ ❊

WHAT IS LIFE FOR, if not to have children? Why am I here? I puzzled over this question a lot in my thirties, even before I did the very deliberate, very deep soul-searching before my hysterectomy.

I won't pretend I came up with The Answer, but I settled on something that works for me: we are all here to make an impact on others, and to leave something behind. For many people, that's producing and rearing the next generation of humans, teaching and guiding and shaping them, and living on in them once you've moved on.

For me, that is also the case, only not in a literal sense. I am here to learn and grow, and to make sense of what I have learned, and to share that with others.

To write it down, in other words. Yes, that's right: the meaning of my life is to write. (grin)

I'm serious, though: I found great comfort when I came to that realization. We are all connected, we humans; and if I am not literally leaving offspring of my body behind, I can hope to leave "myself" in my words. And in the people I shared those words with, whether in person or on paper (or in zeros and ones and pixels).

❊ ❊ ❊

I REMAIN CURIOUS WHY others have chosen to be childfree. I'm glad we're starting to talk about the subject more.

The more we share, the more we learn that we're all different—and we're all connected. That we all matter.

That we're all part of the human race.

Even if some of us decided to be aunties, not moms.

I Posed for Playboy

It started with a small ad in the campus newspaper. "Models wanted." Followed, in short order, by a big article in that same newspaper, decrying the small ad and all that it stood for.

It was UC Berkeley, after all; and even though it was the heart of the Reagan Eighties, Berkeley still held fast to its radicalism.

Playboy Magazine had decided to recruit *nude models* on our proud leftie campus?! Exploitation! Insanity! The very nerve!

I read both article and ad with great interest. They were offering $100 for "clothed," $200 for "semi-nude" (just boobs, I guess), and $400 for "fully nude."

Four hundred dollars was a *lot* of money in those days, my friends. Heck, it's nothing to sneeze at today. Back then, though, it was as much as I made in two months in my work-study job—a job where I was always careful to ensure I was scheduled for Wednesday afternoons so I wouldn't miss Donut Hour, an important part of my weekly caloric intake.

But I didn't do it for the money. I mean, I *did*, but there were other, more complex reasons that drew me…

❈ ❈ ❈

I HAD A BOYFRIEND then, one who would subsequently become known among my friends and family as The Evil…hmm, oh, let's call him Joe. The Evil Joe was greatly in favor of his girlfriend posing for *Playboy*. I guess it would give him bragging rights, or something; I'm not even sure I remember his arguments, because they didn't matter. I didn't want to do it because The Evil Joe wanted me to do it. I already wanted to.

You may know I was raised by hippies on a counterculture commune.

29

We swam naked in the river every summer; kids ran around without their clothes whenever it pleased them—heck, adults did too. I grew up with a very casual acceptance of the body and of nudity.

Of course, I lived in the real world too. I understood, even as a small child, that at school, we wore clothes; at public swimming pools, we wore these stupid binding contraptions of straps and elastic (why, *why*??). But body modesty has just never been a thing for me. (Amusingly, I periodically have the naked-in-public dream, but it's never an anxiety dream. It's always more like, *Oh, gosh, I'm naked, huh, I wonder if I should find some clothes before I make the others uncomfortable…*)

Another thing my hippie upbringing gave me was actual exposure to actual adult magazines…Playboy and Penthouse and, um, other ones. I learned all *sorts* of interesting things from all those publications, which were left lying around the house freely for anyone to read. I have to say, the Playboys always looked the most like art. Like appreciation of the female form. The women were photographed so beautifully; the golden light streaming down from above made them look like angels. They were naked, sure; but there was a soft, gentle aspect to their portrayal.

The other magazines were more, shall we say, *clinical*. That's a good word, we'll go with that. As a young woman growing up, trying to understand who I was and what this world was and what was considered beautiful…I could see it, in the Playboy photos. I had a harder time with the others.

But I could always see the appeal of posing for Playboy.

❀ ❀ ❀

STILL, I NEVER GAVE any of this serious thought till that article in the *Daily Cal*. I was instantly excited, and also nervous. I remember I carried the number around for a day or two until I drummed up the courage to call.

I was told that they would be "interviewing candidates" at the Claremont Hotel in a week or so, and was given an appointment time.

My boyfriend The Evil Joe was ecstatic. Even at the time, I found this a little weird, a little off-putting, but I shrugged it off. (The red flags I ignored in that relationship went *so* much further than this little fetishization-fantasy of his—plenty for another essay, should I ever choose to delve in such unpleasant memories for long enough to write it.)

But that brings me to the most important reason I had for wanting to pose: specifically *as a feminist*, the idea of owning my own bodily agency was foremost in my mind. The idea that *I could decide* that I wanted to do this, for any reason whatsoever—that I thought it was cool; that I liked the magazine; that four hundred dollars was a lot of very useful money; that the moon was in Scorpio; *whatever*—that it was my decision and my decision alone: *that* is what appealed to me the most. Anyone trying to shame me away from it—or creepily pressure me into it—they didn't matter. Yes, yes, I had taken Women's Studies classes where we talked about the power of the patriarchy and its money and how it can control you and the male gaze and all that sort of thing…but hey. I was eighteen.

You don't see things with a lot of nuance when you're eighteen.

❊ ❊ ❊

THE EVIL JOE ACCOMPANIED me to the interview appointment, though of course, he had to wait in the hall while I went into the hotel room to meet the photographer. By now, of course, I was entirely nervous. The Claremont is a super-spiffy resort hotel a few miles from campus, the kind of place parents would stay when they came to visit their kids. Not *my* parents, of course; and not the parents of anyone I knew; but rich parents. Fraternity and sorority parents. Business-school-student parents.

Even so, what was I going to find behind that hotel room door? Was this creepy? Surely this was creepy. But no, it couldn't be. It was *Playboy*, for crying out loud. It was the "Girls of the Pac Ten," it had been in the newspaper, there had been protests, it was a national magazine, they published serious articles too, it was legit…was it creepy? Was this okay? What was I doing?!

I knocked. A fully dressed woman answered the door. Whew! She let me in, introduced herself, handed me paperwork. Of course there was paperwork. Paperwork is very reassuring. I filled out the paperwork.

But I couldn't help noticing that the room in which we sat opened onto a large, fancy bathroom. Sunlight streamed in from a huge window, illuminating a woman with her top off, and a man taking Polaroid pictures of her. Her breasts were HUGE. So much bigger than mine.

They were never going to choose me.

❊ ❊ ❊

THEN IT WAS MY turn. The huge-breasted woman dressed, came out, and left; the man introduced himself as David Chan. He was quiet and unassuming, hardly said a word other than to give me polite directions. We went into the large fancy bathroom, with the door standing open, leaving the main hotel room (and the fully dressed woman with the paperwork) in view.

It was very ordinary. I took off my shirt and bra, and he took Polaroid pictures of me. At least I was premenstrual, so my boobs were bigger than usual, though nothing like that last lady. After only a few minutes, David Chan handed me one and said, "Give it to your boyfriend."

How did he know The Evil Joe was waiting in the hall?

Then I was thanked and I put my shirt back on and out I went, after being told they'd call me if they wanted to do a photoshoot.

Well, that was that, I thought. *At least I tried.*

❄ ❄ ❄

I GOT THE CALL. It would be a one-day shoot, at a private house in the hills far above campus. Since I had opted for the Full Four Hundred Dollars, no need to bring any fancy clothes or lingerie or anything. Also, there would be a hair and makeup person; I was to arrive unadorned.

There are two important things you need to know here. One is that, despite being a student at UC Berkeley and grandly independent and all of eighteen years old, I was a hippie child still. *Hair and makeup?* Ohhh-kay, sure.

The second is that…remember that "premenstrual" business above? Well, now I was menstrual. GREAT. Perfect time for nude photos! But I was so nervous and excited and overwhelmed…*Playboy wanted to take my pictures!!!*…there was no way I was going to ask if we could reschedule.

Anyway, that's what tampons are for, right?

I drove to the remote house in the remote hills. (I must have borrowed The Evil Joe's car; I couldn't afford a car of my own for several years.) I once again worried about whether this was weird and creepy and dangerous. I once again felt reassured when I got there.

This time, there was not only the same fully dressed woman as before—she was the hair and makeup person, as it turned out—but there was also another woman, an assistant of some kind. She dealt with lighting and props and whatnot. It was all very…ordinary. These were people, doing their jobs.

David Chan himself remained mild-mannered, entirely professional, seemingly quite unfazed by what was actually going on here. In fact, when I googled to make sure I had his name right for this essay, I found an adorable, tone-deaf puff piece in People magazine published a few years after I posed. (Puffery aside, the article pretty much told it like it was, although I was chagrined to note that the pay rates nearly doubled in those few short years.) He was just a guy, who took pictures of naked ladies for a living. You know. As one does.

❊ ❊ ❊

BUT THE HAIR AND makeup. Oh my goodness. After the fully dressed woman (I have entirely no recollection of her name) finished with me, I was unrecognizable. At that point, my long thin straight hippie hair fell nearly to my waist; she did something with hot rollers that gave me gentle flowing curls and waves barely past my shoulders. WITCHCRAFT. And she painted me to within an inch of my life—but I didn't *look* painted. I just looked like…someone else.

Then it was time to take the photos.

If you've never modeled, you might not know that it's actually hard work. A natural-looking pose is usually very unnatural, especially if you have to hold it for any length of time. (I've done a bit of artist's modeling over the years, and that's even harder than photography work; it's considered impressive if you can hold a pose for five or ten minutes. True professionals can do twenty minutes, holding perfectly still. Try this at home…it'll surprise you.)

But I did my best, and David Chan had made his name working with nonprofessionals, so he was patient and kind.

Mostly, though? It was boring. I'm so sorry to have to tell you this. It may have been empowering and sexy and daring and naively feminist and whatever-all else it was…but in the moment, it was dull and a bit uncomfortable. It was kind of a cold day to be sitting outside naked, my bare ass on the concrete next to a hot tub.

But boring wasn't the worst of it, it turned out. After an hour or so, the nice fully dressed makeup lady called a break, and pulled me aside. "You'll want to tuck the string of your tampon in…" she whispered. "It's showing up in the photos."

Crap. Crap crap crap. Now they *knew* I was a complete amateur. Why hadn't I asked to reschedule? Jeez. Plus my boobs were all small again. Everyone was obviously just putting a good face on things, going through the motions here. This whole day was a complete waste of everyone's time.

❃ ❃ ❃

WE GOT THROUGH THE day. Everyone remained completely professional. I don't even remember if they fed me lunch—they must have, because I don't remember starving, but I'm sure I didn't eat a lot, or my belly would have pooched out.

What I do remember is *more* paperwork at the end of the day. I was keenly disappointed to learn that a check would be mailed, within four to six weeks…I had somehow expected to walk away with my bounty at day's end.

And then there was the question of the name. In my proud proto-feminism, I had indicated on the initial forms that I intended to use my own name. I had nothing to be ashamed of! The nice fully dressed makeup lady wanted to talk to me about this, to be sure I really wanted to do that. "Most women choose a pseudonym," she said. "Their families…"

"I don't care about that," I said, though my parents weren't hippies anymore, and I knew my mom would be horrified to learn I'd done this—I'd decided I only needed to tell her if the photos actually got published.

"Yes, but your classmates…" she said.

I thought about the issue of the magazine coming out, right when the fall semester began. The new friends I'd make. The new professors… "Okay," I said, chickening out. I chose a grand and foolish fake name.

Then I went home to go back to my life, and to wait and see if they would use the photos. Because of course they wouldn't *inform* anyone. We all just had to wait for the issue to come out.

❃ ❃ ❃

A MONTH OR SO later, I got a phone call from my mom. Mid-week, so I knew something was terribly wrong. "Why is there an envelope addressed to you from Playboy Enterprises?"

My stomach suddenly had that feeling like when the elevator floor drops out from under you. "What?"

"In today's mail. An envelope, for you, from Playboy Enterprises. *Should I open it?*"

"Um…sure…" What had they *done?* I'd given them my campus address! Except they'd also asked for a "permanent" address…the morons had mailed the check to my mom's house!

Her tone was icy. I had to tell her everything, to get her to mail me the check. She was so disappointed, so horrified. Just like I'd thought she would be.

"Well, we won't tell your grandma, unless the photos actually get published," she finally decided, in a textbook illustration of the perpetuation of disgraceful family secrets.

❋ ❋ ❋

SPRING SEMESTER ENDED. SUMMER passed. Fall semester started. This would be (if I remember correctly) the September issue, on the newsstands sometime in mid-August.

I went to the newsstand every day, checking to see if the issue was out. And then. One day. It was.

I bought the issue, without even looking inside. I figured I'd want to own it, either way.

I hadn't yet broken up with The Evil Joe by then—in fact I'd rather ill-advisedly moved in with him—but we weren't doing well. This was not a moment I wanted to share with him.

This was just for me.

I found a quiet place on campus. I opened the magazine. I found the spread: "Girls of the Pac Ten."

I paged through it quickly, and then more slowly.

I did not see myself.

Not even the crazy-curled, painted thing that myself had been for a day.

I went through one more time, reading the captions. Every Pac Ten university was represented, sometimes by a few "girls", sometimes just one photo.

Then I saw the Cal Berkeley photo. Three $100-girls, in full bathing suits, sitting together at the edge of that hot tub where I'd frozen my ass for a day. Smiling at the camera.

❋ ❋ ❋

I WAS *SO* RELIEVED, and *so* disappointed.

Now I wouldn't have to wonder if everyone in my new classes was looking at me, thinking, *Is that her? Have I seen her naked?* I could just be myself, without that whole extra layer of weirdness.

But, why hadn't they chosen me? Was it the small boobs? The tampon string?

Was I just not pretty enough? Not sexy enough?

Had I not measured up?

❀ ❀ ❀

I STILL HAVE THAT issue of the magazine, though I'm not entirely sure where it is at the moment. Probably in one of those boxes on the top shelf in the garage, with all my old journals, and the particularly important school assignments, and other memorabilia I couldn't bear to throw away.

I do joke that if I ever get *really* famous, those photos will surface. Because, beyond that one Polaroid that I dutifully gave to The Evil Joe, I never saw any of them.

I'm not an impressionistic young woman of eighteen any more, though I still applaud my determination to make my own decisions about my own body. I understand with a lot greater subtlety what Playboy and all the other "men's" magazines were for, and the part they have played in making and reinforcing this exploitative, screwed-up world we're grappling with now.

Yet I'm not sorry I did that. It was interesting; it was an adventure; it's given me an insight into a world that not everyone gets to see. It was a rush to get chosen, even if I didn't make it to the finish line. The $400 (when it finally arrived) was *super* helpful.

And I wouldn't be sorry to see those photos someday.

Stop Waiting for Permission

For those of us who are a bit older, it's become painfully clear that so many of us have spent far too much of our lives waiting for permission.

Waiting till all our homework and chores are done before we can go out and play.

Waiting till we have a good job and some savings set aside before we travel the world.

Waiting to get an agent, so we can wait while the agent finds us a publisher, so we can wait while the publisher spends two years getting our book out (or folds before they get to it).

Waiting for him to propose.

Waiting for permission.

❈ ❈ ❈

I ATTENDED A SMALL elementary school in a tiny rural town. I was already a weirdo: the only hippie kid from over the hill, lost among the children of farmers who'd all known each other since birth. The first two grades shared a classroom, which had a single bookcase with two shelves. The bottom shelf held first-grade books; the top shelf was for second-graders.

Well. I was a reader. Our commune over the hill had no electricity, therefore no TV; reading was my greatest joy. I read all the time—at home by kerosene lantern, on the playground at recess while the other kids ran around, on my hour-long bus ride. I read all the first-grade books in the first week, then all the second-grade books.

When I asked the teacher if I could have more, she was startled and unhappy. I'd read two years worth of books in a couple of weeks! Didn't

I know those second-grade books were off limits? Who had told me I could do such a thing?

The message I got was pretty clear: stay on your shelf. Paint within the lines. Don't do anything without permission.

And that was far from the only time I heard that message. Sometimes it seemed like growing up was an endless lesson in how to conform, and why it was terrible if you didn't. My home-sewn and thrift store clothes were all wrong; I could never be one of the cool kids, dressed that way. Later, in high school, I broached the idea of maybe not going straight to college. Parents, teachers, and counselors all quashed that, hard.

I conformed. I complied. I waited for permission.

❋ ❋ ❋

OF COURSE I'VE BROKEN rules. Who hasn't? I snuck out of the house. I went through a spate of shoplifting in my early teen years. I've been divorced twice. Perhaps there have even been illegal drugs, though you didn't read it here.

But through it all, I've largely tried to "be good". Not just be a good person; I still believe that we should all have empathy and compassion for our fellow creatures on this planet, that we should try our best to avoid harming others. No, I'm talking about these scripts that we follow, these permissions we wait for. These life programs: Here are the steps you must take to achieve this, that, and the other thing. This is how it must go. Do not deviate.

You know what? Screw that.

Because all that script-following only left me middle-aged and frustrated, waiting for my turn to shine. Because now I'm looking around me, and I'm seeing a different approach. I'm seeing "kids these days," magnificent creatures in their teens and twenties and thirties who are remaking the world. Just stepping out there and doing what needs to be done.

I am not a political writer, and this is not a political article, but I am so damn inspired by all the bright, brave and daring young people I see not waiting for permission. Like Alexandria Ocasio-Cortez. The old men in power are going blue in the face telling them You're doing it wrong, sit down, shut up, know your place; and they're just smiling—or shouting—as they keep on keeping on.

It's not just famous people. Folks everywhere are making incredible art and posting it online. Writing amazing books and self-publishing them. Going places, doing things, rewriting the rules or throwing them out altogether.

The hippie generation that influenced my parents was all about this too, I think, but with an important distinction. Counter-culture came with a big pile of rules and scripts of its own. "Make love—not war." "Don't trust anyone over thirty." "Resist The Man." My mother escaped the rigid strictures of suburban housewifedom, only to spend all her time cooking on a wood stove, washing everyone's clothes and sheets and towels in the creek, and cleaning a hand-built cabin by lamplight.

❊ ❊ ❊

I'M DONE WAITING FOR permission. In this phase of my life, I'm learning about boundaries—the importance of making my own rules, not mindlessly aping others. I took myself to Italy to visit my auntie a few years ago. I've started writing all the things, and I'm publishing them, and the world is going to love them or not; I can only control my part of that… and keep writing. I've found a life partner who is creative and supportive and kind, who is also working on this same thing.

Here I am: just me, former hippie kid, former trophy wife, still and always a weirdo. Always growing. No longer waiting.

I Don't Want Total Honesty

Idon't want you to tell me the whole truth. I don't want to hear everything you're thinking—about the world, about me. About someone I love.

I don't want to hear about what you'd rather be doing right now, or the specific details about what turns you on (unless I happen to be *married* to you), or what you saw when you looked behind the couch, or what happened to your foot after your roller-skating accident in Golden Gate Park that time (even if I *am* married to you).

Make no mistake: I don't want you to *lie* to me, either; I just want the right amount of truth. Of honesty. Of detail.

It's called discretion. Or being sensitive. Just tell me what I need to know. If I want to know more, I'll ask.

But how much truth is the right amount? It's so hard to tell. We're making mistakes all the time. I know I am.

❋ ❋ ❋

WHEN I WAS IN junior high school, my best friend and I spent a **lot** of time trying to get our hair to express the exact perfect lusciousness of Farrah-Fawcett-wave-curl-flow.

We had the cut, of course. But that was only the start. We blow-dried. We curling-ironed. We hair-sprayed.

Then we got to school and had to do the whole business all over again, in the bathroom, because the damp windy weather had ruined all our home efforts.

I knew that neither of us had achieved Perfect Farrah-ness (my friend got closer than I did), but I tried a few options, and asked my friend which one looked best.

"Actually?" she said. "Your hair looks best French-braided."

Translation: *There's nothing you can do, you might as well just give up. Hide it in braids. Or maybe a scarf! Or shave it off!* (Though Sinead O'Connor was still a few years in the future at that point…)

❀ ❀ ❀

WAS THAT TRUTHFUL? WELL (sigh), probably.

Was it helpful? Did I feel better about my thirteen-year-old self, more confident, ready to take on the world?

No. No, I did not.

All I did was to take decades to reclaim French braids as a viable option for my hair.

French braids are *awesome*. Once I got into a complicated sweaty daily yoga routine, with lots of rolling around and going upside down and all that, I found that French braids were the only way to keep the mop under control—out of my face and off my neck and not in an annoying knot on the top of my head or *anywhere*.

❀ ❀ ❀

MY HUSBAND AND I were just talking about this the other day. I mean, not about my hair; this time, the context was about work situations that get uncomfortable, where things go wrong but everyone's being all polite and just hoping to get through the job without too much unpleasantness. (As freelancers, though it's not the norm, this does, alas, happen to both of us from time to time…)

Sometimes, he's so frustrated, he just wants to *tell them the truth.* "You asked for this, but you didn't know what you wanted, and so when I delivered it you weren't happy, and so I cheerfully put in a bunch of extra hours that I know you're not going to pay for, and still didn't make you happy because you cannot explain what you want, so I tried to *read your mind* and make yet another stab at it, and you hate it worse than ever, and you know what? The problem isn't *me* here, pal. You need to take ownership of *your own project* and come up with at least a vague sense of what you want me to do for you."

But, yanno, that's not the sort of thing a freelancer says to a client. At least, not very often, if the freelancer wants to keep freelancing.

❃ ❃ ❃

IN MY POLYAMORY DAYS, I learned the important distinction of *secrecy versus privacy.*

Secrecy was not okay. Secrecy = dishonesty. Secrecy was, "We have a rule about letting our partner know if we're going to hook up with someone new, but I'm here now and things are getting hot and, ohhhh, let's just go with it, what she doesn't know won't hurt her..."

Privacy was something else entirely. Privacy was, "Thank you for letting me know you'll be hooking up with Wilhelmina this evening. I hope you have a fabulous time, and practice safe sex, and I'll look forward to a phone call tomorrow morning, and I'll probably want to meet Wilhelmina someday if this looks like it's going anywhere." *And don't tell me every detail of what you-all get up to, I'll ask if I need to know anything specific, thank-you-very-much.*

(And meanwhile, I plan to be off hooking up with Horace, which I've already told you about, so we're all super good here.)

❃ ❃ ❃

THEN THERE'S THIS CATEGORY of "polite fictions." One of my favorite polite fictions is "I need a little break."

I had a friendship a while back that started out so nurturing and balanced—in fact, it arrived in my life when I was really in a place where I needed some serious nurturing, but I was also able to give back. It was a really good, really happy friendship.

And then time went by, and things shifted, and patterns emerged, patterns that may have been there from the start but hadn't seemed important, but were now fast approaching deal-breakers; and then they were deal-breakers; but I still had so much fondness and appreciation for the earlier part of the friendship (and, okay, I'll admit it, cowardice about conflict, yes, that's me) that I said, "I need a little break from this friendship."

More recently (and I will be deliberately vague here for obvious reasons) I found myself in another situation where things became toxically untenable for me, but Making A Big Scene About It was not in the cards, so I became "real busy" and "took a little break" from the situation.

These "little breaks," their duration? FOREVER, thank you very much. One little increment at a time.

I mean—unless things change. Not that I expect them to, but, they could? And then bridges won't be burnt. So, there's that.

❈ ❈ ❈

I BELIEVE IN HONESTY. I believe in telling the truth, even if I have not always done so, at every moment in my life. It is something I have gotten much better about over the years, as I've grown more comfortable with who I am, and gained a better understanding of what I need from those around me, and the courage to ask for it.

But I do not always tell ALL the truth, ALL the time, to everyone. Trust me: you don't want me to. You don't want me to tell you your hair looks best in French braids...unless it's clear to me that YOU love the French braids best. In which case—rock on with your excellent French braids!

Because French braids are indeed awesome, and I do kind of look cute in them. (Or at least I did at age seventeen, though I hardly knew it.)

The bangs, though, ugh. That was a different story.

Tattooed and Pierced Fellows in an Upscale London Hotel Gym

The year was 1995. My then-husband and I were on a business trip in London, staying in a spiffy, elegant hotel in Marylebone.

Make no mistake: the *business* was his, as always. I was the spouse, along for the ride, nothing to do but enjoy myself. Oh, sure, I made some gestures toward bringing along writing or something to work on in my "free time" on our many trips; but I was really there for the adventure, the fine meals and finer wines, the shopping, the good life.

❊ ❊ ❊

THE NATURE OF MY husband's business necessitated fancy banquets, late evenings in rich settings with far too much food and drink. Loads of fun; but I felt kind of sorry for my husband, who always had to get up early the next morning to put on his suit and participate in actual meetings about actual work-stuff. I tended to sleep off my hangover (as best I could) and then toddle out to the pool (if we were somewhere tropical) or to the hotel gym (if not), to sweat out the rest of the previous night's excesses, and prepare myself for the excessive evening to come.

And so it was that I found myself entering this entirely empty hotel gym, in this spiffy hotel in Marylebone, at about ten thirty in the morning. Well, empty except for the earnest young attendant around the corner and down the hall, in the gym's lobby. He had a posh British accent, naturally; he checked me in, issued me a fluffy sweat towel, led me into the workout room, and asked if I needed any instructions on the fine glossy machinery.

No, I did not, thank you so much; I knew my way around a gym, hotel or otherwise. He gave me a bottle of water and left me to my own devices.

The first thing I did was weigh myself. Or, at least, I tried to; the scale was in stones, not pounds. Not having any clue what nine-some-thing-something meant, I shrugged and approached the exercise equipment.

The treadmill was easier to suss out; even though the numbers were different, I understood the basics, and I was soon marching along, working up a good sweat and wishing my dull headache would finish going away.

❊ ❊ ❊

THEN A COMPLETELY INCONGRUOUS dude strode into the workout room. He was about my age, which was weird enough already; I was younger by decades than any other guest I'd seen since we'd arrived here (including my husband). It was a stuffy upscale business hotel, and this guy…he had long dark hair, and tattoos, and wore a loose-fitting muscle T-shirt that showed…could that be *pierced nipples??*

"Hey," he said, nodding at me as he went to check out the free weights.

"Hey," I said, noticing his American accent, wondering *what in the world?*

A few minutes later, another young dude strolled in, even more tattooed and pierced than the first guy (which I could plainly see, through his scanty garb). He had dark hair and bold eyebrows, and a well-trimmed goatee/sculpted mustache scenario. He greeted the first dude; they were friends, clearly. (Which was actually kind of a relief. The only way this could have been any *more* bizarre would be if *unrelated* tattooed, pierced, youngish American dudes all wandered in at the same time.)

Because you guessed it: a minute later, a *third* such fellow arrived, wearing a bandanna and equally revealing workout gear. He joined the second fellow at the scale, and they had much fun trying to figure out how stones translated to pounds. I marched on, on my treadmill, pretending I wasn't there, trying not to feel self-conscious about the fact that their stones were fewer than my stones.

They were *fit* dudes, is what I'm saying.

❊ ❊ ❊

SOON THEY'D ALL SETTLED into their workouts. Bandanna Guy was doing a StairMaster-like thing in the row behind my machine; the dark-haired goateed fellow took the treadmill next to me and started it up. He caught my eye in the mirrors in front of us and nodded at me. "Hey."

"Hey."

Then they started talking to each other, around and behind me and over my head, clearly aware of me, maybe even almost playing to me, while ostensibly pretending I wasn't there.

Fine with me. I'd pretend *they* weren't there. Weirdos.

Healthy, fit weirdos.

Apparently there should have been a fourth one, but he was still asleep up in his room, and Bandanna Guy hadn't wanted to wake him.

I wasn't really listening to them—well, I was *trying* not to—but I couldn't exactly ignore them either. And then something caught my attention. I started to get interested.

"We were really good last night," one of them said.

"Yeah," the others agreed. And then something about an audience, how great they were, something like that. Maybe something that sounded like a song title?

That's when it finally started to dawn on me. "Are you guys…like… some kind of a *band* or something?" I asked.

All three dudes laughed. "Yeah," said Goatee Guy.

"Who?"

"The Red Hot Chili Peppers."

"Oh!" I exclaimed, pleased with myself. "I've heard of you!"

✻ ✻ ✻

FORTUNATELY, THEY THOUGHT THAT was quite amusing. Adorable, even. We were all roughly the same age, but I'd been living the life of someone twenty years older—attending fine foreign art films in vintage movie houses, and symphony concerts at the big hall downtown; listening to jazz and NPR while reading my *New Yorker*s and my literary novels. I'd *heard* of the Red Hot Chili Peppers, of course, they were huge then; but I couldn't have named a single one of their songs. (And, clearly, wouldn't have recognized any of the band members if they were half-naked and sweaty in front of me.)

(Or…more than half-naked. They weren't showing me anything more than they'd revealed on stage many times, as I learned later. I've been forever grateful that I had no idea about the sock thing when I met those nice young men.)

Because they were totally nice young men. We all got to talking then, as we worked out, discovering that we were all not only Americans, but Californians. I told them I was from San Francisco. "Ah, we have to live in LA," said Goatee Guy (Dave Navarro, in his brief time with the band, I later pieced together), somewhat sadly. "We love San Francisco though."

We talked about food, specifically the awful food you found in English restaurants at the time. In 1995, your best bets for a decent meal in London were Indian food, or pubs. I told them about pub food, how nothing beats a good Stilton ploughman's plate.

"We're staying out of drinking establishments at the moment," the long-haired one (Anthony Kiedis) said. "Putting our partying days behind us."

I could certainly believe that, as fit and healthy as they looked. (Alas, sobriety was apparently a brief moment for them as well, at that point.)

❀ ❀ ❀

EVENTUALLY, I FINISHED MY workout, said it was nice meeting them, and headed out. The earnest young gym attendant at the front desk asked me, worriedly, "Were those blokes bothering you?"

I laughed. "No, they were fine."

I went out walking later that day and passed a record store. I didn't *think* those pierced, tattooed guys had been having me on. Even so, I was relieved to see a huge poster in the store window. Yep: that was them. Flea was the one who'd stayed in the room, sleeping.

❀ ❀ ❀

I THINK ABOUT FAME, and what it does to people, how it distorts them, and the world around them. I've never wanted to be famous—which is a strange thing for an author to say, but there you go. I want writing *success*, while somehow still staying anonymous. (Impossible, I know.)

These successful, hugely famous dudes clearly wanted me to know who they were, or expected that I already did; yet when they understood that not only had I not recognized them but I had only the vaguest impression of their band, they opened up, becoming relaxed and friendly. Only then did we have an actual conversation, as if we were all just people. People who came from the same part of the world, meeting up in a hotel gym in a foreign city, talking about the local food.

It must be so strange to be famous. I attended a sci fi/fantasy convention once that had the author Neil Gaiman as a guest of honor. He wasn't as widely known then as he is now, but he was already a huge celebrity in our field. A number of us had gathered in the hotel bar the first evening (as one does) when Neil walked in…and you could *feel* the magnetic force as everyone in the room simultaneously noted his arrival, pretended to keep on with their conversations, watched him out of the corners of their eyes, almost held their breaths… Everyone trying to be cool, to act like he was just another author, *just one of us*…while almost imperceptibly straining toward him. He could not possibly have been unaware of his effect, but what was he to do? He talked with the people he'd come to meet up with, as if nothing was weird. As if he hadn't just changed the very atmosphere of a big, noisy bar with his mere presence.

Neil seems to handle it well; but, I think it's no wonder that so many celebrities have so many divorces and drug problems and generalized life chaos. How can anyone live a "normal life" with the world staring at them, breathlessly? I would fall apart under that kind of scrutiny.

I just want to hide here on my island. I want to be a successful, famously reclusive writer. "Oh, Shannon Page? Yes, she grants one interview a decade, in writing only… Here's a photo of her from the 1980s, that's all we could find… I hear she has another book coming out soon, I can hardly wait to buy a couple dozen copies of it for myself and all my friends!"

They say it takes a vivid imagination to make it as a writer…

I'd Rather Not Hide My Scar

One fine Sunday morning when I was a sophomore in college, I went to the campus hospital with severe, inexplicable pain in my lower abdomen. I'd initially thought it was something I'd eaten, but quickly realized it was more serious than that.

A few days went by while they tried to diagnose me (during which time I, perversely, started feeling fine and wondering when they would send me home already); the upshot, however, was that I had a ruptured ovarian cyst and they were sending me to a 'real' hospital for surgery.

I met the surgeon before the operation. I found him calm and reassuring: he just *looked* like the kind of man you'd want operating on your important parts. I even developed a bit of a crush on him—hey, I was just nineteen.

The surgery was successful: the cyst had been benign, and another benign cyst was forming on the other ovary. He removed the cysts and left both my ovaries intact and healthy.

He told me all this when he met with me and my family after the surgery. He was pleased to be able to report all this good news to us.

The thing he was *most* pleased about, however, was that—even though it had made the surgery more technically difficult—he had performed it through a "bikini line" incision, so that I would not be left with an unsightly scar on my belly.

❈ ❈ ❈

EVEN AT NINETEEN, I was bummed to hear this. I wasn't goth or anything formal like that (though I did dye the last inch or two of my hair black),

49

but neither was I a glamour girl, shall we say.

I certainly cared how I looked, just…not in a traditional way.

Now I'd just been through a scary medical thing, freakin' *surgery* for crying out loud. No way did I want to hide the scar.

I wanted to show that scar to *everyone*.

Here is what "bikini line" incision means: After I'd been put under general anesthesia, someone shaved off almost all my pubic hair, all the way down to the top of my labia. Then, about a quarter-inch below where that hair had been, in what might be a natural crease of the skin, the surgeon cut me open. My incision was about five inches long; after the surgery, it was closed up with thirteen staples. Yes, metal staples, just like you use on paper.

They used a metal staple remover to take them out, too, before I went home from the hospital. (And probably billed my university insurance a hundred and forty-seven dollars for it, but that's another article for another time.)

Shaved pubic hair begins growing back almost immediately, of course. Anyone who has ever shaved anything on their body, at any time in their life, is familiar with the concept of stubble.

I'm sure I don't have to spell out in any more detail the discomfort of the process of stubble growing in, in a sensitive, painful surgery site.

❋ ❋ ❋

I, OF COURSE, SHOWED off that scar to every new boyfriend, and to anyone else I felt daring enough to roll down the top of my pants so they could see. But eventually, the hair grew back enough to obscure it. Not completely—even to this day, decades later, the hair there is sparse and weird. It never grew back soft and curled like it was before the shave-and-surgery.

I'm kind of grumpy about that too.

But mostly I'm grumpy that some man—a well-meaning man, a man I liked instantly, a man who did me a huge medical good deed that I am eternally grateful for—decided how I must want my body to look, without even consulting me. Without even letting me know there were options.

"Now you can still wear a bikini," he'd said, as though I would want to hide a scar, an "imperfection," a "flaw."

I want to show my scars. I love the streak of grey in my hair, the lines by my eyes. I've lived on this planet for fifty-three years (and counting), and I've bumped into a lot of things along the way, things good and bad and mixed: surgeries, heartbreaks, books published, pets raised and lost, gardens planted, countries visited. I'm not made of porcelain, nor do I want to look that way.

Life touches you. I'm okay with letting that show.

❈ ❈ ❈

IN MY EARLY FORTIES, I had a boyfriend who had surgery for cancer. The day he got home from the hospital, he invited over a well-known photographer to do a photoshoot of his scars. One of the photos ended up on a book cover. (I'm on that cover too, or at least my cleavage is.)

That was many years after my ovarian cyst surgery, of course, so maybe times had changed; but I wonder if we would have ever seen my (or any other woman's) abdominal scar on a book cover—had I somehow managed to acquire a scar in a non-R-rated part of my body in the first place. My boobs, sure. Boobs get to show up everywhere, whether the situation calls for boobs or not.

But a belly scar on a woman? Unsightly! Terrible! Cover it up!

Do a much more difficult surgery so she doesn't look "damaged" in the first place!

❈ ❈ ❈

I HAD A HYSTERECTOMY in my mid-thirties, and my surgeon used the old scar site. We *did* discuss this before the surgery, in great detail; it was medically appropriate to go through the old incision site, rather than disrupting a different, intact part of my body.

More shaving, more stubble, more uncomfortable healing. Same invisible scar. Oh well.

A little research shows that the bikini-line incision is at least as popular as it was in the 1980s, when I had my first surgery. Though not for medical reasons. The Wikipedia article I read about the procedure informed me that: "It is often used in preference to other incision types for the sake of aesthetics, because the scar will be hidden by the pubic hair."

I wonder how many women are asked about this before their surgeries, even now? How many realize this is even a question, a decision to be made?

A decision that was made for me.

I hope I never have to have any kind of surgery again. But if I do, I'm going to want scars I can show you. A scar is a sign of strength, a message to the world: *I survived this.*

I've survived a lot, over the decades.

I would rather not hide that fact.

Deliciously Invisible:
Being a Straight Woman in a Gay
Neighborhood

In 1991, my marriage ended and I lived alone for the first time in my life.

I rented a studio apartment in a lovely building at the corner of 18th Street and Collingwood, in the heart of the Castro in San Francisco. It was a big studio—an entry hall, a little bathroom, a big main room with a huge closet (which had clearly once housed a Murphy bed), and a decent-sized kitchen with built-in cabinets and room to put a small dining table. The apartment had high ceilings and hardwood floors, and big windows in the kitchen and main room, and a small window looking onto an airshaft in the bathroom.

My rent was $610 a month, which was outrageously expensive for a place that didn't even have a separate bedroom. But I had a full-time job and a tiny bit of savings (even after I'd "loaned" my ex-husband enough for first-and-last-and-deposit on a place of his own so that he'd move *out* already). I couldn't afford the place that we'd shared (it was a two-bedroom in Noe Valley, and nearly $900), and I'd tried the roommate thing and hated it, so, I took the risk and signed the lease.

(How times have changed…I just did a quick online search. A small one-bedroom one block down Collingwood from my old place is currently listed for $3,885 a month. Or you could splurge and get a two-bedroom one block up 18th for $4,950!)

Living alone was terrifying, and glorious. It wasn't quiet: just below my apartment was a bar called The Edge, and just across the street was another bar—I don't remember the name of that one, but it was even noisier than The Edge. (And yes, the city did indeed have a bar called The White Swallow, but that was a few blocks away.) A bus line turned the corner just outside my window, so I also got the flashes and pops of its overhead electric lines. The bars closed at two; the recycle scavengers came through at four; the official city recycle trucks came at six, every single day of the week.

I loved it. I bought a futon bed, a hundred-year-old green Chinese rug from my friendly neighbor upstairs, and a huge used desk from Busvan For Bargains. I was going to come home from work every day, sit down, and write the Great American Novel there.

❋ ❋ ❋

I HAD NO IDEA how to live alone. I mean, yeah, basically it's just like living with other people except without the other people; but really, it's entirely different. You can cook whatever you want, and leave the dishes in the sink until you feel like washing them. And when you *do* clean up, nobody else comes along and makes a mess! You can play whatever music you like, and stay up as late as you want reading—nobody trying to sleep on the other side of the bed.

At times it felt like playing house, except it was real. That apartment was my refuge, my place of peace (if not quiet), *my own space*. I no longer had to worry about what my husband's mood might be, when he finally made it home; I didn't have to tiptoe around his anger, his drinking, his despair. When I got home, that was it: the household was complete.

❋ ❋ ❋

THE CASTRO IN THE early 1990s was very, *very* gay. That changed over the next fifteen or twenty years, but when I lived there, it was pretty much Freddie Mercury-style T-shirts and assless chaps with nothing under them and tight, tight jeans. In the four or five square blocks around Castro and Market Streets, the sidewalks were packed night and day: men, men, men. Men cruising other men. Men going about their business—the video store, the pharmacy, the market. Men on dates at the bars and the restaurants and the movie theatre. Men living their lives, open and out and free.

I worried a little bit when I moved there. Having no car, I needed to be close to transportation and shopping and other amenities, so the Castro was perfect; I just hoped I wouldn't be seen as an intruder. I wasn't even a lesbian, after all.

I needn't have fretted. My neighbors in the building were great—friendly and welcoming—and the men on the street…didn't seem to see me at all. Their eyes passed over me as though I were a blank spot in the landscape.

Until I realized this, I hadn't fully perceived how much, as a young woman in this world, I'd been so continuously *looked at*. Assessed, judged, regarded. Found desirable; found wanting. Even if men in the rest of the world made no comments (and they usually didn't), I realized that they always, *always* looked at me, and that that was something I had to be aware of—something I *was* aware of, even on an unconscious level. And I was always assessing and judging in return: *Is he a threat?* Or even, *Is he interesting, is this attention I want?*

Soon I began joking to friends that I could have walked down my street naked, and would have been in no danger—wouldn't even have been noticed. But it wasn't really a joke. I'm quite sure I could have.

It was really, *really* gay.

❋ ❋ ❋

AND AS SOON AS I got over the weirdness of feeling invisible, I found I just loved it. Ironically, that was the first time I really felt at home somewhere. I could be myself—whoever I was that day. I could experiment with identities, outfits, whatever. *Nobody gave a shit.* I didn't have to conform, or perform, for anyone. Not in my neighborhood, anyway. I could go to the grocery store in my pajamas. Yes, I know people do that all the time these days; but that would have been weird then, in more *normal* neighborhoods.

In the Castro? I was a tiny mouse, a nullity, utterly without color or consequence. I lived amid a huge jumble of humanity, and I was entirely—fantastically—alone.

❋ ❋ ❋

I ONLY LIVED THERE about a year and a half. I had met the man who would become my second husband; he lived just over the hill in Noe Valley (another reason the Castro was a convenient place for me). My trophy wife years were just ahead—I could already see them from there, though I had no idea how they would all unfold.

I wrote and wrote, but the Great American Novel never emerged. Other things did, including (eventually) a novel about my hippie upbringing, and a lot of journaling and introspection and soul-searching.

But I think the best things that emerged were the little, almost impossible-to-explain things. Exploring my embryonic—but growing—self-confidence: watching a baseball game in a bar full of men (I didn't have a TV) and being benignly, comfortably ignored. Walking down the street openly admiring the pretty, well-built men with no possibility of consequence or even conversation. It was a safe place to explore *myself.*

It's not good to be invisible at work, or in a relationship, or anywhere you need to have a voice, to have power. And I've struggled with this: for far too long, I was voiceless, meek, unsure. That's not what I'm talking about here.

Separating out *strangers looking at me* from *important people in my life listening to me*…that's been a lifelong lesson for me. One that got started when I moved into a neighborhood of flamboyant men who did not, in a million years, want to fuck me.

Always a Bride,
Never a Bridesmaid

I'm not Elizabeth Taylor or anything, but I have been married a time or two.

Well, three, if I'm honest. I'm on my third marriage, and really, that's plenty. I don't want to look *greedy*.

I always did want to be a bridesmaid, though.

❋ ❋ ❋

I DIDN'T HAVE A whole lot of female friends when I was younger. I tended to always have one best friend, though more than one of those friendships turned out to be problematic, sooner or later.

There were always a lot of guys in my life. I was as boy-crazy as any teenage girl, of course, but I also had guy friends with no romance involved. By the time of my third wedding, I just went ahead and had male attendants, including my two brothers, and my pal Chaz as my Best Person.

Because guess what? It turns out that *there's no rule about it*! You can do whatever you want, have whatever loved ones you like standing up with you! You can have your dad *and* your stepdad walk you down the aisle! You don't even need to have the same number of attendants as your groom does. *Who knew?!?*

❋ ❋ ❋

SOME OF THOSE BEST friends of my younger days did get married, but it never happened that I was asked to be a bridesmaid. Various reasons, I guess.

Actually, it's not 100 percent true that I've never been a bridesmaid. I did stand beside my mother when she married my stepfather, when I was seventeen. It was a small wedding, so I was her only attendant; my step-dad's twin was his best man. I wore an adorable pale blue sailor dress-suit and didn't have any idea what a bridesmaid was supposed to do.

My mom didn't have a lot of female friends either, come to think of it. (Hmm.) But one of them did organize a little bachelorette party for her, and another one brought us both champagne to calm our nerves when we were getting dressed and I was braiding our hair and weaving baby's-breath into it.

I still have that adorable sailor suit, though I'm twice the woman I was at seventeen, so I won't ever be wearing it again.

It hangs in my closet next to my three wedding gowns, all wrapped in plastic.

❀ ❀ ❀

IT WASN'T UNTIL MY forties and now fifties that I started making more, and better, women friends. By then, of course, most of them were married, or at least not looking for bridesmaids.

But then one of my dearest friends got engaged in my very living room! She and her boyfriend were visiting here when he dropped to a knee and proposed to her. I walked in a moment later; they both looked stunned, and were giggling. "What's up?" I asked.

"He asked me to marry him!"

Of course I asked if I could be a bridesmaid, in the moment somehow forgetting that she has *three adult daughters*, not to mention many wonderful women friends of decades-longer tenure than me. So she very graciously…invited us to the tiny wedding. Where she had decided that one of her oldest friends would be her only attendant—and then somehow forgot to mention it to her.

I guess we're all getting older. The Uninformed Bridesmaid leapt up and did her duties as soon as she became Informed, and everyone had a marvelous time. I brought home orchids, and leftover wine, and excellent memories.

❀ ❀ ❀

WHY DO I WANT to be a bridesmaid? I honestly don't know. I love weddings; it's fun to participate in them, and I've been a bride enough times. I guess I just want to play a different role, at least once. To plan the shower or bachelorette party, to feel proud and excited and joyful and supportive of a friend on her big day.

I suppose it could still happen.

Meanwhile, I'll attend every wedding that I'm invited to, raise a glass, and dance the night away. Congratulations! Marriage is the *best*.

I should know. I'm an old hand at it by now.

A Different Kind of
#MeToo Story

"I *hired you for your brains."*
It was his mantra. My new boss was so excited to learn that I was a recent graduate of UC Berkeley, just across the bay. His wife, he told me during our interview, was a professor there. He informed me on my first day of work that that was why he'd hired me: he liked smart women. He bragged about my brains to the whole office as he introduced me around.

Soon, all too soon, the unspoken second half of his mantra became painfully clear: ...*so why don't you* use *them?*

❀ ❀ ❀

It was a starter job, but a pretty good one; I felt lucky to have landed it so fresh out of college, with a résumé short on work history. The office was on the top floor of a tall building in downtown San Francisco. I would be paid an okay salary, but the benefits were generous even by the standards of the day (the very early 1990s): plenty of vacation and sick leave; the company matched 401(k) contributions dollar-for-dollar; and the free, excellent health insurance even covered psychotherapy, if you can believe it.

I commuted downtown on BART, carrying my high-heeled pumps in my handbag, like the rest of the skirt-suited, sneaker-shod ladies. I even wore panty hose (yes, my young friends, the eighties and nineties *were* a different time). I enjoyed playing dress-up, even though I couldn't afford much, rotating my few outfits as best I could.

Things are always so clear in retrospect. There were signs on my very first day: my predecessors—two of them, most recently—were already gone; apparently no one had managed to stay in the job longer than six months. There was nobody to train me, no instructions left behind.

It was an Executive Secretary position, though: how hard could it be? I had those *brains*, after all.

I went through the desk I'd chosen as mine, then the other one, searching for hints and clues, things left undone. My boss was out much of those first few days, doing business, I supposed. I found a notebook with some information about travel arrangements. There was a Rolodex. I figured out how the phones worked, then waited to be assigned something to do.

I suppose you could say that my boss trained me, but only by making it clear when I'd gotten something wrong. On day three, he dumped a huge pile of mail on my desk on his way back from lunch. "I found this in the mailroom," he said, his voice dripping with disappointment. "Haven't you been checking my box?"

"Um…where's the mailroom?" I asked, suddenly sick to my stomach. Of course there would be mail. Why hadn't I thought to ask about the mail?

He rolled his eyes, took me to the mailroom, then repeated his mantra.

❀ ❀ ❀

ON FRIDAY OF THAT first week, though, he stopped by my desk with a big smile. "Come on, I'm taking you to lunch at Postrio."

I was thrilled and terrified. Postrio was San Francisco's "it" restaurant just then, and far, far out of my budget, a place I'd only read about in Herb Caen's column in the newspaper. So *oh my goodness yes*.

But also: my older married boss wanted to take me, his new secretary, out to lunch in a fancy, trendy restaurant? I may have been only twenty-three, but I wasn't an *idiot*. (Brains, you know.) I knew what this would look like, what it might mean.

He drove us there in his luxury car, even though it was only a few blocks from the office. A valet whisked the car away; my boss led me down a grand sweeping staircase to the most gorgeous dining room I'd ever seen. Lunch was amazing, delicious, incredible. My boss told me stories about all his famous friends, asked me a few perfunctory questions about my studies at Berkeley, and complained about the current trend in upscale restaurants for bringing unsalted butter to the table. "The whole point of butter is the salt," he said.

(He wasn't wrong about that.)

At the end of the lunch, he said, "Well, I'm going to the Bohemian Club for a massage; I won't be back to the office today. Go ahead and take the rest of the day off."

I got home, still trembling. I'd just been given *half a day off*. I'd just been taken to lunch at *Postrio*. What did it all mean? Was I in big trouble here? Was he leading up to making a pass at me?

What was this job all about, anyway?

❀ ❀ ❀

MY BOSS LIKED TO roll in mid-morning, after calling me from the phone he had installed in his *car*—something only super-rich people had, in the very early nineties. "Any messages?" he'd ask. "Any interesting mail?" I'd read off what had come in.

He'd tell me in which order we were to make the call-backs. It was my job to already be dialing as he strode into the office and hung his long black cashmere coat on the rack. "Is Mr. Y available?" I'd ask the secretary on the other end. "Mr. X is calling."

The game is this: these Misters must never be forced to speak to another Mister's secretary. I was only to transfer the call once Mr. Y was on the line. Of course, Mr. Y's secretary understood this as well as I did. (She was, no doubt, hired for her brains.) Victory was me telling a clearly annoyed Mr. Y, "I'll put him on now."

Defeat was a lecture from my boss, and the shaming mantra.

❀ ❀ ❀

THE JOB SOON SETTLED into, as the old saying about war goes, "…long periods of boredom punctuated by moments of sheer terror." My boss traveled a lot. When he was gone, I had basically nothing to do. I began bringing novels to read at work, first sneakily, then openly. Nobody could do anything about it—I made friends in the office, but I wasn't allowed to help anyone with their work. I had to sit by the phone, keep my decks clear, in case the boss needed something. Even from afar. Anyway, Executives don't share their Executive Secretaries.

Sometimes I would gaze across the room at the other desk, the empty one, wondering what the man could have possibly needed with *two* secretaries. Maybe they were there to keep each other company, like when you adopt two kittens so they can play together. I wondered if he now felt he'd come down in the world, with only one idle young *brainy* woman sitting outside his office, playing Spider Solitaire and reading novels.

When he was in town, that's when things got more *interesting*. There were more fancy lunches out—he took me to Lulu, and Aqua, and Zuni, so many places I don't even remember them all; it also amused him to drive us over to the Mission District, to a corner taquería where he'd slurp down a bowl of menudo, grinning at the incongruity of his bespoke suit and my downtown drag in the humble setting.

There was weirder stuff, too. One day, he informed me that I must rush over at once to Saks Fifth Avenue, where his wife (the Berkeley professor) needed some help. You see, she'd just had a manicure and her nails were still wet, but she had to return a pair of Ferragamos she'd bought in Honolulu and decided she didn't like. I had to open her wallet and remove her credit card to hand it to the clerk so they could apply the credit; I also had to carry her bags to her car and put them in the trunk, then hand her into the car, behind the wheel.

I got the rest of the day off after that, too.

He never did make a pass at me. So there's that, I guess. Whatever strange psychological dynamics were going on inside the man, they weren't about sexually fetishizing his young secretary.

Small favors.

❊ ❊ ❊

I THINK IT WAS more about the humiliation. He loved to wield that mantra, setting me up to fail, then announcing loudly how smart I *wasn't* being.

I learned to go one floor down, when I needed to cry in the bathroom, so that no one from our office would know.

Until this job, I had always thought I *was* smart. Hadn't I gone to Berkeley, and graduated with honors—paying the whole way myself, I might add? But now I began to wonder. Was I actually smart, or had I just been…unusually lucky, or something? Was I now being exposed for the horrible fraud I truly was? How did I keep screwing up? How hard could it be, to open mail and answer phones and make travel arrangements?

Oh, travel arrangements. The heart of darkness.

❊ ❊ ❊

GATHER ROUND, MY DEAR young friends, and let me tell you a tale of the olden days. You see, back when the earth's crusts were cooling and your humble narrator was a girl of twenty-three, there was no internet. There were people called Travel Agents, whom you called on the telephone (which was a device that sat on your desk and was connected to a wire that came out of the wall). You told the Travel Agent what flight times were wanted, along with hotel rooms and rental cars and the like; and she (it was always a *she*) took down the information and promised to call you back.

She entered all the information you gave her into a magical device that sat on *her* desk called Sabre, and if she was any good, she knew further magic that she could wield when Sabre didn't give her the results she wanted; and the upshot was, she called you back an hour or two later with flight times and prices.

Now, my boss didn't care about prices, of course, because the company paid for all his (first-class) travel; but he cared a *lot* about flight times.

Flight arrangements were always fraught. Never, ever, ever, in the entire time that I worked for him, was he happy with his flight arrangements. The layovers were too long. The departure time was too early. The return time was too late. The airport was too far from his destination.

For a man who traveled as much as he did, he sure did hate traveling.

There came a day, a fateful day, when he called me into his office to make arrangements for yet another trip. I grabbed my trusty notepad, because I had *brains*; I stood before his desk, my downtown-drag heels sinking into the deep carpet. "I need to visit the office in Melmac," he told me. [City names have been changed to protect the Executive Secretary, here; but they did all start with M.] I wrote down, *Melmac*. He told me the dates and times and other particulars—which specific hotel, what kind of car. I wrote them down.

Dismissed, I went back to my desk and called the Travel Agent. She and I, though we never met in person, were by now very good friends. She made arrangements for my boss's travel to Melmac. He was cranky about the times and the connections, but Melmac is a smallish, out-of-the-way city, and that was the best that could be had.

The travel day approached. I received delivery of the tickets (physical tickets, with carbon backs, hand-couriered from the Travel Agent's office: valuable as gold). I put them in their fancy folder, along with everything else my boss would need for his trip, and put them on the top of the pile to give to him, with his mail, when he came in that day.

He came in. Took the pile. Went into his office.

Then. An explosion. Shouts, a command to present myself **At Once**.

I rushed into his office in a sick panic. "What? What's wrong?"

He waved the tickets in my face. "These are tickets to *Melmac*!" he shouted.

"Yes...?" I replied, trembling.

"I am flying to *Montac*!"

"But...you said..."

"*I! Did! **Not!***" he thundered. "What in the *world* made you think I wanted to fly to *Melmac*? Everything is going *swimmingly* in Melmac. It's *Montac* that needs my presence!"

"I...wrote it down..."

"I don't *care* what you wrote down! I need to go to *Montac*! How could you have gotten this so wrong??! *I HIRED YOU FOR YOUR BRAINS!*"

❊ ❊ ❊

I'll spare you the rest, it doesn't get prettier.

❊ ❊ ❊

I think about Mr. X periodically, what could have been going on there. What kind of person needs so badly to prove his power, his superiority, that he hires an endless string of young, powerless, smart women, then randomly rewards and humiliates them until they flee? I didn't know the term *gaslighting* then; it feels apropos, but only to a degree. What he did was less focused than that. Frankly, I don't think I was even important enough to him for the concerted effort that gaslighting requires.

I don't think he saw me as a person.

Sure, I was a good accessory, with those *brains*; and I proved capable of learning how to open the mail and answer the phones; but to him, I was not a human being. I was a device for tending to his demands, and when I broke down, I could be replaced. There was an endless supply of brainy young women he could, and did, hire.

This is gendered, even if it wasn't #MeToo-level sexual abuse. Yes, women can be executives and men can be secretaries…but even today, that's so not the norm. In 1991, it was basically unheard of.

I'm glad we've made some small progress in breaking down this gendered system, but we've got a *long* way to go.

❉ ❉ ❉

THERE IS A NICE coda to the Melmac story. As I was sobbing in the ladies' room on the floor below ours later that afternoon, a kind woman asked me if I was all right; it turned out she ran a temp agency down the hall, and she—and her agency—provided me the rescue I needed from that job. I temped happily for nearly a year, slowly recovering from the psychological abuse I'd suffered, learning to trust myself and my abilities again.

Eventually, a staff version of my Berkeley student job became available. I returned there with undying gratitude, remaining for nearly twenty years. That time had plenty of its own dramas and stories…but it was a department founded and staffed by all women.

What a difference that made. Oh my goodness, what a difference.

I wish the whole world could be run like that office full of women.

How I Got Fired from My First Job…By My Own Dad

In my early teens, my dad and his friend opened up our little town's first health club. This was the very late 1970s, and health clubs were *hot*. Racquetball in particular was all the rage—Dad's club had six courts, and getting one of the prime after-work slots was a challenge.

The whole club was an instant hit. The aerobics classes were packed with women in leotards and tights and leg-warmers and sweatbands (wrists *and* forehead), like so many extras in a Jane Fonda video. The hot tub was basically a singles bar; you could even take your beer in there, as long as you had the front-desk worker pour it into a plastic glass.

It was a fun place. *Super* fun.

By the time I was fourteen or so, I was already spending so much of my time hanging out there, it seemed natural that I should apply for the open front-desk position.

I'd already been babysitting for a number of folks—sometimes overnight, once for an entire weekend. I'd proved myself reliable. I was too young to get a fast-food job, but I needed spending money. I knew all the regular members, and they liked me.

What could possibly go wrong?

❀ ❀ ❀

IF YOU ARE ACQUAINTED with any fourteen- or fifteen-year-old girls, you probably have some sense of the many, many things that could possibly go wrong.

Yes, I was mature for my age…and no, I wasn't *mature*. I was just coming into an embryonic sense of myself. I was awkward and shy at school, with boys my age; but the older men at the health club flirted with me shamelessly, making me feel pretty, and desirable, and grown-up.

Also, my dad was the owner of the place. So everyone was nice to me because of that, too.

I applied for the job. Maybe I was the only applicant, because for some reason, Dad and his manager interviewed me. They asked me serious questions, like how I was going to get there for my shifts (being too young to drive), and if I would have enough time to do my homework, and the like. I had good answers for all those questions—I had worked out rides with a friend who worked there, and homework was…never much of a challenge for me. (It was a different time. Even high schoolers didn't have a lot of homework in those days.)

So they hired me.

※ ※ ※

I *LOVED* WORKING AT the health club. I loved checking people in and giving them locker keys, and making smoothies and reheating frozen bagel dogs at the snack bar. I loved working the racquetball tournaments we had every few months—folks would come from all the neighboring cities, and it was like one giant weekend-long party, complete with a live band on Saturday night, and dancing till our feet fell off. I wasn't legally able to draw beers for sale or to change the kegs or anything, so I absolutely didn't, unless no one else was handy. I loved the whole social scene of the place—flirting with all those older men, being part of what felt like the best in-crowd ever. And I loved getting paid so much. It was minimum wage—a whopping $3.35 an hour—but that was 3.35 times as much as I ever got for babysitting.

Sure, there were parts of the job I didn't like. It was hard when it was slow but you still had to keep busy; I'd rather just sit around and read, or eat the ice cream we made the smoothies with, or chat with whatever customers happened to be hanging around. I did have to miss some shifts because of school work, or because I was tired, or sad, or there was something else I would rather do that day. And inventory was the freakin' *worst*. Ugggh. We had to *count* all those unsold leotards in weird sizes and colors and *write that all down* somewhere???

So I guess what I'm saying is that I was a terrible employee.

❀ ❀ ❀

STILL, I WAS THE *owner's daughter*. He wouldn't fire me, would he?

Dad did call me into his office a few times to talk about my performance. Yes, the club was a fun, friendly, laid-back place to work, but employees were still expected to actually work. Yes, I was paid minimum wage, but I was being paid, after all. If I just wanted a fun place to hang out, I could do that for free.

I took his little lectures to heart and cleaned up my act each time. At least, I thought so. And everyone loved me. It was all going to be fine.

❀ ❀ ❀

THEN HE CALLED ME in and told me he was going to have to let me go.

I couldn't believe it. My own *dad*? Was *firing* me?

Yes. Yes, he was.

I cried. I was, I don't know, fifteen. A basic gloppy soup of hormones and dramatic emotions and too-short shorts and wanna-be Farrah Fawcett hair.

Dad was very nice. Only much later did I realize *how* nice he'd been, for so long. I must have driven the other employees crazy—though I know at least a few of them actually liked me, despite how awful and immature I was. Dad said he was sorry. He said he still loved me. He said he knew I would be a good worker somewhere in the future—maybe even here at the health club—but that it would be best for everyone concerned if we just agreed that this wasn't working out, right now.

I protested, even as I knew, deep down, that he was right. I hadn't taken this seriously. I'd thought of myself as special—something I hadn't had much opportunity to believe about myself, before then.

What I didn't understand was that I *was* special. Just...not because I was the owner's daughter, or a pubescent girl just exploring her own embryonic sexual power, or anything like that. I was special because I was *me*—which was something I was going to have to spend the next decades (and counting) figuring out.

I've learned a lot since then. I've never been fired from another job; usually, my employers are sorry to see me go. Once, while I was trying to give my notice, I was offered a *stupid* amount of money to stay on, after I'd already lined up another job. (Which bought them another six months, more or less. It was a bad job.)

✷ ✷ ✷

Even at the time, I bounced back quickly. In fact, soon I turned sixteen, and got a job at Burger King.

But that's a whole '*nother* story.

The Power Behind the Throne

A good admin knows where all the bodies are buried

Before I became a freelance copy editor almost ten years ago, I spent nearly all of my career in jobs with the words "administrative," "assistant," or even straight-out "secretary" in their titles. Only in my last two years of day-jobbery did I become, officially, a Grants Analyst…though I was also, not-so-secretly, still the administrative assistant to the department head.

It had always been my goal to get those dreaded words OUT of my job title. To rise above lowly admin work, to advance to a career that was actually meaningful to ME, not in support of someone else.

And yet? The most enjoyable, satisfying, meaningful few years of my pre-freelance career—though I didn't know it at the time—were right smack in the middle of those decades of admin work. I was technically an "Editorial Assistant," but I was the hub of the office, and I *made it all happen*.

Quietly. Effectively. Enjoyably.

❊ ❊ ❊

IT TAKES TIME, INGENUITY, and cheerful, patient persistence to get good at bureaucracy. A huge, old bureaucracy—like the university I worked for—is like a coral reef. The layers farthest in are dead, calcified, immobile. Don't bother going there. They're necessary, to hold the structure together, but they can't help you with anything that needs doing.

The outermost layers are too new. The tiny soft-shelled creatures are easily picked off by passing fish, or damaged by pollution, before they can get established. They are here today, gone tomorrow. Flashy and colorful, sure. But temporary.

The middle layers, though…that's where the movement, the energy, the gravitas, the *life* is.

❄ ❄ ❄

KNOWING HOW IT ALL *works* is a priceless skill in any job environment. Priceless—and completely unvalued, I found, at least by the higher-ups. The people who don't see what you do all day. That's why secretaries and administrative assistants are paid so poorly, and why they (we) are almost always women. (These days, anyway; of course originally, they were all men.)

Women hold the modern office together. Women hold the home together. Women don't just do the emotional labor; they do the cognitive labor.

Women are obviously the secret masters of the universe—

—but I digress. I was really only meaning to talk about administrative work here, about its value, and even perhaps its joy. The universe will have to carry on without me for a little bit longer.

❄ ❄ ❄

WHEN I WORKED AT that huge bureaucracy, that calcified coral reef of a university, I learned, after a few years and a number of frustrating dead ends, how to make things happen.

I learned what rules you could break and what rules you must follow. I learned which committees had power and which were set up to make talentless, meddlesome people feel important, while doing as little harm as possible. I learned who to go to in the controller's office, the librarian's office, even the president's office. Mostly, though, our tiny department tried to stay off everyone's radar.

Bureaucracies work best if departments are just left alone to get their work done.

Once I got familiar with all the *unwritten* rules, though, I prided myself on knowing my way through the labyrinth. Our building itself, in fact, was a physical metaphor for the twists and turns and dead-ends of the administrative structure of the place. There were floors between floors, called "tiers", inaccessible from any public elevators or stairways. There were unmarked doors that led to storerooms full of treasure (if you like ancient manuscripts, that is).

I even learned which drinking fountain gave the best water. (Fourth floor, by the old HR offices: both filtered and chilled. The rest of the fountains in the building emitted something similar in color, temperature, and taste to weak pee.)

I liked knowing how it all worked. I liked it a *lot*.

❊ ❊ ❊

PERHAPS ONE OF THE reasons that my administrative job was so satisfying for so many of the middle years of my day-job career was that my office was entirely composed of women. Even the big boss, the founder of our little department, was a woman.

Or maybe it was because we were a small research office, focused on a variety of intellectually interesting—yet not flashy, not earth-shattering, not *attention-getting*—pursuits.

I don't know. Yet, even though I pined and yearned to achieve a more prestigious job title (and, of course, better pay), I enjoyed my work. My co-workers and immediate supervisors all appreciated me; I believed in the value of what we were doing. Everyone came to me to solve problems, *and I could*. And my hands (however invisibly) were on every piece of research that left that department to go out into the world.

❊ ❊ ❊

I TOILED FOR YEARS, before and after that golden moment, in far less satisfying secretarial work. Jobs where I didn't have enough to do. The boss who made me cry.

Admin work is not coveted, not prestigious. Yet it's hard work; it takes intelligence, and flexibility, and creativity, and strong organization skills. (Wow, could I sound any *more* like a job description here?) It's the invisibility that makes it so…thankless. The "secret" part of "secret master of the universe." If an admin is doing her job well, you never see it. Things just work. And the bosses get all the credit.

❊ ❊ ❊

I SUPPOSE I'M AT least as invisible now, in my work. I mean, do you ever read a book and think *Wow, this was beautifully edited?* No, of course not; you'd only notice if it was poorly edited, full of typos or plot holes or unintentional malapropisms.

Yet I find my work very satisfying, *incredibly* satisfying. I'm sure it's the being-my-own-boss aspect, at least in part; I also appreciate the appreciation my clients give me. *They* know what I've done for their books.

That I get to do it in my own home and on my own schedule is a singular pleasure. I'd probably enjoy this work rather less if I had to do it in an office downtown, wearing pantyhose. I certainly did not enjoy making someone else's travel arrangements while wearing pantyhose in an office downtown. Or taking meeting minutes. Or filling out expense reports. Or ordering office supplies. Or trying to do all of that and a thousand other things while being interrupted by the telephone every five minutes.

❈ ❈ ❈

ADMIN WORK IS MAINTENANCE work. It's like housework that way: it's never done, and only noticeable when left undone, or done poorly. It's repetitive, not creative. And it's *support work*: it's the work of holding the infrastructure together while "the real work" gets done…by someone else.

In one sense, I am the administrator of our little household-of-two—but in another sense, I'm not. I am in charge of the finances, and the laundry, and keeping the hummingbird feeders clean and filled, and making ferry reservations (mostly). My husband, however, does the meal planning and cooking, including most of the grocery shopping; he handles the garden, and the firewood, and home repairs, and pest control, and the garbage and recycling and compost, and cleaning the bathrooms, and the lion's share of the social calendar.

Actually, looking at that list, he does way more of the administration and maintenance around here. That's nice. It's how I get so much work done. Paying work. "Real" work.

❈ ❈ ❈

WHILE THIS ESSAY WAS cooking in the back of my brain, I looked at a whole bunch of articles about secretaries and administrative assistants. I saw a lot of questions about "are secretaries vanishing?" and "is technology going to reduce the need for administrative assistants?" and "will the robots eventually take over all the menial stuff?" and the like.

No. The answer is *no*. There is no machine, no Siri, no answer-bot, that is going to replace the need for a thinking human brain to *handle all the stuff*.

I read a lot of science fiction, and I can promise you, even in the future, when the computer is so smart that it's virtually indistinguishable from a person, we're still going to need humans to pay attention to the details of running the home, the office, the ship, whatever.

❋ ❋ ❋

WORDS ARE IMPORTANT. WORDS matter. When "secretary" began to sound too lowly, began to fall out of fashion, that's when the women who held offices together started being called "administrative assistants" or "executive assistants" or whatever other terminology was in vogue.

My husband and I formed ourselves—our freelance business—into an S corporation earlier this year. Our friend-and-lawyer who helped us set this up told me that we were legally required to name at least two positions: President, and Secretary. "Who do you want to be which?" she asked.

"Who has the most responsibility?" I asked her. "Who does the actual work?"

She laughed. "The Secretary."

So, although we are equal partners, I am the Secretary of our business, and my husband is the President.

That would irritate me if I didn't understand how the world works.

If I didn't understand that the Secretary is the (not-so) secret master of the universe.

But I do. So I'm good.

The Gym Is a Weird Place

Happy new year! It's January 2 as I begin writing this, and I am freshly back from the gym, like so many people with New Year's intentions—or at least, so I hear. Our gym, here on the island, is never very crowded, and today was no exception, thank goodness.

Its quietness led me to reflect upon what a strange place the gym is.

And not just my gym, or any of my previous gyms. I mean *any* gym. They're all just plain weird.

❊ ❊ ❊

First of all, the gym is the place where we go and become naked in front of other people, but only other people of our assigned-or-assumed-or-adopted gender, with the further assumption that this is because we are only attracted or appealing to members of the assigned-or-assumed-or-adopted opposite gender (with the further assumption of course that there are only two genders) and so therefore it is okay to be naked in front of other people in those particular settings, because there will be no Random Stray Inappropriate Sexual Attraction resulting from viewing said naked bodies.

I think we can all agree how absurd those assumptions and presumptions are.

Be that as it may, that's how our society has organized itself, and so that's how it goes at the gym. I go into the locker room with other female-identifying persons and we all take off our clothes in front of each other—to change, to shower, to sit in the sauna. (Except for the people who stay clothed, for whatever reason.) And we all politely avert our eyes from one another's nakedness as best we can, though of course it is impossible to shield one's eyes against one another entirely.

This polite gaze-aversion doesn't always work out for the best. In a minute, I will tell you a story about one time when I really wished I'd been watching another woman far more attentively.

(It's not what you think. Probably.)

❊ ❊ ❊

I ACTUALLY AM QUITE comfortable being naked, and being in the company of other naked bodies. I was raised by hippie parents and spent much of my formative years on a back-to-the-land commune in California, where casual nudity was frequent, particularly at the river. (We had the BEST swimming hole; folks came from miles around to skinny-dip at our beach.) I occasionally have "oh gosh I'm naked in public" dreams, but they're not anxiety dreams; the feeling is more like, Huh, what do you know, oh well, la.

I sleep naked, and have since college. And I love swimming naked. I've said it before and I'll no doubt say it again: I still think it's ridiculous to put clothes on to go swimming. Sadly, most gyms, including my current one, do not agree with me. So I squeeze into a bathing suit, and bring the wet thing home in a towel, and spend forty or fifty or eighty dollars to buy a new one when it wears out, harumph.

I realize I'm in the minority here. But I still think it's weird that it's okay to be naked in front of other female-identified persons (but only in the locker room! Never at, oh, say, book group!)—and of course, small boys too, if their dad isn't there to take them into the men's locker room—but I must remain clothed in front of male-identified persons, as they must do so in front of me.

(Oh, and more on *that* in a minute too, come to think of it.)

❊ ❊ ❊

SO I WAS SHOWERING after my swim a few months ago when a woman who was clearly in a hurry came in. She hung up her white towel and turned on the water and jumped under it before it could even have had a chance to get hot, and began quickly and efficiently soaping up and all that. I'm not sure exactly everything she did, because of course, though we were barely two feet away from one another (the showers at our gym are kind of stupidly arranged, all bunched together at one end of the gang shower area), I was doing the polite gaze-averting thing.

Which is how it came to pass that she had turned off her shower and grabbed MY white towel and wrapped it around herself and scurried off to the locker area before I'd entirely become aware that she'd taken my towel, leaving hers behind.

By the time I *did* realize this, I knew she had almost certainly thoroughly dried herself off *with my towel*. So even if I did want it back (*eww*), it would be wet (*ewww*) from *her* body (*ewwww*).

What to do, what to do?

I finished my shower—washed and conditioned my hair, soaped up, whatever—all the while staring at *her* towel. See, our gym doesn't provide towels; this wasn't some fresh standard-issue gym thing. This was her personal towel that she brought from her own house. Just like my towel was my own fabulously anciently soft raggedy worn-out thing that was just a few threads shy of being demoted to rag status.

But it was *mine*. And she'd *stolen* it.

The more immediate problem, however, was that here I was, sopping wet (including waist-length hair), and only *somebody else's towel* to use. (*Ewwwww!*)

Well, I used it. If it is possible to gingerly towel oneself off while making minimal body contact with said towel, that's what I did. I had to wrap my hair up in the dumb thing; there's no way to get dressed under dripping waist-length hair and have any garment remain dry.

Her towel was awful: scratchy, nasty, smelled like some weird detergent. (Joke was on her, though; I don't wash my swim towels all that often.)

I came home, complained about it on social media (cue a chorus of '*ewwwwwwwws*' from all my friends) and tossed her terrible awful no-good very bad towel on the rag pile.

I miss my soft raggedy worn-out towel, but, oh well. I guess I survived.

❊ ❊ ❊

BUT THAT WASN'T THE weirdest thing to ever happen to me at a gym. That was just an inattentive woman in a hurry, and a temporary squicky experience.

The most bizarre thing I ever saw at a gym has to be the guy in the swimming pool at my first gym back in Portland. This story isn't the reason I left that gym…but I'm not saying it had nothing to do with it, either.

I was just swimmin' along, minding my own business, in my own lane, when some…odd movement…caught my eye from the next lane over.

I glanced over, looked again, trying to figure it out. Even as clear as the water in that pool was, it's still sometimes a little hard to figure out what you're seeing, underwater, through swim goggles.

But a lap or two later, I was quite sure.

The elderly man in the lane next to me had rolled his little Speedo down, freeing his, er, water snake, and said water snake was bobbing and flopping around freely as he swam. I mean, as freely as a water snake attached to a body can bob and flop.

I'm sure you have a mental image right now, and I'm sorry, but also not sorry, because at least you didn't have to see it in person, in the lane right next to you, and wonder what in the *world* to do about it.

We were the only two people in the pool at that moment. Being a freelancer, I have the freedom to go to the gym during the quiet hours, so I do; and 99.9% of the time, that's a marvelous thing.

Until some random water snake pops up in the next lane.

So, my options were:

- Confront him. (Awkward, certainly uncomfortable, probably not dangerous but who knows?)
- Go to the front desk and tell on him. (Logistically quite complicated, given that I was wearing a bathing suit and was sopping wet, and the front desk was a good distance from the pool, basically across the entire huge gym.)
- Change lanes.

I opted for #3, moving to the farthest lane in that five-lane pool.

He followed me, taking up residence in the lane right next to me.

Okay, this was officially creepy. I cut my swim short, considered again option #2, but I was still sopping wet and the front desk was still quite far. So I showered and dressed, and told on him on my way out, but by then of course he was long gone, and there was nothing anyone could do about it.

I mean, on the one hand, it was so dumb. Of all the people in the world to flash (if that's what he was doing), he picked the hippie child who'd seen a great many water snakes in her time, and would be swimming naked herself if only society allowed it?

But society doesn't, at least not here-and-now-in-these-circumstances, so what he was doing was bizarre and weird and vaguely threatening, although the man was eighty years old if he was a day, and…why? That's what I'm left with, even all these years later: Why? It couldn't even have been comfortable, the Speedo rolled down like that.

I dunno, man.

Life is mysterious, and gyms are weird places. But I hope your New Year's resolutions are going, er, swimmingly!

Listening to that Small Voice
Inside Me

I got married young, too young, the first time. I was twenty-two; there are definitely people in this world old enough to get married at twenty-two, but I was not one of them.

It was a tumultuous marriage. It barely lasted two years, though it would have been even shorter if I'd been willing to listen to what I already knew.

Heck, if I'd been willing (or able) to do that, we wouldn't have married in the first place.

But we did, because I was in love, and I was sure, so sure, that this love was different and real and true. And it was! I had never had a relationship like that one. There was so much that was so good about it, even to the end.

The things that *weren't* good, though; maybe such things are fixable in marriages that weren't ours, but they didn't get fixed in ours, and at some level, I knew it. Those things were always difficult, and then they became unbearable, and then I asked for a divorce.

❀ ❀ ❀

EVEN IN THE EARLY days of that marriage, I had a line that would run through my head. Do you do this too, or is it just writers? I narrate the story of my life, internally; I make sense of what's going on in my life by telling it back to myself. I mean, not every moment, but a lot. A *lot*.

It's like a rehearsal for telling others whatever-it-is, or writing it in a journal. But just in your head. The shaping of the narrative.

Anyway, I found myself referring to my husband, just privately in my own head, as *The husband of my youth*.

❀ ❀ ❀

THE FIRST TIME I caught myself doing that, I was mortified. What was I thinking?! Was I implying that we wouldn't be together forever, that there would be *another husband*?

(Why yes, yes I was. I was implying exactly that. But I couldn't know that.)

I told myself that was terrible, and that I shouldn't think that way. That whatever was going on between me and *the husband of my youth* at that moment, it wasn't some tale that would be told over gin and slender cigarettes in my elegant literary salon in Paris when I was forty-five and jaded and wise; it was happening right now and I needed to deal with it, not fantasize about some future when I would no longer be unhappily shackled to that man, after somehow magically not having to go through the hard work of either fixing the relationship or leaving it.

I was ashamed of my thoughts. I tried not to think them. I tried not to let *the husband of my youth* travel through my brain.

Guess how well that worked?

❀ ❀ ❀

AND IT WASN'T EVEN true, really. Because I asked for the divorce after barely two years, and immediately fell in love with the man who became my second husband, I spent a great deal of my "youth" married to the second man.

That was a much more successful marriage. It lasted longer; it was far less tumultuous than my first. I thought it was The Marriage, that we would be married for the rest of…well, the rest of his life.

Because you see, he was a lot older than me.

This time, the small, quiet voice in my head began spending a lot of time thinking about what my life would look like when I was a young widow.

❀ ❀ ❀

I MEAN, NOT AT *first*. Not even for a while—years and years. But when things began to get uncomfortable, when I began to feel shaped, silenced, squeezed, unheard; when I got smaller and smaller and still wasn't quite small enough; when he would travel out of town occasionally and I would take a deep breath and unclench my shoulders and maybe even leave a dish in the sink; when I began to say to myself quite sternly that I was NOT going to get *divorced twice*...well, I began to let my mind roam to a fantasy future when I lived in that lovely house alone.

Well of course I was horrified to be having such thoughts, and I forbade myself from having them, and, you know, like that.

Things waxed and waned. It was, in a lot of ways, a good marriage. But neither of us were very adept at understanding our needs and feelings, or articulating them; we were really no good at letting one another change or grow; and we were terrible about conflict (as in, we just didn't fight, even when we really should have). So there came a time when I looked around the house, the lovely house, the house I adored, the house we had remodeled together, expensively and gorgeously and also with our own hands, and I thought, *I can't leave, I would really miss this house...*

That, actually, was the moment when I knew I had to leave.

❊ ❊ ❊

I'M MARRIED AGAIN. I have in fact been divorced twice, and married three times. This is a good marriage, a happy marriage. An excellent marriage. Different from any other marriage—any other relationship—I've ever had before.

Nothing is forbidden here, nothing *cannot be said*, cannot be thought. My husband and I, we went through such strange times at the beginning of our relationship. It wasn't supposed to lead to marriage, to anything permanent—we were, by definition, supposed to be a temporary fling. Everyone knew that, including my very serious (and very polyamorous) boyfriend at the time, who set us up.

This husband says things to me like, "This is wonderful, but if it ever stops being wonderful, we should move on. I don't want it to end, I sure hope it doesn't—but if it does, that's okay."

I'm not sure anyone has ever said that to me before, in any relationship.

If there is a small, quiet voice in me now fantasizing about life after this one, I'm not aware of it. (And I'm not just saying that because there's a slender chance he'll actually read this essay. Because of the nothing-is-forbidden thing, I would say everything I'm writing here to his face. In fact I *have*.) I suppose it's possible that the voice is so quiet that I can't even perceive it; or that self-deception is clever and tricksy, so that when you catch on to one of its moves, it shifts tactics, works behind your own back in other ways.

Maybe? How would I know?

But my shoulders are not around my ears, and I do not tiptoe around my partner's moods. I do not feel small, or unheard, or stuffed into a box. In fact, I feel as though I can be me even if I don't have *me* figured out yet; I feel that my husband in fact is interested in who I am today, and tomorrow (and yesterday!); I feel that it is okay to explore, to stumble, to experiment, to breathe. To think and to feel. To be wrong.

I feel loved, and known, and safe.

I feel like this might be The Marriage.

Though, in the interest of full disclosure, I will say this: he is ten years older than me, and women live longer than men do. When he dies, I am totally selling his Magic cards.

Adventures in Polyamory
And Other Romances

The Ex-Girlfriends Club

There are so many of us.

After my fifteen or so years as a trophy wife had come to an end, I spent a period of time in the intimate company of a gentleman who was, shall we say, fond of the ladies.

This is not to speak ill of the man: quite the opposite. He was always clearly, openly honest about his romantic life. It was called polyamory, he explained to me; he had a number of partners, all of whom knew about one another—they were polyamorous themselves, enthusiastically on board with the concept. Some were married or partnered up, others were free-floating on the dating scene.

What was more, he explained, I myself should feel free to seek other partners, if I wanted. In fact, this man encouraged that. Introduced me to his like-minded friends. Gave me a copy of *The Ethical Slut*, the then-current bible of polyamory.

Long story short, after some initial (pretty brief, I have to admit) soul-searching on my part, I decided that all this sounded like a fantastic idea.

What followed is a very long tale which I will tell in another essay, perhaps, someday. I only tell you this much so that you can get some sense of how many ex-girlfriends this man had.

This man had a *lot* of energy. Six hours of sleep a night was generous for him; he often needed only four or five. He had a demanding full-time job, a complicated social life (as you might imagine), a deeply involved creative project (which would have been a full-time job for us mere mortals), and offspring.

Part of that complicated social life was his large handful of current girlfriends, but he also had a *huge* list of ex-girlfriends.

And guess what? All of them were crazy! Not the ones he'd dated briefly, and they moved out of each others' orbits, for one reason or another. No, all the girlfriends who'd been serious partners—*and* his two ex-wives—all crazy. All of them.

Astonishingly, I was different. I was The One. No crazy here. Nope.

❋ ❋ ❋

I'LL SPARE YOU THE lamentable details of how I also became Crazy. You certainly saw that coming; and that is not what this story is about.

What I really want to do here is honor this man, to thank him, for how *many* marvelous women he brought into my life.

Even though he is no longer here to read this.

❋ ❋ ❋

THE FIRST TIME I realized what a large Ex-Girlfriends Club I had joined was, amusingly, at my wedding shower, a few years after we parted company. Every woman in attendance had dated this man—except for one, and only because she had turned him down. She knew him well, yet she had always been, somehow, resistant to his charismatic charm.

As we got to know each other, as we all processed our experiences, I am sorry to say that we failed the Bechdel Test (two women discussing something other than a man) pretty flagrantly at first. Every new woman I got to know in this circle, all our early conversations were about this man. What he had done and said, what we had learned about him from others, what he was doing now. We discussed his social media presence and his art, his current lovers, which of his friends were "in" and which were "out".

But you know? We got past that. The conversation moved on.

And you know what else? Astonishingly, I found that none of these women were actually crazy.

❋ ❋ ❋

MOST OF MY BEST friends today came to me via this man. He really did have excellent taste in girlfriends, I give him kudos for that. These women are clever, creative, funny, warm and wise. I write books with one. I have deep, true conversations over bottles of wine with any number of them. There is a particular intimacy that comes from having been intimate with the same man. We don't talk about *that*, for the most part; but we know each other in a way that few more casual friends ever reach.

He had a huge collection of marvelous men friends too, as well as women (like the holdout at my wedding shower) who resisted his romantic charms but happily called him friend. Lots of these folks remain in my social circle. I am no longer polyamorous, but I cherish the people I met in that community—who I would have never encountered if it weren't for that energetic, charismatic man.

All that energy had a cost, if you are inclined to look at it that way. He did not even live to be fifty. But oh, how he lived!

❋ ❋ ❋

THIS MAN ALSO INTRODUCED me to my husband. I feel I should, in the interest of full disclosure, mention that as well.

Thanks, dude. You left us too soon. But you left us all better off for having known you.

I've Never Online-Dated

Though I am often pretty good at disguising this fact, I'm really not very normal.

For example, I grew up on a backwoods hippie commune without (among other things) television. I had to learn about the real world mostly through reading books. I've never been able to participate in those conversations about all the shows everyone loved in childhood. Fortunately, at my advanced age (I now qualify for AARP…my goodness), those conversations are less common than they were when I was in high school and college—when it seemed like that was the only way people bonded.

I was one of the first people I knew with access to a computer, though, and with an email address, due to my job at a university; email is rather less interesting when there's no one else to write to. But despite this early exposure, my actual computer expertise is pretty rudimentary.

Even so, I probably could have figured out how to sign up for, and use, online dating apps. But I never did. Instead…

❋ ❋ ❋

Barrington Hall: Not as High-Toned as It May Sound

I MET MY FIRST husband before there even was an internet, so online dating wouldn't have been an option.

I was a student at UC Berkeley, and, after two years of relocating every few months from one crappy living situation to another (the dorms only accommodated about 10 percent of the freshman class in those days; the local housing market was *very* tight; one of my most memorable moves

90

involved leaving a drug dealer's house for an ant-infested home owned by an alcoholic pornographic-comic-book fiend who needed most of the rooms for his collection but deigned to rent out one or two to desperate college students), I moved into the notorious co-op Barrington Hall (it has its own Wikipedia page, you can look it up) in the spring of 1986.

M. lived across the hall from me. I was super interested in his roommate (one of the "notable Barrington residents" mentioned in the Wikipedia entry, as a matter of fact), so I spent a lot of time in their suite, in the process getting to know M. as a friend. M. was interested in another lady who lived in the house, though her feelings about him remained rather opaque—to all of us.

M. was also the Kitchen Manager, for which he received full room and board, in addition to covering his workshift duties. I was a Head Cook, which satisfied my five-hour-a-week workshift requirement. His position meant that he was essentially my supervisor, although it doesn't really work that way in a co-op. He was responsible for planning and ordering the food for three meals a day, seven days a week, plus snacks and beverages and incidentals, for a house of 182 people; I, with a crew of three assistants, was responsible for the preparation of one dinner a week.

One evening, I was in the kitchen, thirty minutes till dinnertime, and some essential ingredient could not be found. Nor could the Kitchen Manager be found. (Remember, 1986: not only no internet, but no cell phones either. Barrington Hall had a switchboard, manned by oft-blown-off workshifts, and which closed altogether at night. Oh, such different times…) I was frantic, improvising—

—and then in walked M., in a black overcoat, charcoal trilby hat, and heavy engineer boots with lots of buckles on them, looking dapper and sullen and cranky and irresistible. How had I never noticed before what a fine, brooding, goth-ish man this was? Dark hair, darkish skin, bright green eyes… *And* he immediately solved the dinner-ingredient problem. My interest sparked.

Within the week, M. and I and the lady in whom he was interested had planned to see a movie together (*Brazil,* playing at the art-house second-run theatre near Barrington). I was still under the impression that I was rooting for them. That I was interested in M.'s roommate.

But when the lady backed out at the last minute, and M. and I went to the movie alone together…well, we emerged from the darkness as a couple.

Blame Terry Gilliam, I guess.

❊　❊　❊

What Color Is Your Parachute?

DESPITE SO MUCH CLEAR evidence that this man was lifetime-partner-ship material (trilby hat—which he soon left behind on a bus; bright green eyes; a deep and abiding passion for The Cramps and Bauhaus and Siouxsie and the Banshees; a persecution complex; an insane cat), I wait-ed until a full week after graduation to actually marry him.

Within two years, we were on the rocks.

I didn't really recognize that, at first; I thought I was feeling stalled out in my career. Well, I *was*; it's just that that wasn't the only problem.

But that was the one I focused on. That was the *safe* thing to confront. I bought the latest version of the then-popular career self-help book *What Color Is Your Parachute?*, read it carefully, and began following its advice.

One key piece of advice (at least in the probably 1990 version I read; I have no idea what it recommends now) was to do "informational inter-views" with people working in the professions you think you might be interested in. That way, not only can you ask somebody actually doing the job what it's really like; you will also have a friendly, well-placed connection in the field should it come to pass that you begin job-seeking there. Clever!

I was interested in a certain type of business career. Fortunately, a friend and business associate of my father's was well-established in just that career! And his office was only a few blocks from mine. I phoned him up and made an informational-interview lunch date. I even planned on paying for the lunch.

We met for lunch, this kind older gentleman and I. He answered all my questions, and then regaled me with a number of amusing anecdotes about his clients and associates. *And* he picked up the tab for lunch, over my objections.

I was impressed and encouraged. So much so that I decided I hadn't re-ally learned everything I needed to know about that profession. I phoned up the charming gentleman once more and proposed another lunch date.

We began lunching regularly. After all, we worked so close, and en-joyed one another's company so well. And I really did want to grow my career. I began taking postgraduate educational courses in the field designed to lead me there. The charming gentleman advised me on this coursework—what classes to take, where to focus my efforts.

Meanwhile, my husband and I were doing worse and worse. He, too, had a job he hated; it also put him on the road a lot. He drank more, and talked less. My entire coping strategy at that point in my life was "run away," so I found myself focusing more and more on my new friend. Who was only seventeen years older than me…that wasn't so inconceivable, was it? And he was so mature, so *adult*…what a mistake it had been to marry my college boyfriend.

Thus began the trophy wife era of my life.

❉ ❉ ❉

Take a Hard Left Turn

THIS NEXT CHAPTER'S ORIGIN story might be the closest I ever came to "online dating," though it actually wasn't that at all.

Fifteen-plus years down the road, I was again (or still?) at a crisis of identity. I wanted to be a writer: I now realized that was *always* and *only* what I had ever wanted. After I married the charming older gentleman, I dropped out of the business training; instead, I sort of took the path of least resistance, staying in a low-key, comfortable job, enjoying my Trophy Life until…everything started eroding.

The nice easy job grew more toxic. The marriage faltered. I…employed my old go-to solution: "run away."

I had begun following the blog of a prolific, highly social writer when I learned he was going to be one of the instructors at a workshop I'd signed up for. He was charismatic and well-liked, and he wrote about literary and genre topics as well as politics and food and the writing community and his fascinating travels and his entertaining friends and his deeply interesting polyamorous life. Also, he wore colorful socks, and had long hair.

By the time the workshop rolled around, I was primed and ready to take a hard left turn, veering off the straight, safe road I'd been on for so long. (I'd even bought myself a midlife-crisis red roadster.)

This man, though *technically* still married to his third wife, was absolutely on the market. A starry-eyed wanna-be writer, lonely in her marriage and desperate for recognition and encouragement, was absolute catnip to him.

We took long walks on the beach. He praised my writing and seemed impressed that I'd brought *New Yorker* magazines to read. He *also* drove a red convertible. I was doomed.

I found the whole polyamory thing intriguing, and scary, and exciting, and weird, and fantastic, and world-changing. I dove into it with great enthusiasm.

My marriage, of course, ended.

I had never wanted to be *twice divorced*; I could not think of being married a third time. Fortunately, Writer Man was already (technically) still married, so, no problem! We would just be primary partners, and have other partners on the side. My restless soul, my wandering eye, would be satisfied by this arrangement. Why, that had undoubtedly been the problem all along—I was never meant to be monogamous. I'd finally found the answer!

❊ ❊ ❊

Lancelot, Guinevere, and Arthur

WRITER MAN ENJOYED FINDING men for me to date. He had *lots* of friends; he introduced me to many of them, encouraged me to hook up with anyone I found interesting.

I did. It was great. And he was doing the same thing, with all the women in our community.

Good times.

One of the men I found myself interested in was a good friend of Writer Man's. We'd hit it off, and he confessed that he had found me attractive from the start, but he was understandably wary of the whole poly situation. He initially—and repeatedly—told me he'd rather just be friends.

Eventually, when *both* my boyfriend and I managed to convince this sweet, fascinating, lovely man to give it a try, he agreed, under the condition that he was always, and ever, going to be the "Lancelot" to our "Guinevere and Arthur." That is, he would never seek to remove my primary partner from his place of primacy; he would be content—even delighted—to remain "tangential and temporary," as he put it.

He knew about my relationship history—I'd told him everything. Nothing in my past bothered him, but as for going forward, he told me, "The minute you decide you like me better than him, you'll lose both of us."

He *meant* it, too. I know that's hard to believe. But it's true.

I had no problem agreeing to that. It wasn't going to happen. Everything was different now. This would be a life without secrets, everything out in the open without those quiet discontents, the things you can never speak of, that tear down relationships… We were all free to date anyone we wanted, our only boundaries those of total honesty, consent, and safe sex.

❊ ❊ ❊

Nobody Expects the Spanish Inquisition

SO THE PERSON WHO blew up *that* situation, naturally, was King Arthur.

As part of the fallout, Lancelot also removed himself from the scene. And I found myself single, quite unexpectedly, for the first time in my adult life.

It was awesome, actually. I mean, not every minute of it; I was confused, and lonely, and heartbroken, and I missed both men; but I also… learned how to be alone.

It didn't last a terribly long time, my period of singledom. Not long enough for me to, oh, want to explore online dating, say. Just long enough to get really comfortable with my own company. With silence. With *myself.*

Through it all, I'd stayed in touch with Lancelot. Nothing had gone wrong between us; just the situation had become untenable.

But now the situation had changed. And, before long…we started dating again.

We took it slowly, though. And monogamously. Our cities were three hours apart; we saw each other every few weeks. Spent the rest of our time alone—busy, living our lives.

After a year or so of that, we moved in together.

After another year, we were married.

And *that*, dear reader, is why I have never online-dated.

The Long, Long Reach of Gaslighting

Back in my dating days, I had a relationship with a man who put me on a pedestal. That was marvelous, at first; I'd been starved for that kind of attention for a number of years before I met him. I wholeheartedly welcomed his adoration, his delight in taking care of me.

Outside of that intense, passionate relationship, my life was pretty challenging at that point. I was in the process of blowing up everything—career, a lengthy marriage—leaving family and friends behind to move out of my home state and start over. These were all things that needed to happen, and I wasn't then and am not now sorry about any of it, but I'd be lying if I said it was easy.

So it was great to be taken care of. And not just by him: he had a huge community of friends and admirers and fans and lovers. They all welcomed me into the fold, helping me with so many things, introducing me to the nuances of polyamory, making me feel like I had finally found a community where I belonged.

I let my guard down. In the face of all this warm, loving affection, it felt really good—it felt *crucial*—to become vulnerable. To trust, to show the weakness and uncertainty I was feeling.

This period of my life was a turning point in so many ways. I couldn't have become who I am today without going through that time. I made so many deep, loving friendships then—including with the man I am now married to—that I wouldn't trade for anything.

But I also put my trust in some people I really shouldn't have.

❊ ❊ ❊

HE CALLED ME A princess, that boyfriend of mine; he said it adoringly, and I tried to take it in the spirit in which he meant it, but it always gave me a little bit of a shiver, and not a good one, even at the best of times. I was a grown woman in my forties, after all.

I am sensitive—emotionally and physically. I feel things strongly. I have a very low threshold for pain; I'm quite somatic, and I love bodily pleasures. I am not tough or mighty, in any traditional sense, though I don't believe that makes me weak. I have endurance, and patience; a quiet strength. I am good at pursuing what I want and following through with things I decide to do.

But I stress out over things; I cry when I'm angry, and I shrink and cringe and want to run away whenever anyone else is angry. If I'm under any kind of ongoing stress, I am unable to sleep, which of course only makes things worse. I am not sure I have ever shouted at anyone in my entire life. I will be one of the people who dies in chapter one of any post-apocalyptic book.

My boyfriend saw all this. He made sure everyone understood how sensitive I was. That I couldn't handle the tough stuff.

His other girlfriends (who I really liked—a number of them are dear friends to this day) were recruited into taking care of me. I'm sure many of them did so because they saw how stressed I was and knew that I needed some help. And they liked me. Others…had other motives.

This is hard to talk about.

This man, my boyfriend, told stories about all of us. And about himself. He was a master storyteller; he had rewritten the narrative of his life—without changing any facts—to tell a heroic tale. A tale of overcoming huge struggles and awful adversity and achieving self-awareness and happiness. His life was clear evidence of the veracity of his tale. He was popular, and well-regarded, and successful.

So if he said I was a princess, it must be true. After all, I knew I was sensitive. I had never been comfortable with conflict. Even as a child, I had been spooky and quiet, nearly friendless.

❊ ❊ ❊

THINGS BETWEEN US GOT crazy. Slowly, and then all at once. My instinct—as ever—was to run away, but I wasn't going to do that this time.

I was going to stay and fix this.

My boyfriend was convinced that I was unhappy. That I wanted to leave him. He told me so, many times.

I didn't want to. But I wasn't happy, he was right about that. I wrote short stories with thinly disguised him-and-me characters. I talked to friends. I second-guessed myself. This man had defined me—literally. He told me who I was and what I wanted and what I liked, all the way down to the food I ate and what I liked to wear.

And he told me I was leaving him.

At last, he wore me down. I broke up with him. He wept and raged, professed astonishment and despair, and then presented me with a box of "my stuff" that he'd already packed into his car and brought with him that evening, including some other woman's underwear. It sounds amusing and histrionic when I tell it like this, but it was awful, and I second-guessed myself so hard.

Was I a selfish, weak princess? Was I not willing to do the difficult work of a relationship? I'd already been divorced twice, after all; this relationship was supposed to be my redemption, my change of path.

❀ ❀ ❀

It took a while for me to see all the gaslighting for what it had been. The many tiny ways this man brought me down, chipped away at my strength and autonomy even as he was setting me up on that pedestal, telling everyone to admire and coddle and baby me. I was far from alone in this; so many of his ex-girlfriends were "crazy", in his mind—having broken out of that narrative of his. He sought out the vulnerable: women who weren't sure of who they were and who they wanted to be; or women who were in transitional places, exposed to the elements, in the process of shedding one skin and not yet safely encased in another.

It was a talent he had.

He's gone now. Beyond the veil, and fondly remembered by so many people. I'm even no longer quite so angry, though I'm still processing the many lessons from that time.

And I'm still suffering from the gaslighting. I'm so much stronger now, so much more in possession of myself, and in a relationship that is so healthy and nourishing. But when I receive any criticism—even mild "corrections" to something I post online—I feel sickened, I cringe and flee and feel I cannot abide it. If someone tells me they are unhappy with something I've done, I try and face it bravely, to listen, apologize, atone, learn; but again, I feel it as a physical queasiness, the certain knowledge that I have *done wrong*, that I have been selfish and princessy.

That I am worthless, and weak. That I must apologize for being here.

That is what gaslighting does. It takes the normal interactions and negotiations of being human and amplifies them all out of proportion. It renders its victims incapable of trusting themselves, believing their own experiences.

And it doesn't go away when the initiating situation ends. You carry it with you, like a stain on your soul. A little quiet voice inside you, whispering, *What if they're right?*

That relationship was not the first time I'd been gaslit; it's just the most recent, and the most clear. It probably wouldn't have worked so well on me if I hadn't already had those deep wounds. The channels in my heart, already cut, ready to take the toxic message, to own it. Ready to apologize for being myself.

I will probably be wrangling this forever.

I Thought I Had a Daddy Complex

From my earliest days of being attracted to men (far earlier than was appropriate, I'm sorry to say), I have been drawn to *older* men.

This made perfect sense, of course: my parents divorced when I was pretty young, and it was my dad who went away. Far away, a plane flight away, which was a big deal to a family with as little money as we had. We didn't even have a telephone.

Dad wrote me letters every now and then. I cherished them, treasured them, read them over and over. I loved his half-printing half-handwriting; I loved how he abbreviated words ("nite", "lv" for love) even though he knew perfectly well how to spell.

I did get to visit him occasionally, and briefly, flying as an unaccompanied minor on one of those PSA planes, the pink and orange ones with the smiles on their noses, all the way to his faraway city. He would pick me up at the airport in his big car that had windows that went up and down with the push of a button.

We had *so much fun* together. He bought food Mom never would feed me and my brother—fig newtons dipped in lemon yogurt; ice cream, Wheat Thins. He would laugh and tease and joke. He had a TV. He let me stay up late.

It was never enough, my precious time with Dad. I had to go back to Mom far too soon, sullen and mopey and complaining about "But *Dad* did…but *Dad* didn't…" (You can just imagine how much she enjoyed this.)

❊ ❊ ❊

SO OF COURSE I crushed on older men. All through my teenage years, I would drape myself in front of them, trying to catch their eyes, my heart a-flutter when they would flirt back. To the credit of most of these men, they didn't take this seriously, they didn't step out of bounds, though I was convinced that I desperately wanted them to.

(To the shame of a few…well, that's a story for another day.)

I did have a few age-appropriate boyfriends, but truly, my heart was with those wanna-be substitute daddies. And of course, I later married one. He was even a friend of my father's.

Yes, this all made perfect sense.

❊ ❊ ❊

ONLY QUITE A BIT later did I begin to put together what was really happening here. I'm sure the therapist I saw in my twenties pointed it out, but it's hard to hear something you're not ready to hear—something you're deeply invested in *not* hearing—so if she did, I clearly tuned it out.

It wasn't until I developed a devastating crush on my boss, when I was well into my thirties, that I began to get it. He was (yes) an older man, intelligent, well-spoken, successful in his field—our field. He was published, tenured, respected; he was confident in his place in the world, and unafraid to ask for what he wanted. Yet he was also kind, and encouraging, and inclusive. He would listen—to anyone, everyone, giving his full attention to whatever issue you brought to him. I had never before felt so heard at work. Or, heck, anywhere.

Ohhhhhh I soooooo wanted him.

I was back in therapy at this point, and of course I moaned and whined about my desire for this man incessantly. My new therapist carefully, patiently explained to me what *she* was seeing. Eventually, after hearing her say it dozens of times in dozens of different ways, I began to see it too:

I didn't *want* that man. I wanted to *be* that man.

❊ ❊ ❊

NOT LITERALLY, MIND YOU. I wanted to be the kind of person he was. I wanted to be powerful but gentle, successful yet comfortable. I wanted to be strong and self-confident, and sure of my place in the world. I wanted to have a voice, and to know how to use it. I wanted to be listened to. Respected.

I wanted a seat at the table.

I wanted it to be assumed that I *deserved* a seat at the table.

I had at that point seen very few models of women in such roles. There are more now, yet they're still the minority, and there's clearly very little ease or comfort in it. There is not the general assumption that they deserve to be there. Women in power...well, I don't really have to explain how fraught that is, do I?

I'm not a psychologist; I can't explain why my attraction to the kind of person I wanted to *be* got expressed in a sexual and romantic desire to *take that kind of person and put him inside of me*. Because that was safer? Because it was how the world, and my place in it, was presented to me from my earliest days? Because I really did miss having my own actual dad around while I was growing up?

I don't know—probably all of that, to one degree or another.

❀ ❀ ❀

My husband, the one I'm married to now, is ten years older than me. Yet our relationship is very different from any I've had in the past. There are at least as many areas where I'm the expert and he defers to me as there are the other way around (though I remain *totally* willing to teach him how to drive a stick-shift). Our give and take feels really balanced.

I feel like a *person* here. Not a junior partner, or an aspirant, or... well...his trophy.

It probably helps that I'm the major breadwinner these days (even if it would be great if there were rather more bread). I am finally feeling like I have some authority, some responsibility. Some *say*.

It's scary. But it's also awesome.

And hey, it only took me fifty-two years to get here.

The Astonishing Power of
Male Anger

My husband and I have very different responses to stress. He gets angry; I get anxious. Sometimes I even cry, if I am feeling particularly frustrated.

I know this is not an unusual male-female dynamic. In fact it's so common, it's stereotypical. Neither he nor I decided to be this way; it's just how we are. These are our equally honest, equally valid emotions.

The trouble comes in the fact that his anger frightens me. When he's just entirely pissed about something, his voice becomes sharp, the words bitten off and spat out. He steps heavily; he might slam a door, cuss at an inanimate object; his entire body stiffens up. He's scary. I don't want to be anywhere near him when he's mad.

And yet he has never hurt me. I truly believe, all the way down, that he *won't* ever hurt me. My husband has never raised anything other than his voice in my presence. Furthermore, when he does get angry, it's almost never *at me*. Yet I'm usually the only one there, and I feel it almost as a physical sensation.

He knows this, of course; and so he tries very hard not to let his anger out, to be gentle and considerate of me. He feels terrible when his anger causes me to cringe and flee.

But that just puts him in a no-win position where he's not allowed to express—or even have—emotions. Where he has to stuff himself, never vent his frustration. And then, on top of that, if he does slip and let himself feel something, he then has to take care of me—all scared and anxious because he got angry.

I brought this dynamic up online the other day, and I got a lot of interesting responses from my friends. Women friends, that is, in much the same situation with their partners. One friend said, "We've been married for thirty-four years, and for thirty-four years he's felt like he can't get angry." It seems it's a common theme in relationships between men and women.

I've been with my husband for ten years now. As I said, I *know* he's not going to hurt me. So why is that raised voice, that palpable anger, so scary?

I'm not trying to be disingenuous here—I understand that men are, for the most part, bigger and stronger than us. I also am quite familiar with the statistics on partner abuse, rape, and murder. A number of my friends, including the thirty-four-year-married friend above, were abused in their early lives. These experiences mark a person, leaving one wary, alert to the danger of a raised voice.

Yet I had no such childhood terrors. My father is a calm, steady, peaceable man. Loving and kind and gentle. I don't believe I have ever heard him raise his voice. My mom had to do all the disciplining of us kids; there was no "wait till your father comes home..."

Granted, after my parents divorced, I did briefly have a terrible stepfather, when I was around ten. He shouted and stomped and drank and swore; he hurled our dog off the high front porch; he slapped me in the face once, hard. But my terror of male anger was already well in place by the time he came along, and Mom divorced him soon after that slap.

❀ ❀ ❀

As curious as I am about why even us women who don't have a history of abuse are frightened by male anger, I find myself in even greater wonder about those few women who are *not*. They exist: I know several. I've seen them in action. It's *amazing*.

When I was nearing the end of my relationship with the polyamorous guy I mentioned in "The Ex-Girlfriends Club," we asked some friends of his to come over one evening and help us work through the issues we were having. (The poly community is big on that sort of thing.) His friends were a married couple, also polyamorous—just marvelous people. They sat across the table from us, and the wife asked just a few mild, but pointed, questions. My boyfriend soon became enraged at the direction this was going. He had done nothing wrong! He was the great polyamory guru and I was the neophyte! These were *his* friends; why was she attacking him?

Finally he got up and stomped out of the room, and proceeded to bang around in the kitchen. I felt dreadful—frightened, embarrassed, worried what these nice people might think. (Yet also, I have to admit, just the tiniest bit vindicated...)

After a few minutes of this, the wife said to him in a perfectly calm, serene voice, "When you're finished with your tantrum, we can continue."

He did come back in, and he blustered at her, hard—leaning forward, getting in her face, nearly shouting. He dramatically refused to eat; this whole situation was just making him sick, *sick*. She did not flinch. She did not budge. She just gazed back at him, utterly unruffled. "You're not frightening me," she said at last. "Now, where were we?"

I thought, *When I grow up, I want to be her.*

I still do.

❀ ❀ ❀

I LEARNED LATER, WHEN I got to know her better, that that amazing woman did not escape her own childhood unscathed—far from it, in fact. So how did *she* come out so strong, so unflappable?

How do *I* learn how to do that?

Or is that even possible, at my advanced age of fifty-two? Am I already pretty much the person I am? Part of me really does believe that; I have long held to a sort of "90–10" theory about people. (Or 85–15, if I'm feeling optimistic; or sometimes 95–5, if I'm not.) That is: 90 percent of who we are is just intrinsic. It's not going to change.

But, I do think, we've all got maybe 10 percent of ourselves with which we can make dramatic adjustments. We can go to therapy and delve into why we make the same stupid relationship mistakes over and over, and learn to make different choices; we can go to Toastmasters and work on overcoming our stage fright; we can write every day and join critique groups and submit to publications and grow as writers. I can work out at the gym and become stronger, but probably not much more than about 10 percent stronger; I'm not going to build muscles like a man, or even like a twenty-year-old woman. (And at my age, I'm probably not going to try out for any Olympics team, no matter how hard I push myself.)

Is my strong, unflappable friend the way she is because of something fundamental in her makeup—something she was born with? She is certainly living fearlessly right now, or at least it looks that way from here.

Could I ever learn to be so fearless?

Or maybe, could I even learn to fake it reliably?

※ ※ ※

MY HUSBAND AND I are working to address this unfair emotional imbalance—where I am free to have my "female" emotions but it's too dangerous and scary for him to have his "male" ones. This is something that's available to me, in my 10-percent leeway. I can learn—I *am* learning—to recognize when he is having a bad or frustrating day, and to remind myself that it is not about me. (Unless it is, but that would be a different set of responses on my part, to explore in a different essay.)

I am learning that it is all right for me to think, and even to express, *This is uncomfortable for me to be in the same space with. I'm going to remove myself from this environment and let him vent his anger.*

Then later, when everyone is calm again, we can either talk about it, or just put it behind us—whatever seems appropriate.

※ ※ ※

THAT'S ALL WELL AND good, with the man who loves me, who has committed to spending the rest of his life with me. But what about in the wider world? What about the man who screamed abuse at me from his truck when I rode my bike through a green light while he wanted to make a left turn? That left me shaking and terrified—almost more from his angry man-voice than from the objective threat of truck versus bicycle. That was several years ago, but I still remember every moment of it like it was this afternoon.

I am a woman on the internet...but I am a very quiet woman on the internet. It's no accident that I keep my virtual voice small; my Medium articles are the loudest I've dared to get. And I did receive a few angry responses to my most widely read article, "I Was a Trophy Wife." (They were all from men, in case you were wondering.) I didn't respond to them; I didn't even "clap" to let them be more visible to readers, and I eventually figured out how to go in and delete them, though that felt kind of cowardly of me.

My unflappable friend probably would have engaged them—or maybe she wouldn't, who knows? I've rarely (if ever) seen anyone convince anyone else on the internet, come to think of it. Probably she's smart enough to not feed the trolls.

❊ ❊ ❊

I WOULD LIKE TO become more brave. And yet, when I really reflect on it, I *am* more brave—far braver than I was when I was younger. In my early twenties, I was too frightened to go anywhere by myself. My therapist at the time actually assigned me homework along those lines: go write in a café alone for an hour; take myself to dinner alone; then a movie alone; then, the grand finale, she had me take myself out of town and stay two nights in a hotel.

None of that would faze me now—I've traveled overseas by myself, more than once; I go anywhere I feel like without giving it a thought.

But men's anger still scares me.

What can I do to become stronger?

❊ ❊ ❊

I KNOW THAT MEN have emotions besides anger. The men I know are tender, thoughtful, creative, sensitive, smart, funny, vulnerable, sometimes also frightened—men have all the emotions women do, of course they do. Yet anger seems to be the only one that is permitted—even valued—in our troubled culture. Anger, aggression, strength, a manly bluster; men aren't served by this rigid dichotomy any more than women are.

No wonder they get mad.

❊ ❊ ❊

I DON'T HAVE A great conclusion here. I don't know what the answers are. I'm just going to keep on working on getting both a little tougher and a little more understanding; and wishing for more peace and gentleness in all the world around me.

We could certainly use it.

Don't Tell Me What I Like

There was a man in my life, a loving man, an intelligent man, I would even venture to say a sensitive man.

He was also a damaged man, but I didn't understand that at the time.

This man came into my life at a time when I was vulnerable. In crisis, actually, though I also didn't know that at the time. I thought everything was *fine*.

He was loving and intelligent and, as I say, sensitive; he *listened* to me, he seemed to get me, he thought all my quirks and eccentricities were assets, not liabilities.

No one else at that point in my life listened to me. (I did not realize that I was barely whispering; there were *so many things* I didn't understand then. *So* many.)

This man listened to me. He listened so carefully, and then he told me the story of myself back to me, in a way that was validating, and articulate, and intense, and irresistible, and really, *really* affirming.

(I know you know what's coming.)

❋ ❋ ❋

I LIKE PERSONAL RITUALS, the little things you discover—by accident, maybe—and realize you like them, and then do them again, and then create a little routine about them.

(I *love* routine.)

I had a day job then, when I met that man, that sensitive man; I had not enough to do in that day job; I developed a personal ritual during my days at that job wherein I would take the elevator down a dozen floors to the vending machines sometime in the long slow mid-afternoons, and I would purchase a package of peanut M&Ms, and I would take the elevator back up a dozen floors to my office, and I would open the package of peanut M&Ms and dump them all out onto my desk, and I would organize the peanut M&Ms by color, and I would count each color, and then I would eat them, in order, color by color, least-plentiful-to-most-plentiful.

I could consume an entire hour doing this.

❋ ❋ ❋

SOON, I DISCOVERED THAT it was even more fun—and took even more time—if I shared my findings on social media. It was not quite John Scalzi's taping bacon to his cat, but the three or four people who read my little LiveJournal blog back in the day seemed to enjoy my candy haruspicy. Candyruspicy? M&Mology? What did it *mean* that there were so many orange ones today?

Anyway. It was silly, and it was fun, and yes, I enjoyed the snack, because peanut M&Ms are great; but…it was just a *thing*, you know? Not even a big thing.

Most important of all—it was *my* thing.

(I *know* you know what's coming.)

❋ ❋ ❋

THIS MAN, THIS MAN who listened to me, this man who was caring and sensitive and generous and thoughtful—this man divined that I liked peanut M&Ms.

I mean, that's great! Right?

Of course it was great. Don't we all want a partner who knows what we like, and don't like? "Oh, just get me something, *anything*," you can wail, when you're too hangry to think, and they'll return with (say) peanut M&Ms, or Cheetos, or Mounds, and not something with *caramel* in it (blecch)—that's wonderful. That's being taken care of. That's being *known*.

This man…began showering me with peanut M&Ms. When I flew to his city to visit him, he COVERED his dining room table with peanut M&Ms. When, a year later, I moved to his city, he brought GIANT ECONOMY COSTCO PACKAGES of peanut M&Ms to my house.

"Thanks, I'm good," I kept saying, recognizing the love in these gifts.

The *knowing* of me. "It was…actually a thing I did to make the long afternoons pass at work. You can stop now." I smiled, I felt chagrined, I felt heard…and also not heard.

"But you *love* peanut M&Ms!" he would protest, and bring me more, and more, and more. Tossing a package into my lap when we stopped at a convenience store because his daughter needed a snack. Being astonished if I ever chose anything else. Insisting that he knew what I wanted.

(And here it comes.)

❀ ❀ ❀

I STARTED LETTING THEM pile up. I didn't eat them. I'd stuff them into my kitchen cabinets, next to his juicer, where he couldn't help but notice.

I stopped liking peanut M&Ms. They just made me…annoyed. They *meant* something—something I hadn't brought to them.

I eventually threw pounds and pounds of them in the trash.

❀ ❀ ❀

WHEN I TELL YOU something about me, I still own it. I am not giving that to you. I am allowed to change my mind. When you take what I told you and present it back to me under your own conditions, you're taking ownership of it. You're trying to take ownership of ME.

If that man were still here, I would say all that to him. Because I know it, now. Then? I couldn't quite articulate it, couldn't quite understand it. I couldn't figure out how I had come to the point of throwing away something I actually liked, because even just seeing it pissed me off.

Something so petty as a type of candy had become fraught, and emotional, and triggering. It now stood in for everything that was wrong with that relationship—every way that man tried to tell me who I was, what I wanted to do in bed, what I wanted to write about, how I wanted to dress.

Which had all come from things *I'd* told *him*!

Except, also, *not*.

When he did that to me, he stopped having a partner and started having a creation, an echo, a mirror. A living, functioning relationship leaves room for growth. For each party to change, and for the relationship itself to morph, to expand, to adjust.

Life changes us. Our tastes mature, evolve; we grow tired of things, or want to try new things. We learn, we experiment, we shift.

A relationship needs to make room for this.

❄ ❄ ❄

I LIKE PEANUT M&Ms. They have chocolate, and protein, and salt; they are sweet but not too sweet; they come in fun colors. I no longer have long, boring afternoons that I need to fill with candyruspicy—but, I am happy to report, after some years, I can enjoy them again.

When *I* decide to.

I Found Truer Love When I
Stopped Trying to Change Myself
for It

My parents came up to the island to see us this past summer. It was a great visit—we cooked and went to the beach and kayaked and generally had a marvelous time. Near the end of the week, my stepmother pulled me aside and said, "It's wonderful to see you so happy. This marriage is so good for you. You used to just chameleon yourself, turning into whatever man you were with. I'm so glad you're not doing that anymore."

I knew what she meant, and she wasn't wrong. She would know, too: she's been my loving parent since I was a pre-teen, so she's seen basically every romantic relationship I've ever had.

I've been thinking about that conversation ever since. I'm glad that she noticed, and that she is happy about my life now. (I am too!) But I've also been wondering how I kept getting into those situations, and what's different now.

I'm realizing that it's not quite as simple as it sounds.

❀ ❀ ❀

I HAD A HANDFUL of important relationships before this marriage, with men who all differed greatly from one another. Lining these up next to each other, you might think that, when one relationship failed, I immediately sought out a partner who was the exact opposite of the last one. There's probably something to that.

First was the college boyfriend who was a serious distance runner but also a serious party dude, a frat-boy type. I went from him to a dour, pudgy, goth-ish, alcoholic line chef. From there it was the much older man, wealthy, mature, established, lover of fine wines and travel. Hmm, I see alcohol as a common element in those three, but wait: Because next was the flamboyant polyamorous author who basically didn't drink at all. And the man I'm married to now also only has a glass of wine on rare occasions. My permanent "designated driver."

To one degree or another, I changed into each man along the way. The runner got me to take up running; I drank, cooked, and wore all black with the goth-ish dude; I became a trophy wife, frosting my hair and traveling the world with the older man; I turned polyamorous and wore corsets and tall sexy boots to sci fi conventions with the author.

The thing is, though: all these "roles" and "poses" actually appealed to me, different as they were. I suspect I wouldn't have been attracted to each of those men if I hadn't found something fascinating about who they were and what they were doing. I never chameleoned into something that didn't speak to at least some facet of who I was or—more likely—what I wanted to explore. What I was curious about.

The trouble came, for me, in throwing myself so thoroughly into those roles that I got lost in the process. Trying on new identities like so many garments in a mall dressing room, looking at myself in the mirror, imagining being that person…

I didn't know who I was. So I dressed up in other people's lives.

Even married a few of them.

❄ ❄ ❄

SOMETHING SHIFTED FOR ME, round about the intersection between the polyamorous writer and the man I'm married to now (who was one of my "harem," in my poly days, though we are happily monogamous now).

I started…becoming me. I started finding my voice, independently of who I was with. Ironically, I believe that polyamory played a large part in this. When I had *several partners at once*, I couldn't be all of them. I had to figure out who I really was, underneath all the masks and costumes and distractions.

I had to be me.

❄ ❄ ❄

I like being me. I'm not done figuring out who I am now—I'll probably never be done, there's just too many possibilities, too many interesting things to do and explore and try—but I have a much better grip on the basics.

I've kept pieces from all those relationships, the pieces that fit me. My joints don't let this ole body run anymore, but I hike and swim and play racquetball and do yoga, and I love kayaking. Most of my clothes are still black. I enjoy and appreciate luxuries that are beyond my means (sigh). I still go to the occasional sci fi convention, and I wore a corset to a local performance of *The Rocky Horror Show* just last weekend (don't ask me how it fit!).

The man I'm married to now…he's different too, different from all those other men—and not just in the surface details. I have learned and grown over the decades, certainly, so I am not the same person I was when I embarked on the other relationships; but this man is not like any of the others. He is unusually—I struggle with how to put it, to convey what is unique about him—flexible? Accepting? Not-imprintable-on? Yes, all those things, but more, and more complicated.

He doesn't have an agenda about who I should be. He's interested in the journey we are *all* on—not just him and me, but everyone. He knows who he is, but he's open to learning more. To changing his mind.

The connection we have feels truer, deeper, and somehow *safer* than any love I've had before. More real. Because he's interested in who I am now and who I might become, I feel a freedom I've never felt before.

I sometimes feel sad that we didn't meet earlier in life—we could have had so many more years together!—but we both know that wouldn't have worked out for us at all. I was too insecure and un-self-aware; I would have found him not at all appealing. (He assures me he was very unsuitable as a younger man, that we wouldn't have liked each other at all.)

I think we met just when we were supposed to.

When I was ready to be who I am, and love him for who he is—without having to turn myself into some uncomfortable, ill-fitting echo of him.

I'm not a chameleon. I'm *me*.

Creativity as Work

Writing Through the Fear

Writing the truth is so scary.

Yet my rawest, most real writing only comes out in the pieces where I dare to reveal the deep stuff…to bare my soul. Fiction or nonfiction, it doesn't matter; it's the stories that tell the truth, stories where I open myself to the vast unknown universe…and (so much worse) to the people who *know* me. To my FAMILY.

It's terrifying. It's smothering.

I'm so scared when I force myself to write all the way down to the hard stuff. The meat and the bones and the viscera. It's so tempting to back away, to stay safe. To hush myself.

But I also can't stop. Something keeps pulling me in.

❋ ❋ ❋

THE SINGLE MOST IMPORTANT thing I have learned, over the years, is to get the audience out of my head. OUT. To somehow remember how to write for myself alone.

Because it wasn't like this at the very beginning. When I first felt drawn to writing, it was because I couldn't *not* write. The words boiled out—tiny crabbed letters in a black-bound diary, all the angst of my pre-teen *feelings*, feelings about *everything*. It was never supposed to be for anyone else. Writing was *mine*.

But then, no doubt inevitably, I got proud of something I'd written. Or maybe I gave a school assignment just a little something extra. I don't even remember when I first showed someone my writing. When I first let someone else in. I didn't get shut down with criticism; probably my work was praised, maybe even encouraged. It doesn't even matter what the actual reaction was.

What happened was, suddenly it wasn't just me anymore.

Now I had the notion of an AUDIENCE.

❊ ❊ ❊

I MAJORED IN RHETORIC in college. Really, that's actually a thing you can do. It was a great major—it was smart and wide-ranging and endlessly fascinating—but what's important here is that that was the first time this notion of an **audience** was codified for me: when there was finally a name to put to this formless, vaguely terrifying awareness that something huge and intrusive had taken over what had once been a private process.

You must always keep your audience in mind when you write, we learned.

All your arguments (that's what they call the form of a Rhetoric essay: an *argument*) are meant to persuade, to convince, to draw the reader along to an inevitable conclusion. You must choose each word with this aim clearly before you. Write as though you are speaking to a skeptical, imaginary person who disagrees with your *premise*, as you build an airtight case for your *thesis*. So airtight that when they reach the end of your piece, they leap to their feet and exclaim, "Yes! That's right! What a fool I was to ever believe otherwise!"

Yeah, okay. That was fine for a college paper, I suppose; and thinking about who your reader might be isn't a bad approach for later in the editorial process, either. I will admit that I did become a much better writer during the course of my education. But…I would argue (haha) that this is only a small part of becoming an honest, meaningful writer.

A writer whose stories people actually want to read.

❊ ❊ ❊

WHY DO WE DO this, anyway? Writing is a weird thing. For me, at least, it comes from a strong desire to communicate, to share, to be known—alongside an equally strong desire to hide, to slowly and painstakingly shape a pile of pretty words that I let speak for me, leaving *me* in the shadows. *Look over there*, I say. *I built that; it is what I really want to say. Please don't train your gaze on little vulnerable me over here…*

I spent so many years being so careful with my writing. Not wanting to "out" my innermost fears and desires, my embarrassing misdeeds (past and present). Constructing something safe and sensible.

Boring.

Who wants to read safe and sensible? I don't. I want to read the raw stuff, the bleeding stuff, the *real* stuff.

❈ ❈ ❈

OKAY, SO WE JUST need to banish the audience from our raw process. Great! Now what?

Very funny. The audience, alas, is Pandora's Box: there's no putting it away again, once you really understand it's there. Even my later journals are full of self-conscious little asides addressed to my "future biographer," which of course I didn't (and don't) believe there will be one, but *just in case…* It's the embarrassed, ashamed, explain-y little instinct for self-minimizing, apologizing, waving away the inconvenient and the weird and the awkward. The editing that intrudes on the writing.

Yes, I'm also a professional editor. Make no mistake: there is absolutely a time and a place for editing. But editing does not belong in the raw process of the first draft.

I know I am so, so, *so* not the first person, or even the hundredth, to make this observation. "Just write the words, let them flow" is such basic advice, it's why all the creative writing books ever published give some variation of it.

It's not that easy, though, is it? If it were, we wouldn't need so very many writing books. We wouldn't gobble them up like each one was finally going to be *the one*, the golden ticket, the one piece of secret code that will finally unlock the great mystery of just *how* to do this ineffable thing.

Every once in a great while, I find it, that ineffable thing. I have experienced, more than once, the joy of opening myself to the river of words within, the thoughts and emotions deep inside. I have just let them all out, without watching them, without censoring. Words extruded from my fingers, covering the page, the screen. They've come out as fast as I can type—and I'm a *fast* typist. And, in those rare and golden moments, the words have turned out to be awfully damn good. I've gone back later and not had to change a thing.

I can remember only a handful of times in my mature writing life, getting into that zone, where I tapped into something that felt like it wasn't even me, it was so uncensored. One time it lasted an entire half-hour. It's *that* rare.

✻ ✻ ✻

IT BEGINS AND ENDS with the honesty, though. I'm convinced of that. When we come here and say true things to each other. When I write an essay telling you about how I married a man with a lot of money and it didn't actually make me happy. Or how I later threw myself into polyamory, choosing lovers like they were delicious dishes on a giant buffet. Or how I grew up on a hippie commune where all sorts of crazy things happened. Or even how I had a bad boss once.

With each of those pieces of writing—and so many more—I felt the fear even as I was composing them. *Should I say this? Should I soften it, choose my words more carefully, think about how people might react?*

The thing is? Nobody's going to love everything you write. My strongest pieces get the strongest responses—good *and* bad. Of course we want more good than bad—we're *human*, after all—but we cannot control what happens to our words after we publish them. "The story belongs to the reader," one of my mentors used to say, and I know he was quoting a mentor of his own. Once you let it go out into the world…it's there, and your readers, your *audience*, will bring their own experiences and frames and biases and emotions to your story. They will make it theirs.

That's a *good* thing. You *want* that.

✻ ✻ ✻

IT'S CRAZY, ISN'T IT? It's the craziest thing I know. This private-public, hiding-revealing, personal-universal creative urge we get, this drive to write all the way down to our bones… I can't make sense of it. I just *do* it. I would do it even if nobody ever read my words. And I *really really* want so *many* people to read my words. There were times in my life when I wanted to be published so badly, I honestly couldn't think of anything I wanted more. I could *taste* it, the yearning. I still have that fantasy of being on an airplane and looking over and seeing my book in the hands of a stranger.

(Hasn't happened yet—but I have signed the author wall at Powell's bookstore in Portland, so there's that!)

✻ ✻ ✻

WHATEVER THE REASON FOR this madness, we do it. We open up our hearts and our souls and tell the big bad secrets, and the little embarrassing ones…and we hope for some kind of human response out there from the other side. Some sign that we're not alone.

We hope to touch, to entertain, to amuse, maybe even to change minds. I want you to confirm my humanity, by giving me a few moments of your attention out of the jumble of your crazy life. I want you to smile, or think, or pause.

I want to reach you.

…And little by little, I promise, I will dare to tell you all my darkest, scariest truths.

The Novels I Won't Finish Writing

I'm full of ideas. Ideas are the easy part—there's always *way* more stuff bouncing around in my brain than there is time to even get it all down in words, much less developed into a finished piece of writing, polished and ready to share with the world.

I start lots of pieces, way more than I ever finish. That's no big deal if it's an article, or a short story. I've got *so many* files on my computer with a page or two or three of a story that never ended up going anywhere. Maybe the idea wasn't so interesting once I started to flesh it out; maybe I got stuck and didn't know how to resolve the story's conflict (collaborators are super helpful here, I find). I always think maybe I'll revisit those stories someday. I suppose it could happen, but, like I said, I've always got a shiny new idea or three popping up.

Novels, however, are another matter. Two abandoned pages of a short story represents, what, an hour of "wasted" time? Maybe less? And it's not even really wasted; I think all writing is worth something. Failures can teach you even more than successes, if you're paying attention and willing to learn.

I have a handful of novels that each reached several hundred pages. Novels I worked on for months, even a year or more. Novels that I thought were "done," and that I inflicted on critique groups (and what did those nice people ever do to me, to deserve such poor treatment?).

It's time to acknowledge that I am never going to revisit these novels.

❉ ❉ ❉

The novel about the little creatures that live in people's heads and share their thoughts

THE LITTLE CREATURES HAD a made-up name that I could never settle on, but the book's characters referred to them casually as "demons". So the novel was called…wait for it…*Demonhead*. I had a whole magical world worked out as to where these creatures came from, and why they had to go live in human heads, and what they got out of it; and none of it made any sense.

Also I set it in a post-apocalyptic San Francisco Bay Area (though I never exactly settled on what caused the apocalypse), largely so I could write a lengthy, well-researched, mind-numbingly dull scene involving the main characters walking under the bay through the abandoned BART tunnel.

Also I loved to put gratuitous graphic sex scenes in my novels back then, so this one had the main characters taking an abrupt time out from all the crisis and drama in order to go at it in a bathroom, while the other characters waited outside for them to get back to the story.

Only much later did I read Stephenie Meyer's *The Host*, which starts with a similar idea (at least about little creatures in peoples' heads), but which actually works, as a story. I had already long since abandoned *Demonhead* before I learned that someone else had already written it much better.

❈ ❈ ❈

The novel about the haunted house

HAUNTED-HOUSE NOVELS ARE SOME of my favorite spooky books to read. I love the mystery and the suspense; I love a story that slowly reveals whatever it was that made the ghost angry, that made them stick around and mess with the living. So I tried to write one.

I used a different process in planning and writing *One Eleven Primrose* than I usually do—the Snowflake Method, if you want to look it up; lots of people love it and swear by it—but it sure didn't work for me. By the time I'd gone through all the steps and was actually drafting the novel, all the mystery and discovery had been sucked out of the creative process for me. I was bored by my own novel. Even the gratuitous graphic sex scene involving the main character's husband and the angry ghost-lady wasn't very interesting.

❈ ❈ ❈

The novel that was a poorly disguised love letter to the

man who is now my husband

IT WAS OSTENSIBLY ABOUT fairies. Make of that what you will. *Hobgoblin* is the only novel on this list that I'm even the teeniest, tiniest bit tempted to revisit someday. It took place in San Francisco (where I lived at the time), and it had to do with the interface between the hidden fae community that lives underground—literally; you access Fairyland through a portal on the hill in Buena Vista Park—and the human world.

As with *Demonhead*, I didn't really have a good reason that the fae would be interacting with humankind like I needed them to for the story to work, and I also didn't have much of a vision of what Fairyland really looked like, or what happened there. Just, you know, pearls and fancy clothes and beauty and royalty and magic and all that.

The main reason I really know that I am not going to return to this book (however tempting it may sometimes feel) is that I later read "A Tiny Feast," by Chris Adrian (in *The New Yorker*), which is the loveliest, most haunting, most beautifully told fairies-who-live-under-San-Francisco's-Buena-Vista-Hill story you'll ever find. I actually hunted it down online and printed it out and keep it in my file of Really Excellent Writing. *Hobgoblin* was never going to come close to that short story (even if I had finally grown out of the need to insert a gratuitous graphic sex scene) (and I had! The book has plenty of romance, but no *bwow chicka bwow wow*, as my crit group used to call it).

❊ ❊ ❊

So why not delete the old files?

ARE YOU KIDDING? WHAT if…I don't know…the idea well ever runs dry? What if my published and forthcoming novels sell so well that my public starts clamoring for more, more, more? Surely it would be easier to fix what's wrong with those earlier novels—now that I'm a more experienced, competent writer—than to draft something completely new? (Spoiler: NO.)

But I can't delete the old words. Just like I can't get rid of the seventeen different versions of *The Queen and The Tower* that preceded the book that actually got published. That's my history; it's the journey I took to get here…and wherever I'm going next.

Besides, some of those gratuitous graphic sex scenes were *hot*. Surely I'll write a novel some day that needs some ghost-on-human porn…

How I Became a Full-Time Freelance Copy Editor

Once upon a time I had a full-time day job outside the house, with retirement and benefits and all that; I was also married to a man with a great income.

Then that part of my life came to an end. But that's another story.

Today, I am a full-time stay-at-home copy editor and proofreader. I have a large stable of fantastic, loyal repeat clients, and occasionally take on new ones. Even more wonderfully, I also turn *away* potential clients—I did that just last week, as it happens. It feels sort of terrifying and marvelous and irresponsible and unreal; I haven't quite gotten used to that part yet. I'm still emotionally in the days of *what if there will never be another client, never another gig; I will never work again; we're going to starve...*

Even if I haven't actually been in those days for several years now.

✳ ✳ ✳

I CAN'T TELL *YOU* HOW TO become a freelance copy editor/proofreader so successful that you can pick and choose your clients. I can only tell you how *I* did it. As with any personal narrative, there will be parts of my story that are just random luck and happenstance—but, I think there are some things that are generalizable. Things you can control, if you think you want to *try this at home*, as they say.

The first thing I can identify is that, from the start, I've lived a life that has left me very qualified to do this kind of work. I am a reader. (I'm a writer too, but that's also another story.) I grew up without television, and very few other kids around to play with, so I turned to books. I *love* to read. I get paid to read books all day, and when I go to bed, I…read books. I see these "reading challenges" on Goodreads and the like about how "you can do it, you can read **six** books this year" or "a **dozen**!!", and I think, *Oh, sweet summer child*. I read one hundred and forty-eight books last year. Of course, only sixty-four of them were for "fun"; the rest were for my work.

So that's one piece. Luck or planning? Let's call that luck, since nobody was exactly mapping out my future career when I was a hippie kid reading library books by candlelight at home on the commune.

❀ ❀ ❀

I DID WELL IN school, as you might imagine. The American public school system is absolutely set up for people like me: folks who are comfortable with the written word. I am not quite as conversant in math and science, but I muddled through those well enough while excelling in language skills. (I'm one of the only people I know who scored higher on her English SATs than on math.) I liked school, and I liked knowing that the teachers found me smart and talented.

As a result, I got away with stuff. In high school, I was busy reading Michener's *Hawaii* when we were supposed to be writing a book report on something from a prescribed list in our Social Studies class. I just didn't get around to reading a qualifying book (*Hawaii* is very long, and I was a teenage girl with a teenage girl's social life) so…I invented one. The novel I made up was called *Owyhee: Story of the Islands*, by Arlo Hutton. Arlo was the family dog of the Huttons, for whom I babysat regularly (don't bother Googling him, *Owyhee* was, sadly, Arlo's only novel). I invented the whole plot of the novel, and the publisher, and the date of publication; I wrote a book report on *that*. Somehow, that seemed easier than choosing a book from the teacher's silly list.

I got an A.

Speaking of education: I also managed, later, to attend a really fine university. This part was entirely luck, of the temporal and geographic variety. UC Berkeley was our "local" school (two hours from where I grew up), and, though admission wasn't a shoo-in in the mid-1980s, it was a heck of a lot easier than it is today. (Especially if you had good SAT scores.) Also, it was priced like the state school it is (and still should be, alas), so I was able to put myself through college without help from my parents, or crushing student loans—just part-time jobs. That was impossible even five years later; and it costs as much as a new car now, *per year*.

So, okay. I got lucky in the education department, and I'm a weirdo reader-writer-book fiend. If you are not that thing, you might want to consider whether a career working with books is right for you.

❀ ❀ ❀

THE NEXT STEP WAS getting jobs that featured editorial work. I've actually never had a job with the title *Editor*, but all my work had to do with manuscripts, publications. Words, in one way or another. I transcribed oral history interviews in college (one of those part-time jobs that funded my education); later, I worked as an Editorial Assistant in that same department. Sometimes the editors would have me proofread the interviews before publication. I even worked in a lab in a medical school—but again, helping the department head with the scientific papers, grants, and patents he was writing.

It was then that I discovered my freakish superpower. I spot typos. A misspelled word just *looks* wrong to me. It's the wrong shape; it sticks in my craw; it feels itchy on my skin. I can't explain it, and I would have no idea how to teach anyone to do it.

I'm one of those people who finds typos in published books. I've had to work hard to not get irritated by it. (Okay, I lie: it always bothers me.)

But it also, perversely, cheers me up. There will always be typos! There will always be a need for proofreaders!

❀ ❀ ❀

THE NEXT PART OF the story is how this became my actual full-time job. It went like this: when I left the old life and job behind, I had a little bit of financial cushion, which gave me space to figure out what to do next. So I looked very carefully into my heart and soul, at the things I loved to do, at what would be satisfying to do all day, for years on end, and I decided...

...that I wanted to become a realtor.

No, really. I went through hundreds of hours of training, aced my state's licensing exam, interviewed at a number of local realty offices, and accepted an offer at one of them. I built a list of potential clients, held open houses for other brokers, even upgraded my wardrobe and started wearing makeup again.

I tried that for an embarrassingly lengthy period of time. During which time I never sold a house; never even landed a listing or a client.

Meanwhile…being a writer, I had a lot of friends who were also writers. Back when I was still doing the real estate training, one of my friends had a book coming out from a small press. They'd sent him the galleys to look over; I offered to help, since I was good at that sort of thing. I found a lot of typos. We corrected them and sent them in.

I kept trying to be a realtor. I really liked being able to look up all the behind-the-scenes information on houses for sale. I loved the magical device I had that enabled me to open up any lockbox city-wide; I walked through *so many* vacant houses. I even took a friend through dozens of houseboats on the river (she was interested in the houseboat lifestyle, though she had no money to actually buy one).

My writer friend's book came out. It was gorgeous. Some time later, I met the small press owners at a convention. (I was going to lots of writers' conventions in those days, hoping to meet agents and editors and publishers, so they would publish my books.) The small press owners congratulated me on the typo-finding I'd done on my friend's book, and said if they ever had any freelance work available, they'd keep me in mind.

More time passed. I didn't sell any houses. My savings dwindled. I was going to have to figure out what to do.

The small press did contact me! Months later. They sent me one gig. I worked so hard on it, trying not to let myself read too fast, trying to find *every single typo*. I have no idea whether I managed that or not, but they liked my work well enough to send me another book to proofread a few months later.

And then another one a few weeks after that.

Soon, I was working for them fairly steadily, but it was nothing like enough to pay the bills. But then they asked if they could send my name to another small press! I said yes, of course. So now I had a second client.

I met another author at another convention, who was starting a small press. I told him I did proofreading. He asked if I did copy editing too. "Sure," I said, promising myself I'd go home and look up the difference between copy editing and proofreading.

(Here's a secret: these days, they're kind of the same thing. In the olden days, a copy editor worked on a draft manuscript. They came after the developmental editor, and the structural editor, and the line editor—also functions that can and do get combined these days. The copy editor was the second-to-last line of defense, looking for typos of course, but also infelicities of language, overuse of crutch words, detail inconsistencies—someone's eye color changes, or they get up and storm across the room after they already got up and paced to the window—and what I like to call the "forty-five-hour afternoon," which usually happens when an author moves things around in the manuscript and forgets to keep track of time.

(The proofreader, on the other hand, traditionally is given actual printed page proofs: an already-typeset manuscript ready to go to the printer. She checks for typos (again), headers and footers, placement of the text, and other things like that. Ideally, nothing she finds should change the pagination; it's been *set*. After the proofreader, the traditional book is printed, bound, and sold.)

❀ ❀ ❀

So, I STARTED COPY editing too. Just as much fun as proofreading! That author-friend with the small press referred me to a friend of *his*, who was a successful self-published writer. That was new to me, and I was a little skeptical, as at that point in my life, I was still laboring under the outdated delusion that people self-published because they weren't good enough to publish traditionally. *Hahahahaha*. Trust me, I have long since been set to rights there. (In my defense, once upon a time, that was actually true. Don't make me show you my grandfather's self-published book, *Reprieve from Chaos*, about how aliens abducted him and gave him detailed instructions on how we're supposed to remake our society into a utopia of their own design. He actually wrote it as a science fiction novel to make it more accessible.)

That new client, the successful self-published client, was part of a group of other self-published writers, and she asked if she could give my name out...and thus started a fractally branching system of referrals that hasn't stopped to this day.

❀ ❀ ❀

IT WENT ON LIKE that. Until there came a day when I had to stop what I was in the middle of at home—copy editing a fascinating book—to put on my realtor clothes and go into the office for "desk time," answering the phones and being the office presence to nab any walk-in business.

And I realized, *Wait a minute. This business is booming. Real estate is entirely not happening. Why don't I...do this instead?*

So I quit real estate, though I kept my license active just in case. And I leaned into doing what I actually love: reading books and making them better. I handed out business cards at conventions, to other small presses and indie authors. I told my clients I was open to referrals. I updated my website, and published my rates.

It was scary, and a little dicey, at first. You will no doubt be astonished to hear that I am not as wealthy as a successful realtor (though I'm doing way better than a realtor who has no clients or listings). But I make enough. Enough, in fact, that I have spent large spans of time being the major and sometimes only earner in my marriage. We trade off; sometimes he makes the big bucks. (The two-freelancer marriage: I will have to write *that* essay some day...)

But it worked. When two years had gone by and it was time to renew my real estate license, I let it lapse. (I was very sad to give back that magical door-opening device, but alas, it had to be done.)

I love how my career found me, and not the other way around.

❀ ❀ ❀

So: You want the freelance lifestyle, hm? You want to sleep till you wake up, and go to the gym in the middle of the afternoon when the pool is empty, and eat lunch every day at your own table? It's pretty sweet, I won't deny it. Yes, there are downsides: with all that farting around, your workday better not end at 5pm, or you're going to run out of money fast. You do have to be the kind of person who can be disciplined, without a boss looking over your shoulder. You have to stay on top of your expenses, and pay your taxes quarterly—EXTRA taxes, I'm sorry to inform you, because you're also paying the employer's share. And health insurance... all I can say is, "Thanks, Obama!" We'd be toast without the ACA and its life-saving subsidies.

But if you're up for that, here's my advice:

1. **Have a cushion**. This never would have even had a chance to happen accidentally if I hadn't had a little savings at the outset. So, don't quit your day job. Or, if you have a spouse or partner who can cover the household income needs for a while, that works too.
2. **Network, network, network**. Tell everyone what you're doing.

Ask for referrals. Don't be shy. Give your gorgeous business cards to *everyone*.

3. **Do spectacular work, and deliver it on time, or early**. Be an adult, be reliable, be professional. Your clients will keep coming back if they know they can trust you.

4. **Keep track of your hours**. I charge by the job, not by the hour; but I log every hour spent doing the actual work. (Not the time spent drumming up the work or messing around on Facebook or going to the post office or whatever—I'm not a *maniac*.) That way you can be sure you're being paid what you need to be paid.

5. Related to that: **Make sure your rates are competitive**. I'm fast, so my rates are lower than the industry average, but that still works out for me.

If that sounds workable to you, go forth and freelance, my friend! I wish you much luck, happiness, and success.

❊ ❊ ❊

Coda: I am 100% certain that, having written a cheerful, detailed article about what a whizz-bang copy editor and proofreader I am, there will be a typo or ten in here. Because the world is just cruel that way, and it's really, really hard to proof your own work. I just wanted to put that out there. Be kind. ☺

Finding Errors in My Own Books Makes Me Crazy

I've just sent the draft of *Orcas Investigation*, book **three** of my cozy mystery series The Chameleon Chronicles (co-written with my dear friend Karen G. Berry), to our editor for his inputs and emendations.

As I was putting the finishing touches on my part, I naturally had book **two**, *Orcas Intruder*, by my side so I could refer to it, to help me remember all the little details that tend to slip an author's mind: *Had we given Lisa's ex-husband a name yet? What weird vegetables did Paige bring to Cam's house the first time? Which recipes did we include at the back?*

And then I noticed the great big heading at the top of the "sneak preview" chapter at the back…offering an advance look at "*Orcas Investigation*, book 2 of The Chameleon Chronicles!"

Argh! In what kind of circular universe does book 2 offer you a sneak peek at book 2!?

I'm a professional copy editor and proofreader, for crying out loud. I formatted and laid out that book myself. How could I have missed that?

Or another of my books that I also formatted (I swear I'm going to get better at this with practice…), the print version has a big chunk at the end of chapter five that is somehow still in draft-font and not fancy-final-book font…and I carefully looked over the proof. Sigh!

Or an earlier book, which was put out by an actual publisher who was not me, and used a proofreader who was also not me… I was slammed with other work at the moment it came to me (with a very tight turn-around) for one final proofing, so I just…didn't. Well, I glanced through it, but that was it. And, well, it has typos. But honestly? If I didn't see them every time I edited and re-edited that book before I turned it in, or during one of the many rounds of edits after that, I likely wasn't going to see them then.

Not like I see them every time I open the published book.

❋ ❋ ❋

IT'S *SO HARD* TO proof your own words. I mean, when it matters: I see them like glowing neon signs whenever I glance into any of these poor imperfect books. They just leap off the page and strike me in the eye.

And it *hurts*. I pride myself on my attention to detail. I think I'm actually a pretty good copy editor and proofreader. I find typos all the time, in published books; my clients all tell me how happy they are with my work, how amazed they are at how many things I've caught. I've actually been hired to re-proof already-published books.

This is what makes it all the more painful to let mistakes in my very own books go out into the world.

It's like they're a walking advertisement for my own incompetence.

❋ ❋ ❋

I'M SURE I'M BEING too hard on myself here. We're all human, right? Mistakes get made. After all, there's all those typos I keep finding in books put out by major publishers—and even in *The New Yorker*, if you can believe it.

(I had a friend years ago when I lived in San Francisco who would circle errors in her *New Yorker*s, because they were so rare. If she's still doing it, I hope she bought a good supply of red pens.)

Oh, but oh, errors hurt.

I love each and every one of the books I copy edit and proofread, *yes I absolutely do and don't let anyone ever tell you otherwise*, but some I love even more than others, and sometimes I'll give one of those to my husband to read, because I think he might enjoy it too.

The first time this happened, we were lying in bed reading together, me all happily watching him out of the corner of my eye, thinking *Oh I can't wait to see him loving this book, such an amazing and fabulous book*, when he leaned over and held up the book and said, "Look, a typo. You missed one."

I gritted my teeth and said, "Huh. Look at that."

A few minutes later, he pointed out another one.

"Okay, stop," I said. "I don't want to know. It's like you're stabbing me in the belly. I can't stand it."

My husband is a smart and compassionate man, and he has never again pointed out a typo in something I proofread.

Later, of course, I decided that the publisher was at fault. Surely they failed to make all the corrections I told them to; no way would I have actually missed those things. There! Now I could sleep at night.

❋ ❋ ❋

No, SERIOUSLY, IT'S GOOD to stay humble. To know that I am not perfect, no one can be perfect. It's why copy editing and proofreading are two *separate* steps, to be done by two *separate* people. It's why several of my more well-funded clients actually pay for two rounds of proofreading, by two different proofreaders—after all the other editing and copy editing steps.

(Even so, I've found errors in *their* published books, books I didn't work on.)

But there is a particular madness in seeing a mistake that *I* made, in my *own* book. One that got past every round of editing.

Oh well! I just have to keep trying.

It's good to have something to strive for, I suppose.

This Week I Got a Four-Book Deal and Cleaned Rooms at an Inn

Today I will leave a few minutes early for my gig cleaning guest rooms at a B&B across the island, in order to stop at the post office and mail off this signed contract to my new publisher.

Because yay, I got a four-book deal! Outland Entertainment is going to be bringing out my Nightcraft Quartet. The first book, *The Queen and The Tower,* came out as an indie book last year, but I really want what a publisher can bring me for this project: marketing and promotion, editorial input, and the ability to get into bookstores beyond the one here where they know me.

Also, just the structure of a real deadline is going to be *so helpful.* I was supposed to have the second book out in the world by now. Instead, it's still a messy pile of manuscript and notes on my desk (don't tell my new editor).

The re-released *Queen & Tower* comes out this fall; then, a book a year starting next summer. Woohoo!

❅ ❅ ❅

MEANWHILE, LIFE GOES ON around here. As in, you know, that gig cleaning rooms. Because, as thrilling as the book deal is (and it *is* thrilling), any money from it is going to be a long time coming. That's just the way publishing works.

But we have to eat this week, and next week, and the week after that.

So I edit and copy edit and proofread; I write articles and copy; and, yes, there are those guest rooms.

❀ ❀ ❀

IT'S ACTUALLY VERY PEACEFUL, to clean rooms at a little B&B on the water. Mostly, the work is not that onerous; the vast majority of inn guests don't leave a lot of nastiness behind. (Yeah, sometimes they do; my husband and I worked a whole winter at that inn a couple years ago, and there were a *few* memorable occasions…but pretty much, if you're cleaning a bathroom every day or two, it doesn't have a chance to get that bad.)

The first thing I like to do is the beds. Strip them and get laundry going (if Mr. Owner hasn't already started that); then bring up the clean sheets and remake the beds. I know "real" housekeeping staff probably save the beds for last, but I like how the room looks nearly finished when the bed is made, even though I've just started.

Don't forget to look under the beds. When Mr. Owner was teaching us how to run the inn that winter, he lifted the bedskirt in the first room he showed us and—yep!—there was a bottle of lube.

(Just throw it away. Nobody is going to come back for it.)

Then I make a pass through the bathrooms, gathering the towels, assessing the situation. Take the towels down to the laundry. Start a trash bag… and then get into the real work.

❀ ❀ ❀

IT'S QUIET AT THE B&B. When I'm tired from carrying laundry and the vacuum cleaner up and down the stairs, I take a moment to look out at the harbor. To catch my breath, to enjoy the beauty of the setting. Usually, all the guests are out for the day, hiking or shopping or eating out. Yesterday, one guy was in his room, on a lengthy phone call. The walls are pretty thin. It sounded like a fun phone call.

I didn't need to bother him; we only clean the rooms when they turn over. It's not a hotel.

❀ ❀ ❀

THERE IS SOMETHING VERY satisfying about physical work. Even if it's repetitive—weeding, washing dishes, mowing the lawn, cleaning rooms that will need to be cleaned again after the next guests leave—it's also tangible, visible. Everything looks better when you're done. You can stand in the doorway, making one final sweep with your eyes to make sure you didn't miss anything. *Yes. All is in order now.*

Proofreading feels tangible in that way to me; the deeper forms of edit-ing do not. A typo is a typo is a typo. An infelicitous sentence, a slippery point-of-view, an author's tendency toward lengthy soapbox speeches by his "characters" who are really just stand-ins for the author himself—those are always judgment calls. As an editor who is also a writer, I am a true believer in *author voice*. I mess with an author's style as little as possible.

Many writers hate being copy edited, most particularly. They're hap-py to have their typos caught, and most of them seem grateful to have large structural problems brought to their attention (even if it means more work in the rewrite). But copy editing occupies that weird middle ground where *voice* lives, I think.

So I do try and take a light hand there.

❊ ❊ ❊

Tomorrow was supposed to be my last day cleaning rooms, but a few minutes ago (while I was writing this essay) Mrs. Owner texted asking if I want to do two more days after that. *Yes,* I wrote back, without hesita-tion. We can always use the money, and I do enjoy the work.

Also, it will likely be some of the last moments I ever get to spend at that inn. Unless the new owners need occasional help...our friends, the old owners, are selling the place. Escrow closes in a few weeks.

Of course, I said yes.

❊ ❊ ❊

What I like about my life right now (one of the many things I like) is the variety. I love having many different projects going on. If I get stuck on one thing, there's another right next to it, one that's shiny and excit-ing, full of life and energy, calling out to me.

What I *don't* like about my life right now is...there's too darn much going on. I can't quite keep up, and that stresses me out.

But it's all great stuff! Book deals, and essays, and fascinating books by other people to proofread and edit, and the other book I'm working on, and yes, even guest rooms to clean. How can I say no to anything? But I *have* to. I'm just too busy, and it's overwhelming. But I can't. But I have to. But...

I'll let you know if I figure out an answer.

It Scares Me When the Creative Spark Dims

Sometimes my writing just pours out of me. Ideas bubble up in my head faster than I can scribble notes about them all. I can have six or seven or ten files in my drafts folder, in various stages of completion, because the urge to write each of those stories *just couldn't wait.*

Other times...I go look at those draft files and think, *There's a story there? Really? Because I'm so not seeing it.*

You'd think I'd be used to this cycle of hot-and-not by now. I've been writing, in one form or another, for over forty years.

But when the well goes dry, it scares me every time.

❊ ❊ ❊

I BELONG TO A Facebook group of prolific professional writers. It's an amazing, supportive, uplifting, informative group of people. We support each other, cheer for each other, have each other's backs; we share tips and opportunities and data about our audiences and earnings. Of course not everyone is at the same level in their careers—and not everyone even has the same goals for their writing careers. A number of the members of the group write full-time, and a number of *those* folks do really well at it.

I don't write full-time. Writing is a quantitatively small, though emotionally crucial, part of my life. It's work, yes, but it's also my art and my creativity and what keeps me sane and in touch with myself. Earning money from my writing is a very happy bonus, but it's not the major goal. I don't even actually want to be a full-time writer: I love editing and copy editing and proofreading too much to want to give them up entirely. Sure, it would be nice to be able to be choosier about the jobs I take on, but by and large, it's pretty sweet work.

When I'm in a creative and prolific space, writing and publishing a few essays a week, I find I also spend a lot of time in that Facebook group, putting my work out there, reading and responding to the work of others, feeling great about it all.

When I'm in a dry spell…the group feels like a rebuke. Not because of anything anyone there says, not at all; this all comes from me. It feels like a party I didn't get invited to, but that I can hear in the next room. *Look how productive everyone else is*, my jerkbrain tells me. *You should just sit down and crank out a story. It'll be great! You know you can do it, look how fast you wrote the last one!*

You'd think by now I'd learn not to try to write when I'm not feeling it. It *never* works out well. The writing comes out stilted, forced. The spark isn't there.

It's obvious to me, and worse, it's obvious to my readers. "Do your homework" articles get far less reader response than "I can't *not* write this!!!" articles.

That's why I say it's not writer's block, exactly. I can *always* make words come out. They just aren't always good words, or interesting words. Living words.

❀ ❀ ❀

I THINK WHAT SCARES me most profoundly about the dry spells is that they feel like being silenced.

I have a lifelong history of pain around being silenced. I was never very verbal to begin with, at least not that I can remember; I suppose it's possible that I was a chatty child when I was really small. But by the time I have memories from, I played alone a lot, and read books. I was shy and quiet, both by preference and because I knew I was supposed to be quiet.

There were not a lot of other children around, where I grew up. My parents were very busy and very distracted doing adult things. And even when I went to school, all the kids there already had made friends; I was the odd one out.

It's left me with this strange mix of being happy in my own company, craving peace and silence; and a sad and lonely sense of not being heard. Never having been heard. This carried into my own adolescence and adulthood, into a number of relationships. I am no good with confrontation. I practically whisper my needs and desires—and it feels like screaming.

❀ ❀ ❀

I TURNED TO WRITING early on as a way to reach out. A *safer* way. It was an attempt to get my thoughts and feelings down, yes, but then—more importantly—to share them with others.

It's a way of communicating, fundamentally. Even my private journals (which I started keeping at age eleven) are written with the thought in the back of my mind that somebody, someday, will read them. Or sometimes that's in the front of my mind: "Dear future biographer," begins more than one entry…only partially tongue-in-cheek…

When I get upset, when there is conflict around me, even if it isn't aimed directly at me (but especially so if it is), I "lose my words." My throat literally feels like it's closing; my eyes fill with tears; my mind floods with emotion and I cannot speak. Writing allows me to circumvent that silencing—safely. Privately. In writing, I can choose my words; type them and delete them and rearrange them, not having to show them to anyone until I'm ready. Or ever.

But I *do* want to show them to people.

❀ ❀ ❀

WE HUMANS ARE SOCIAL creatures, even us introverts. We want the connection with like-minded souls, with people who care about us, people who might find us interesting. People who can learn from us; people who can teach us something.

We want to be known.

I write because I'm a human and I want you to read my words.

When the words are sludgy and they don't want to flow, I feel like I'm a small child again, being told to be quiet. Being told I don't belong.

If I push through that and put the "wrong" words out there, to deafening silence…that feels even worse. That feels like a confirmation of the not-belonging. Like I crashed that party I wasn't invited to, only to stand in the corner, ignored.

It's easy to find other things to do than write.

❀ ❀ ❀

AND HONESTLY? THAT REALLY has to be okay. That's really the answer here, I think. I am not on some kind of schedule in the "write and publish personal essays" department. Nobody has assigned them to me, or given me any deadlines. If my forty-plus years of writing has taught me anything, surely it has made it clear that the urge to write *will come back*. The spark, the magic: it's not dead. Even if it goes dormant. Even if it does so for a long time.

I've gone years without writing, in decades past. Years when I was busy, or blocked, or too sad, or too happy to stop and write it down. Years when I was pouring my creative energy into other stuff—both stupid stuff and worthwhile stuff.

It didn't matter. Writing always came back.

I can write at my own pace. I can be open to the spark and let it happen when it shows up; what I need to work on is being gentle with myself when the flame burns down to embers and then ashes, for a while.

I can refill the well. The quiet times: those are times to read. I can still go on my lovely, supportive Facebook group and read everyone else's essays. I don't have to compare myself to them: their productivity, their easy floods of words.

I write my stuff, for me. And for anyone else who might like to connect with me. Human to human.

Hi, fellow human.

How to Write a Novel in Three Weeks

Y ou've heard of the National Novel Writing Month—NaNo WriMo—where the goal is to hit 50,000 words in one month. But what if you don't *have* a whole month?

Over the past two years, I have written five novels in three weeks apiece. (Don't bother looking for them; none were published under my own name.) The reasons for the tight timeline varied, but the process did not.

Here's how I did it.

Start with a killer outline

I DID NOT BEGIN drafting until I was very, very clear about the story. I needed to know the world, the characters, the conflict, and the resolution. That meant working out ahead of time what all the rules were—did the setting contain magical elements, and if so, how did they work? What sorts of things were impossible, and (more importantly) what things just *seemed* impossible?

How did the characters fit into this setting? I needed to know in great detail every major character's back story—even if this never got told in the novel itself. They needed to make sense as believable, real people, who would be facing credible situations (even ones involving spells and potions).

My outlines could run to many pages, sometimes containing scene-by-scene descriptions. Until the story worked in outline, I wasn't going to be able to write it.

But don't let the outline constrain you

When a story starts really working at a deep level, sometimes your characters will come up with a different plan of action than the one you sketched out ahead of time. Don't let your characters bully you, but do listen to them: if they're pushing to go somewhere else that will still get you to your resolution, go with it.

Set, and keep, a daily word count goal

For these novels, my target was 65,000–70,000 words. As with NaNoWriMo, just take the total word count and divide by the number of days you have, and there's your goal. I had to produce at least 3,000 words a day, seven days a week, to make my deadline.

When I was in that crunch mode, I sat down at my computer right after breakfast and wrote. It typically took me between one and two hours to hit my goal. If things were flowing, I'd write more; but most days, 3K was about where my brain would run out of steam.

A few times, interruptions made it impossible to write in the mornings, but I never went to bed without having done my word count. Daily momentum, and my good outline, meant that the words would always show up when I sat down to write them.

Let your imagination play in the details

I said earlier that I need to know every *major* character's back story before I begin writing. The opposite is true with the secondary characters. That's where a lot of the fun is: the crazy folks who bust into the story and give it flavor, texture, life. Let them stymie, frustrate, and delight your characters—and your readers.

Save the editing for later

It's one thing to read back over the last page of yesterday's writing to get ramped up for today's. It's quite another to start messing with what's there, rewriting and polishing and distracting yourself. Unless you've strayed into the weeds so far that you can't find your way back to the story, just press forward. You—and your editor(s) after you—will fix it all later.

Sit back and enjoy your accomplishment

Congratulations! You've written every day and now you have a big messy pile of words. But if you've stuck reasonably close to your outline, that mess has an underlying structure. Give yourself time to get a little distance—and to pat yourself on the back—and then dive back in and polish that baby into a *good* book.

And after that? Why, start on your next outline, of course!

Let's Bring Back the Glory Days of the Reclusive, Mysterious Author

When I'm not writing personal essays, or copy editing other folks' books, or messing around in the kitchen, or any of a double-dozen other things, I write fiction.

Now, obviously, I'm not a famous author or anything. But one of my book series, cozy mysteries set on Orcas Island, where I live, sells pretty well at the bookstore here on…Orcas Island, where I live. (Crazy, I know, right?) And by "pretty well," I mean hundreds and hundreds of paperbacks just over the last year or so. My co-author and I are not quitting any day jobs or anything, but this is respectable enough to encourage us to keep writing them.

Besides, they're a kick to write, and I get to collaborate with a dear friend to do so. Remember how much fun it was to play make-believe when you were a kid, inventing crazy stories for your characters to live? That's what it's like to write with a smart and funny friend.

❀ ❀ ❀

So the local bookstore, the one that's always calling and asking me to bring in another twenty or thirty copies, invited me to do a reading and signing when the third book in the series came out. I agreed, though I am not a great lover of public speaking, of being on stage and having to look and sound intelligent. It's gotten better over the years—I no longer feel sick and nervous for days in advance, or throw up before speaking events—but it's never going to be my favorite thing to do. It's never going to be comfortable.

But, a reading at the local bookstore! What an honor, and a great way to promote the series, right? So of course I said yes.

We set the date. I told everyone I know. I put it on my website. I put it on the Book of Face, several times. The bookstore put up signs, and put it on all of their social media sites. A notice appeared in the weekly Chamber of Commerce news blast. I reminded everyone I know. I told my neighbors when I ran into them on the road on my way to check the mail. I posted about it several times the day of the event, as I was starting to get too nervous to do much else. (I certainly couldn't write all day; my brain felt like it was being squeezed smaller and smaller—though I didn't throw up!) As the time approached, I changed out of my Work At Home Uniform (sweats, ancient tank top and sweatshirt, fuzzy socks) and into Fancy Author Reading Clothes. My husband drove me to town.

Can you guess what happened? I bet you can.

When we got to the bookstore, we were greeted by the owner and her mother, who were setting out cheese and crackers and wine, and a few dozen chairs, in the otherwise entirely empty store. A little bit later, our longest-time island friends, B. and C., arrived. Then my writer friend E.

That was it.

Eventually, I read to my husband and our three friends and the bookstore owner's mother. Then we all (without the owner's mother) went out to dinner at the Lower Tavern.

※ ※ ※

THIS IS NOT A story about how disappointed I am that I got dressed up and nervous and went out to read to a bunch of empty chairs. In all honesty, that was easier—for someone with stage fright like me—than reading to a lot of strangers staring back at me. Those five people really enjoyed the reading. And I do actually like reading aloud; it's the audience part I don't love.

I didn't even get the feeling I got earlier in my writing career, that old familiar *I'm a terrible writer, nobody likes my writing, nobody likes me, I should just give this all up, what am I even thinking* refrain. Because, as I mentioned, these books do sell pretty well—in that tiny store on our tiny island. I feel pleased and confident about the books, and about my writing in general.

I also am plenty familiar with the *I gave a reading and nobody came* experience. I have read to audiences of two or three people before, plenty of times; a few years ago, at a big regional convention, I had a reading to which not one person came. Not even my husband—he was manning our booth in the dealer's room. *That* was a terrible feeling, I can assure you—even though I know it's happened to every writer. That made me cranky and peevish and ready for a glass of wine at noon (and we've never been back to that convention since).

This wasn't that, though. I felt bad for the bookstore owner, who had hoped for better results; I felt grateful to my friends who showed up, and dinner out was fun.

No, this has all led me to wonder…why do we do this sort of thing anyway? Is this really the best way to find new readers? So much in the writing world has changed; nothing functions like it used to. Why do authors have readings at all, anymore?

Does anyone want to go out and listen to an author read?

❄ ❄ ❄

THINK ABOUT THE LAST reading you attended. Or the last ten readings. Why did you choose to go to that one, to those ten?

Have you ever discovered a new favorite author at a reading? Maybe you have; maybe you're more adventurous than me, more willing to try new things. I haven't, though. I go to readings for a) people I know, and b) authors I am already a fan of.

In other words, people whose books I'd be buying anyway.

I don't even get to all the readings in those categories, either. The last convention I attended, it seemed like I had friends reading every half-hour. I…couldn't attend them all.

What about readings at the lovely little bookstore here? I think I've been to…one. Maybe two. In the two-plus years since we moved here.

I'm not sure why we do this.

❄ ❄ ❄

ONCE UPON A TIME, authors were spooky, reclusive, mysterious creatures. Okay, maybe not *all* of them, but there were certainly plenty. J.D. Salinger. Harper Lee. Thomas Pynchon.

They didn't need to do author readings, or social media, or show up at conventions, or—well, anything but write.

We spooky weirdo introverts *become* writers in the first place because we don't want to go out into the world and be all social and whatever. And yes, there are exceptions (I'm looking at you John Scalzi), but I think for the most part, we'd rather stay home and write.

I know for my own personal self, my time would have been much better spent staying home and actually getting some writing done, rather than being all nervous, getting dressed up, and going out to read to my husband and my friends (and the bookstore owner's mom). And then buying ourselves dinner.

Bring back the mystery, the magic, the rare-and-preciousness! Make writers invisible again!

We can do it, gang! Who's with me?

The Power of Saying "I Can't"

You know that sweet feeling when you're not sure if you can do something, but you give it a try, and it works out?

Or even, you give it a try and it doesn't 100 percent work out, but you think you can see your way clear to figuring it out, so you practice and research and try again, and you get better at it? And then, after a while, there's a new thing you can do?

So much of my career has gone that way. Even all the way back to my first real job. My boss quit, and the higher-ups asked if I was interested in applying for the position. *No way!* I thought, and politely declined. I was terrified of supervising people, and though I knew a lot of the parts of her job, there was a bunch of other stuff I didn't know. Besides, I was happy where I was.

So they hired someone else, and it was a nightmare. The details are a story for another day, but when we finally got rid of her, I said, "I'd love to take the job."

Now, I wasn't perfect at it, but (to my knowledge anyway) nobody ever added the suffix "-monster" to my name. Like we did the last one.

I'm going to call that a win.

❋ ❋ ❋

THE SAME THING HAPPENED when I went freelance. I love proofreading, so I did it for friends for free, and then a real publishing company offered to pay me real money to proofread a real book. I was excited and terrified, *What the hell do I know about professional proofreading?* But I did it, and they liked my work. I'm still proofing for them today, ten-plus years later.

When I started writing personal essays and publishing them on Medium, I didn't really know what to expect. I'd blogged, back in the days when we all blogged; this was clearly something like that, but also different.

I experimented; I tried some things that didn't work, and didn't do them again; I tried some things that *did* work, and leaned into them. Now it's this nice thing that I do, when I have the time and inclination—I compose a little article, about a thing that interests me, and people read it, and that's just super great.

Some of my articles have gotten more attention than I ever expected (which is even *more* super great); a few of these have led to paid writing opportunities in other places (most super greatest of all!). I leaned into this too, enjoying the wider visibility, the larger platform. (Not that I'm a *household name* or anything, nothing like that; just, actual strangers reading my words, woohoo!)

❈ ❈ ❈

AND THEN CAME AN assignment, an article I *proposed*, on a topic I'm fascinated with—money: specifically, freelancing and retirement—and I jumped into it with gusto. I did a ton of research, both online and asking everyone I know nosy questions about their personal finances.

I assembled all that data, made my point, sweated and strained to get the piece down to the contracted word count; enlisted my husband to help with editing/rewriting; and, at last, sent it in to the publication.

Who eventually got back to me with a *ton* of edits.

Now, edits are fine, in fact more than fine. I'm always a little leery when someone asks for no changes at all to something I've written. A good editor is worth their weight in gold. No matter how good the writer, an editor can always make a piece better.

But these edits...

Well, I was busy, so I didn't get on them right away. I did glance at them, and saw that they wouldn't be quick.

And then I kept being busy. Kept not getting to them. Even glanced at them again, even got started with them...but so many of them were "more research needed here" and "what exactly is the point you're trying to make here" and "need a better source for this assertion" and...

Oh gosh, how busy I was.

Finally one day, I set aside the morning to really, truly, tackle these edits. It was getting embarrassing. And I tried, honest, I did. I did some more research, and read more articles, and rewrote where asked—all the while feeling a sick sense of dread and failure. I mean literally sick: working on this project was making my stomach hurt.

So I pulled back again and really looked at myself, and at the situation. I got honest with myself, despite not wanting to do that—not wanting *so hard* to admit that I couldn't do this.

And then, I withdrew the article.

❊ ❊ ❊

THE PROBLEM FUNDAMENTALLY WAS that I am not a journalist. And that's fine! Journalism is a specific skill set. Journalists study—in school or on the job or both—to learn the ropes.

I've not done that.

I'm a writer: I'll own that, and gladly. I'm a writer of fiction, in several genres; I'm a writer of personal essays, as I am discovering. I am not, however, a reporter who can write a well-researched, well-argued article on business matters—even business matters that interest me greatly.

Now, I could *become* a journalist, if I wanted to. I've pushed myself in the past to learn new things, and I grew in the process and enjoyed picking up new skills, and that's all great.

But I can't do everything. I'm fifty-three years old, and already too busy doing far too many things that I love. I've got more proofreading and copy editing than I can keep up with. I've got several novels going, in various stages of completion; in fact, I've got novel edits sitting in my inbox right now that I *am* excited to get to. I've started a memoir. I want to write more articles on Medium.

I don't even actually want to learn how to become a journalist, too.

❊ ❊ ❊

MY EDITOR AT THE publication was *so* understanding. She made it clear that they're still open to pitches from me anytime, that they've loved my other work, that the door is still open.

I felt such a sense of relief, after my little bout of "failure-shame" died down. And it's helped me learn more about myself.

At a certain level, I can't know what I *don't* want to do unless I give it a try. I mean, some things are clear—I know I don't want to climb Mt. Everest, or program computers, or raise Highland Coos, or become a dentist. But I didn't know what particular kinds of writing I didn't want to do until I tried and "failed."

Because this doesn't actually feel like failure. It feels like refinement: refining my focus. Becoming more fully myself.

Just one more step on this lifelong road to figuring out who I am.

The Headline Isn't the Whole Story

I'm embarrassed to admit this, but I get a LOT of my news from headlines.

But, now that I've outed myself, I'll ask...don't you? I subscribe to two online newspapers (*NY Times* and *Washington Post*) and one print magazine (*The New Yorker*), and I read a lot on Medium, and I scroll through Facebook at least as much as anyone else. I could spend all day doing nothing but reading lengthy articles, or even short ones; instead, I'd say 90 percent of the time I just look at the headlines and move on. If I did read the pieces—even just all the articles that caught my attention—would I be better informed?

Because even an in-depth, well-researched, well-written article is still only part of a story. *Everything ever written* is only part of a story. My husband is currently writing a series of blog posts exploring one small—admittedly key, but still fractional—portion of his life. He has been at it for nearly eight months, and is barely getting into the crux of the issue, and keeps going back to explore aspects he forgot...even while admitting that he's only focusing on a narrow question, leaving out giant parts of his life story.

If a dedicated, thoughtful, thorough writer can only scratch the surface when writing about *his own life*, what does that say for any of us trying to stay informed about the rest of the world?

❋ ❋ ❋

I DIDN'T FULLY APPRECIATE the problem with headline-skimming, though, until I started writing more articles myself. More specifically, when a few of those articles were handed in to publications which edited—or completely replaced—the headlines I put on my own stories.

I'm not going to give you the actual examples, because each time I have had a headline rewritten, that has also meant that my writing was being presented to a much larger audience than I'd have reached on my own. My work was being featured or syndicated, or the article was commissioned in the first place. In case this isn't clear, these are GOOD THINGS, and I don't want them to stop.

So I'll give you a fake example. Let's say I wrote an article about, oh I don't know, our losing battle against garden pests. In this article, I mention the aphids on my roses, the squirrels who eat all the blueberries before we can harvest them, the deer who pulled up the *irises* if you can believe it, and the river otters who invaded our pond and ate all the koi last year. I title the article "The Challenges of Sharing Our Space with Nature."

The article is (dare I say!) witty, balanced, and fun to read, and concludes that there's really nothing to be done about the problem; if we want to live in nature, this is just part of the price.

The article gets picked up for wider distribution. Yay! It gets a copy edit, maybe a new illustration, and…the headline becomes "Why River Otters Are the Devil's Own Creatures, and What You Can Do About It."

❧ ❧ ❧

I GET IT, THOUGH. I understand what a headline is for: to get your attention, to get you to click, to read. And the rewritten headline above isn't entirely *wrong*, exactly—river otters *are* the devil's own creatures—but it's not actually true to the gist of my article, and it's certainly not how I would have put it. Further, my theoretical article contains no actual advice on dealing with the river otters (because this is an unanswered question for the ages). So anyone who did click through is going to be disappointed—if they make it to the end of the article at all.

And yet, even understanding this…I still skim headlines, and tell myself I know what's going on in the world.

Don't you?

The Roads Not Taken

When I was in college, I learned about a study-abroad opportunity, an internship for a publisher of travel guides. They would send you to Europe or South America or somewhere else exciting for four months; you would live there, explore it, and write about it. There would be some training and supervision, but mostly you were on your own.

Learning. Living. Writing.

It sounded *amazing*. I wanted to do it *so badly*. I already had a passion for writing; and at that point in my life, I had never really traveled anywhere, and thought I had a passion to do so. (As opposed to now. I'm so over traveling now, I'm a horrible homebody. If I never had to leave the house again, it would be too soon.)

But…I never even filled out the application form.

Why not?

It's a little embarrassing to admit it now, but it was because of a man. My boyfriend was a sweet man, and he loved me so much. I'd made his life so much better, he told me all the time.

I knew, even before I got home on the day that I'd found out about the program, that he wouldn't want me to go. I already felt the small, sad sense of dread of telling him about it.

But, since I wanted it *so badly*, I made myself bring it up that evening.

I showed him the flier. I downplayed my enthusiasm, shrugged, said something mild like "Oh, look what I heard about today, it sounds kind of interesting, don't you think?"

He looked puzzled, and sad, and worried. "You would leave me to do this?"

I didn't say, "I never said anything about leaving you." I didn't say, "It's only four months, grow up." I didn't say, "You would make me pass up an opportunity like this because of your insecurities?"

I did say, "Well, I'm just thinking about it, is all."

The flier sat on my desk, and the application deadline passed, and that was that.

❀ ❀ ❀

IT'S NOT THAT I was a shoo-in or anything; if I had managed to apply, odds are I wouldn't have gotten it. I didn't have any publication credits, and my writing skills were…shall we say, rather less polished than they are now.

But I didn't even try.

❀ ❀ ❀

AFTER GRADUATION, AFTER THAT boyfriend, when I was engaged to the man who would become my "trophy wife" husband and working at an abusive, low-paying job I just hated, in a fit of desperate frustration I answered an ad for a job that sounded much better. They called me for an interview; the interview went great; they offered me the job.

I wanted to say yes. My would-be team was an exciting, dynamic group of people. Yes, they worked hard—often late into the evenings, and sometimes on weekends. Food would be brought in; deadlines would be made; big stuff would happen and the team would celebrate. And, oh yes, *all that overtime would be paid.* It sounded ideal. (Remember, I was in my early twenties. I would have had the energy for such a thing.)

But…I said no. My soon-to-be husband allowed as how he would be sad to lose so much of my company, while I worked those nights and weekends. (Never mind that his own career demanded exactly that at certain times of the year.) Besides, we wouldn't need that kind of money once we were married; he made plenty.

I did, at least, tell my boss about the job offer (and its salary), and he did give me a bit of a raise and was a little bit nicer for a while.

Yay.

❀ ❀ ❀

I HAVE SO MANY of these examples, and they don't always feature men feeling sad about something I wanted to do, though an uncomfortable number of them do. I'm not actually blaming the men here. They did not, in fact, tell me not to do the things I wanted to do.

I told myself that.

I would go so far as to say that I used "he will miss me, he doesn't want me to do this, I will stay home and preserve this relationship" as an excuse for not taking a chance. Not doing something scary—something challenging and new and different—even if I wanted to do it *so badly*.

"When you *really* want something, you will figure out how to make it happen." That's actually diet advice I got once, but it's true much more widely than in the realm of counting calories and getting one's lazy self to the gym. If I had *really* wanted to go overseas and write for a travel guide, I would have kissed that boyfriend, told him I loved him very much, and filled out that damn application. And if I'd gotten rejected, I'd have sought out other ways to travel and write, not stopping till I'd succeeded.

If I'd *really* wanted a high-stress, high-reward job in my twenties, I'd have done that too.

I know this because I really, really, *really* wanted to become a published writer. I'd always wanted it, but the desire became profound—obsessive—by my thirties.

More on this in a minute.

❊ ❊ ❊

I DON'T FEEL REGRETFUL about those passed-up roads, those forks not taken. I do wonder, though, what would have happened if I had followed them. What if I had gone overseas in college? Would I have found my writing career a lot earlier? Would I have fallen in love with a different culture (or a different man), and stayed?

Or if I had taken that job. Would I have hated it, burnt out; or would I have felt like a high-powered financial success in my own right? How would that have shifted the dynamic of my "trophy wife" marriage? (Would I have regretted losing the time to write?)

I love my life now, though I am always too busy and there's never enough money and something's always broken/in crisis/interrupting me/late/falling apart. I know the path that I did take led me here. Not all the steps along the way were easy, or comfortable, or fun; but they all had to be there, or I would have ended up somewhere else.

But I do wonder, every now and again.

❈ ❈ ❈

So WHEN YOU DO get what you really, really, *really* want: then what?

We humans are creatures of imagination. We can visualize things that don't exist, whether absurd and impossible, like fairies and unicorns and talking giraffes; or merely aspirational, like, oh, becoming a published writer.

As I mentioned, I deeply, madly, *obsessively* wanted to get published. *Anything*, I thought. *If I could publish just **one short story**, it would make all the difference. Just seeing my name in print would make me **so happy**.*

So I worked at it, I worked so hard at it. I wrote, and revised, and submitted, and got rejected.

I worked harder. I revised further, tried new stories, joined a critique group.

Eventually, at long last, I sold a story. *I got published.*

Was it all I imagined? Haha, funny story, that.

❈ ❈ ❈

I MEAN, SURE, IT was at first. When I got the acceptance, I jumped up and down and ran around the house shrieking with glee. That evening, my husband and I went out for a fancy dinner to celebrate, with champagne and everything. Never mind that the dinner and champagne cost far more than the story was going to pay—this was just going to be the first sale in a brilliant career.

While I waited for the anthology to come together, I wrote more stories and sent them out.

Let me tell you, the first rejection after the first acceptance is *brutal.* "What is this bullshit?" you think. "I'm a *published writer!* Didn't they *see* that line in my cover letter?? DON'T THEY KNOW WHO I AM???"

Yeah, well. Turns out, editors don't give a flying banana split whether you've sold one short story about something creepy happening down by the river in Memphis to an anthology being put together by a small publishing house in East Barsoom, if the story you sent *them* doesn't fit what they're looking for.

That was a hard lesson, but I absorbed it and went on. And eventually made more story sales!

Guess what? The first rejection after your *second* sale doesn't feel a lot less awful than the first.

❁ ❁ ❁

THE STORY SALES DID slowly accumulate, and my brag shelf started looking respectable, or at least not pathetic. And yet, I wasn't famous. My stories didn't get nominated for any awards; rejections were still far more frequent than acceptances; and I couldn't get an agent for the life of me.

Because that had been my goal all along, I now realized: I wanted to sell a *novel*. I wasn't really a short story writer; that had been a means to an end. The reason I'd really wanted to sell short stories was to build my pub credits to attract an agent.

(Amusingly, that very first story sale…never actually came to pass. The anthology, and its tiny payment, were delayed and delayed and delayed. Eventually I withdrew the story. It's never been published anywhere.)

I won't belabor the details of the next few years, because you can probably see where this is going…I did, at long last, get an agent! She was a nice lady but she ultimately didn't work out, and we parted ways. And then, at long last, I sold a novel! And it got published! And then another one! And that one even got nominated for an award! And was named one of *Publishers Weekly*'s Best Books of 2014!

And still, I wasn't famous, or even rich.

A writer mentor once described to me the concept of "trading up to a better class of problems," and this is it. The problems he was having then—his high-powered New York agent was having trouble getting his fancy New York publisher to agree to a bigger advance for his new series than they had for his previous one—looked like *pretty good problems* to me.

But my problems—*I've sold dozens of short stories and several novels but nobody's ever heard of me and I'm still not making anything like a living on this whole writing thing*—yeah, Past Me would have given her eyeteeth and at least one big toe for such a calamity.

It's as if your vision shifts when you enter a new landscape. You see things you could only imagine before.

And, as potent as our human imaginations are…they kind of suck at predicting what happens in the real world.

❁ ❁ ❁

I'M SURE BIG SUCCESS changes people…but maybe not as much as we think it does. (I'm having to use my imagination here, though, not being a big success myself; so take this with a grain of salt.) Everything that's happened to me in my life—good and bad—has had its impact on me, has changed me and educated me and (I hope) helped me to grow…but I'm still *me*.

I've long had a "90–10" theory, or even a "95–5" one: that fundamentally, we are who we are. Hard-wired, or laid down far too early in life to unlearn, I don't know; but we have only a relatively small area, that 5 or 10 percent, that we can fiddle with. Our basic personalities, our core likes and dislikes and opinions and tastes and emotional set points, are pretty much what they are.

Now, that 5 or 10 or heck maybe even 15 percent (why not go crazy here) can look huge. I've been a vegetarian hippie and a wealthy trophy wife and a polyamorous party girl and a bookkeeper and a fantasy fiction writer and a secretary and a (failed) realtor. But I was always *me*, throughout those roles. I've always been a reader and a non-arguer and a cheese eater and (once I grew up) a wine drinker and a bit of an introvert, with ticklish knees. And all the stuff underneath that, which I can't even put names or characteristics to: the stuff that makes me who I am.

❊ ❊ ❊

So if I somehow break out and become a huge literary success, I feel pretty sure that I won't just sit there basking in the pride and delight of my own mighty accomplishments as I gaze upon my brag shelf laden with glossy, best-selling tomes. (Okay, I totally will for a few minutes, but then life goes on, does it not?) I'll be doing the next thing, and the next, and the next. Writing the next work; dealing with the "better class of problems" that will inevitably pop up.

I'm fine with that. I mean, it's all been good so far—even when it hasn't.

It's led me here, after all.

It's Weird that You're Reading This

I mean, it's weird to write, at all. Isn't it?

I'm alone in my room here, typing words with my fingers—words that I hear in my head—imagining "you," my reader...reading these words. Hearing them in *your* head.

Hi.

Forgive me for stating the obvious, but...this is kind of magical.

❀ ❀ ❀

I READ ALL DAY long. I mean it: *All. Day. Long.*

I'm an editor by profession—copy editor, proofreader, line editor. And I'm a writer, by second profession. Plus, I read for fun, believe it or not; at the end of the day, I read without getting paid for it. Reading is pretty much my favorite thing to do.

Many of my friends are writers. I'm reading a book by a friend right now; I can hear his voice in my head, as my eyes move across the page. I can almost see him smile when he reads the funny parts. It's a great book, about fairies and gnomes and magic and a world gone awry, in clever and amusing and painful ways.

Oh, and I'm editing a book by another friend right now, and I can hear *her* voice in it as I read. This book is about families and betrayal and desire and deception and love and honesty and loss and the beach. And a million other things. It's breaking my heart. I sent my friend an anguished text last night, when I got to a particular moment. She just sent back a smile.

160

For work, I recently finished a book about a terrible childhood; and a book about climate change; and a book about identity and tech and the future; and a book about an evil clown; and a book about communicating more clearly; and a book about alien civilizations and universes outside of the universe; and a book about weather. On deck, I have a book of stories about monsters and ghosts and danger. At least, I think so—I haven't started it yet, so I'm not entirely sure.

I understand that we, as humans, have the ability to conceive of ideas in our brains, and write those ideas down, so that they are conveyed to other humans, humans that we may never meet. I understand further about the internet—that these words will fly off into a magical realm and may never see paper—that other humans on the other side of the planet might see them, moments after I hit "publish."

I get all that. And yet. I still, sometimes, am struck by this.

❊ ❊ ❊

I AM "INTROVERTED," BY which I mean that I really like people and also that being with people makes me tired. Particularly if—no, actually, it's really as simple as that. People, in my space with me, make me tired. I recharge when I'm alone.

But I really like people, I do. I even love some people; quite a few, actually. I would be sad if there were no other people in the world.

(Unless all the people *really insisted* on *always* making eye contact when we're talking.)

I love to communicate with people.

WRITING IS AN AMAZING WAY TO COMMUNICATE WITH PEOPLE.

And yet. Here I am, alone, writing these words. The thought that other people…are going to read these very words?

Ooh. That's…weird.

❊ ❊ ❊

IN FACT, THAT WAS *so* weird that I stopped writing this essay after that last line and walked away from it for a few days. I wrote a fairly impersonal piece about how to get started doing freelance copy editing, and did more paying work.

Is this a shyness? I don't know, I don't think so; I write many more personal and vulnerable things and publish them.

But somehow, really visualizing the world peering over my shoulder, imagining you all *in here*, in my little writing cave—it scared all the words away, for a bit.

You're not here, though, are you? You're in your little reading cave, whatever that looks like.

And my words are running through your head. If you know me, you might even be hearing my voice.

Hi.

We're not alone. We might be by ourselves, but we're not alone.

I think that's wonderful.

Island Life

My Cassoulet Obsession

I can pinpoint almost to the day the first time I ate cassoulet. It was the month of September, 1994. It would be the third week of that month, within a few days one side or the other of the 18th.

I know this because my now-ex and I were in Paris for our one-year wedding anniversary.

It was the day we landed, and "jet lagged" hardly begins to describe it—it's a looooong flight from San Francisco to Paris. We landed in the morning, and we weren't going to be able to check into our accommodations until much later in the day.

So we had the brilliant idea to just walk around Paris all day—lugging all our stuff—hoping the excitement would stave off exhaustion.

❀ ❀ ❀

IT *SORT OF* WORKED. I had never been to Paris before; he had only been briefly, many years prior, on a trip where he had no control over the itinerary.

We took a taxi from the airport to the Île Saint-Louis, right in the center of the city, and began exploring. It wasn't long before we needed sustenance. We found an adorable, quintessential Parisian café, went in, and studied the menu.

Oh, sorry, *la carte*.

I was trying **so hard** to be sophisticated. You see, this was only one year into my being a trophy wife. I knew I didn't belong there, but I wanted to belong there, and damn it, I was going to try.

I'd taken one year of high school French, plus a *lot* of Spanish; I didn't understand how a simple café *carte* could be so bewildering. Plus, I was exhausted, so any brain I had wasn't functioning all that well. And I was far too embarrassed and self-conscious to ask for an English-language menu, or for any help.

I saw a word that looked vaguely familiar. "Cassoulet." That must be French for casserole, right? I like casseroles. I ordered it.

❋ ❋ ❋

WHAT CAME FROM THE kitchen was the most amazing creation. A big hot dish of creamy white beans, smothered in various meats and sausages and—oh my god, that wasn't chicken, it had to be *duck*—all under a crunchy-savory crust. It was rich and incredible and hearty and I ate up every bite of it. (This was before I had to work so hard to stay trophy-wife thin; I was pretty young then.) (Plus, we were on vacation! In Paris!)

And then I was sick for three days.

I mean, not *sick* sick, just…vaguely uneasy in the tummy. I probably hadn't ever eaten anything so rich in my entire life, and my system just had no idea what to do with it. I grew up vegetarian; though I'd been eating meat for a few years by then, I'd never eaten anything remotely like that cassoulet.

The rest of the trip is kind of a blur, culinarily. Oh, I remember the basics: croissants ("*chaud, s'il vous plaît*") and café au lait at the corner bar every morning; ice cream anytime; red wine and dry white wine and kir; discovering that we liked bistros better than stuffy restaurants.

But that cassoulet. Oh, that cassoulet. I never forgot it.

❋ ❋ ❋

AND I NEVER HAD another one quite like it. We didn't ever go back to that first café—I guess my husband hadn't liked what he'd gotten, whatever that might have been. We traveled to France a number of times after that anniversary trip, and I tried again, but nothing ever exactly matched up.

Forget ordering it in the U.S. I tried a few times, when I lived in Portland, Oregon; my now-husband and I had a favorite restaurant there that served very authentic French food, including crepes and *salade niçoise* and chicken cordon bleu and all that—but the few times they had a cassoulet special, it was…not right. A skimpy portion of undercooked white beans, a sad little sausage, a dry duck leg, all arranged on the plate as though they'd never met before that moment, and weren't sure what they were supposed to do with one another. NOPE.

❀ ❀ ❀

Now my husband and I live on an island, and we're learning to make so many things for ourselves. Lemon curd; ice cream; shrub; almond cake. I can roast a chicken—good ole Costco rotisserie chickens are an hour ferry ride plus a half-hour drive away.

He bought me a cassoulet cookbook a few Christmases ago. It's a lovely book, gorgeously illustrated, and tells the story of every ingredient and every piece of equipment in loving detail.

From this book, I learned about the *cassole*, the One True Vessel for making cassoulet. It must be deep, and wide—wider than it is tall—and made of thick clay, capable of holding heat; and it must have two handles, and a small pouring spout.

Several lengthy searches, both online and in brick-and-mortar stores, have yielded up the result that if we want to own such a vessel, our options are: 1) Go to France and buy one from the One True Vessel Makers, or 2) Commission one from a local potter and hope for the best.

Once I explored all that, I sort of gave up for a while.

But then, I joined a mail-order bean club.

And in my first shipment came…cassoulet beans. Beautiful, creamy white Tarbais. "Classic Cassoulet Beans," read the label.

Surely, it was a sign.

Right?

❀ ❀ ❀

So I went back to the lovely book, and was again daunted. I made the caballero beans from my shipment, and then the black-eyed peas, and some popcorn.

I looked at the bag of cassoulet beans.

I thought about it. I read the posts in the bean club's Facebook group.

And…someone posted a recipe for "Confit Chicken Thigh and Andouille Sausage Cassoulet." I looked it over carefully. I'd already seen other people mention how chicken thighs work well in the Cassoulet Universe. I like chicken thighs; they're one of my favorite meats to barbecue.

I thought, *I could make this.*

❀ ❀ ❀

So I did.

I made the chicken confit part mid-week. (Believe it or not, our island grocery store had a jar of juniper berries. They were eight dollars, but hey! Now I can make gin; the confit only needed four berries.) Then I stuck it in the fridge.

Last night, the rest of the story began. I got out my pots.

Four of them.

I cooked the Tarbais beans in our big red dutch oven. I probably over-cooked them—I had pre-soaked them, not realizing how much faster they would be than the caballeros. Oh well. Probably not a disaster.

We have a smaller red/orange dutch oven, which is where I made the chicken confit.

Then there's an old oval hand-me-down brown dutch oven. This was where the whole business was going to go, when it went into the oven.

And the fourth pot was more of a skillet, containing some of the fat from the confit, ready to fry up the onions and garlic and tomatoes and beans and etc.

(The tomatoes were a very funny prank, actually. "Add tomatoes, crushing with your hands," the directions say. Ha! ha! I crushed four canned whole tomatoes with my hand. Three crushed fine; the fourth bathed me in tomato juice.)

After I cleaned up from my tomato bath, I marched forward. I simmered, I preheated, I nestled. Soon, my concoction was ready to go into the oven.

And then we waited.

"It's smelling very good down there," my husband remarked, when I went upstairs to tell him dinner would be ready soon.

"I sure hope so!"

It came out of the oven looking gorgeous. Sizzling and fragrant, the bread crumbs making a nice golden crust, the chicken skins crispy: *Oh*, it looked good.

And nuclear-hot! We let it rest a bit while he made a salad.

When we dished it out and took it to the table, it looked just perfect. You couldn't tell any more that the beans were overdone; it had all come together in a perfect-looking harmony.

The proof, however, would be in the tasting.

❊ ❊ ❊

Reader, it was *amazing*.

No, it wasn't the dish I had in Paris in September 1994. Chicken is not duck; my oval dutch oven with the silly 1960s-graphic lid is not a *cassole*; I am not a Frenchwoman who has been making this dish—from beans I grew in my garden and birds I raised myself—since I was a girl.

But, oh, oh, oh, was it good.

It was hearty and warm and rich and soothing and delicious…and my husband loved it as much as I did.

We're having the rest of it tonight. I added more bread crumbs and put it back in the oven; I can smell it now, ready to pull out and scoop nuclear-hot onto our waiting plates.

Sadly, I used my entire supply of Tarbais beans on this dish. You can be sure I went online to my bean purveyors last night, intending to order more; alas, they are sold out. (So I ordered more black-eyed peas and more caballeros, because of course I did.)

❋ ❋ ❋

THE EXPERIENCE OF A dish, as I am not the first nor even the hundredth or thousandth person to point out, it grows in your memory; it takes on larger-than-life proportions; it comes to stand for all the things that were happening in your life when you ate that notable dish, things generally and specifically; my first cassoulet on the first day of my first trip to Paris on the anniversary of my first year of marriage to a complicated man who wasn't a bad man but who ultimately (and probably always) was not the right man for me: that cassoulet can really no longer be said to be about white beans and poultry (however amazingly confit-ed) and sausage and lengthy skillful stewing and seasoning and baking, and perfectly turned out, alongside a glass of sturdy red wine.

No, for me, cassoulet is all the hope of that marriage, of that new life that I was never going to fit into but *damn it* I tried; it's the desire to be the kind of person who travels to Paris, learns Paris, knows Paris—but mostly because that somehow *meant* something to me, something that was going to make me more okay in the eyes of other people. "We're going to Paris." "I bought this jacket in Paris." *Going to Paris* is more than just getting on a plane and flying to another place. *Going to Paris* is not a thing that hippie kids who grew up poor get to do. (At least not like we did, my wealthy husband and I.)

I mean, Paris is marvelous, and I would love to go back someday; but *going to Paris* meant something else entirely. Something aspirational, yet always just out of reach.

Cassoulet was all that stuff, but it also was just about the yummiest thing I'd ever eaten. As a vegetarian hippie kid, I'd grown up on beans: but this was *beans gone wild*. This was beans and *animal fat*. And someone who knew how to put it all together and make it sing.

For me, reclaiming cassoulet—I won't say conquering it, mastering it—I may never find a *cassole*, I may never go beyond this "riff on a classic cassoulet [which] skips most of the exotic ingredients and elaborate preparation," but reclaiming the astonishing deliciousness, the surprise of that jet-lagged day, my first day in Paris, when I was so sure I didn't belong anywhere in that story—that city, that marriage, that life—but I knew without a doubt that that dish belonged in my belly.

(Even if my belly did grumble about it for three days afterwards.)

My belly is happier now. It's after dinner, the second night; it was at least as good left over and reheated as it was the first night. I belong in this life, figuring out all these things as I can—this marriage, these things I want to learn how to cook, these words I am writing—it's all okay.

"…it's all okay…with cassoulet…"

Who Ever Said We Have to Wear Bras Anyway?

I don't even know where or how I came across the arcane information. I was a hippie child, living with my folks and a bunch of other feral freaks out on a back-to-the-land commune. We didn't have a phone; we didn't have TV or get the newspaper; the internet was decades in the future. We were ten country miles from the tiny town where I went to elementary school. Summer vacation was, for me, like traveling to another solar system; I didn't see anyone from school, ever, between June and September.

And yet. Somehow, some way, before I entered the sixth grade, I knew enough to tell my mom that my new-school-clothes shopping (meager though it was) needed to include a "training bra."

I didn't have breasts. Ha! Not even sort of. That summer, I had developed a sort of smallish lump on the right-hand side, followed alarmingly later by a sort of smallish lump on the left-hand side (and I was SO worried they'd never even out). These lumps were tender and sensitive, and they only encompassed the nipple and areola, none of the surrounding flesh. You could barely find them with a magnifying glass. A thin T-shirt would have obscured them completely.

And yet. I *had* to have a bra.

❀ ❀ ❀

MOM ACQUIESCED, BLESS HER, and my several new items of clothing that fall included a stiff, itchy, ugly white thing that covered my little proto-breasts. No lace. No ornamentation—well, maybe there was a tiny twist of pink fabric where the straps met the cups, meant to indicate a rose or something. Maybe.

But. I had a bra!

❁ ❁ ❁

IT WAS THE FIRST day of school. My sixth first day of school with the same twenty-five kids. A girl I didn't know very well (because I had basically one friend through all those years, because I was a weirdo hippie kid), let's call her May Adamson, was going around the class, whispering to all the girls, making stealthy notes on a folded-up sheet of paper.

At last, May got to me. She leaned in. She whispered, "Are you wearing a … B…A…R?"

Yes, that's right: she misspelled a three-letter word.

Clever me, I knew what she meant. "Yes," I whispered back, and she made a note on her grubby little tally sheet.

I looked over her shoulder as she wrote (probably wondering what else she might have misspelled). Every single one of us was sporting a bra. (Or a bar, I suppose. A bar might actually have been more comfortable.)

Somehow, some way, an entire classroom of breastless eleven- and twelve-year-old girls had known that they now needed to cover their nonbreasts.

❁ ❁ ❁

OVER THE YEARS, MY little lumps grew into actual breasts. For a long time, they weren't especially large breasts—well, they aren't *especially* large even now, but they're bigger than they were when I was in my twenties. As is the rest of my body. But even at my thinnest and smallest-breasted, I wore a bra religiously. It was just part of getting dressed in the morning. I would no sooner think to leave off the bra than I would forgo underpants. *Eww.*

And then—

Well, there's no "and then." I'm wearing a bra right now, even though I haven't left the house today, and have no plans to. *And then she was fifty-two years old and worked at home and saw an article or two online about celebrities going braless and the backlash and the back-backlash and she thought, Wait, why exactly am I wearing this thing?*

It's a sports bra that I'm wearing right now, one so old and saggy that it's basically no support at all. Just a layer of fabric between my skin and my shirt. But it still digs into my flesh a bit. I still have marks on me when I take it off at night.

I almost never wear bras with lace and hooks and underwire these days, unless I'm dressed up fancy for some reason, although, now that I think of it…*shh don't tell anyone*…I didn't wear a bra on my wedding day, five years ago.

❀ ❀ ❀

I DID SOME RESEARCH. Turns out there's no medical reason to wear a bra, and it's actually pretty awesome to not wear them, and maybe people will notice but that's really on them, isn't it?

I could just…not wear them. It would take some getting used to, I imagine, even going from these nearly-dead sports bras to *nothing*.

There are definitely still times I'd want one. Whenever we go somewhere in our old beater pickup truck, if I don't have the girls seriously locked down in one of my smaller, tighter sports bras, I have to hold them with my hands or it *hurts* every time we go over even the tiniest bump in the road. Those smaller, tighter bras are also the ones I wear when I play racquetball; I don't think I could ever comfortably run, or ride a bike, without support.

But honestly? I haven't ridden my bike in two years. I haven't played racquetball in, hmm, months maybe.

And another thing? The area immediately below my breasts is covered in skin tags—has been for decades. I never even really wondered about it, but guess what one of the major causes of skin tags is? *Being rubbed by clothing*. I had to have one of them removed by a doctor once a few years ago, because it got inflamed and painful.

Yet here I am, wearing these dang things every day.

❀ ❀ ❀

IF YOU WANT TO get really depressed, just try searching "bra" on your favorite stock photo site. Go ahead, I'll wait.

Wasn't that fun? Don't you feel sexy and empowered? (And why so many pictures of asses, hmm?) I almost gave up and snapped a photo of my own floppy little sports bras to illustrate this article with until I found a picture of a grinning young woman holding a potted cactus in front of her chest.

I like her attitude. *Here, look at my prickly cactus and my black nail polish, not my boobs!*

I think I'm gonna go take this bra off, pour a glass of wine, and try to get used to my newfound freedom.

Anniversary

Six months ago today, in the wee hours of the morning, my mother took her last breath.

It was too soon; and she had suffered too long. It was a relief and a tragedy.

It still is.

She was far too young: seventy-three, and vibrant and healthy. Except for the cancer. Just that little detail.

The little details that make all the difference.

❊ ❊ ❊

I'VE DREAMED OF MOM a lot, particularly in the first few weeks after she died. She appears sort of tentatively in the dreams: already sick, and far too thin; but also cheerful, even kind of inattentive. I ask her, Do you have to die again?

She doesn't answer.

❊ ❊ ❊

I WAS THERE FOR her last two weeks. And for chunks of time before that, as well—chemo sessions, surgery recoveries—but those last weeks, when she was truly dying, when everyone knew she was dying…if you haven't lived through such a thing, it's almost impossible to describe it. To convey what it's really like.

Time becomes unmoored. Everything is about what is happening, day by day, moment by moment. Will she eat? Can she swallow? Will she poop? Does she want more morphine? Does she want visitors? Is she asleep? Is that okay?

A month or so before she died, we sat down with my laptop. I asked her questions about her life, typing as fast as I could while she reminisced. I was going to write her life story. She had a very interesting life, and you'd never know it; she held onto "normal, ordinary, nothing to see here" with a firm grip.

We only got partway through the story before she grew exhausted. And by the time I returned, for what turned out to be her last two weeks, she was too sick for interviews. That's all right. I got the parts I hadn't been around for, before I was born; someday I will fill in the rest from what I know, and from relatives.

Not yet, though.

❋ ❋ ❋

DURING MY MOTHER'S LAST full day alive, I copy edited an entire novel for a freelance client. Mom was already in the last sleep; the awful phase of "terminal restlessness" had come and gone, under the coaxing of the good strong drugs the hospice nurses brought. On the morning we woke up to a world without Mom, I typed up the style sheet and sent in the book, after posting Mom's obituary on Facebook, and notifying the mortuary.

The client still doesn't know this.

❋ ❋ ❋

WHAT *ELSE* WAS I GOING TO do in that last day?

❋ ❋ ❋

I PROBABLY DON'T HAVE to make it clear that I loved my mom, and that I miss her terribly, and that we had a complicated relationship. I think that's just the way it is, with parents. She had me so very, very young; I was her firstborn, when she was barely past being a child herself. We were so similar, and so different. (I just wrote that last sentence in the present tense, then had to go and correct it. It's these stupid little things that ambush you.)

When my first husband and I had a terrible fight and he stormed out, and I decided to not sit there waiting for him to deign to come back, but went to Mom's house instead, she sent me right back, wouldn't even let me in. "What if he comes home and you're not there?!"

When I had a hysterectomy in my mid-thirties, she took time off from work to travel hundreds of miles to take care of me when I got home from the hospital, helping me in and out of the shower and putting my clean underwear on me and cooking my favorite dish, her signature enchiladas.

✻ ✻ ✻

WE WERE ALL SUPPOSED to travel to Italy together, to attend the wedding of my cousin—her older sister's son. It would be the first time we would all travel together: Mom and Stepdad, my brother and his family, my husband and me. It was going to be magnificent: Mom and Stepdad were avid, seasoned travelers; Auntie is a spectacular cook and hostess; my cousin and his now-wife are both marvelous, part of the arts scene in their northern Italian city, with access to the very best restaurants that tourists would never find.

But the cancer came back. First Mom and Stepdad, then my brother and his family canceled their trips. My husband and I went, so that Auntie and Cousin would at least have *some* family representation.

The wedding was gorgeous, the food was all it should have been and more, the light and the wine and the gelato and the sun...

I flew back from Italy and went straight to Mom's, without going home, for what turned out to be her last two weeks.

✻ ✻ ✻

WE DANCED.

That's what I took to calling it, when I would help her out of bed, or out of her wheelchair, or off the couch, or off the porta-toilet. I'd lean down and say, Dance with me. She'd put her arms around me and hold tight while I'd stand us up, lifting her without pulling on her. We'd rock from foot to foot, slowly dancing her into position, wherever she was headed—the wheelchair or the hospital bed or the porta-toilet or, sometimes, a chair out on the deck, where she could enjoy a few minutes of sunshine. I danced her across the room, if no one else was there to position the chair, bed, toilet, wheelchair.

No one else could lift her like I could. Stepdad was too strong; he could easily lift her with his arms, but that would hurt her frail body. Even the marvelous attendant, sent by hospice three times a week to bathe Mom in her bed (and who delighted in asking me direct, personal questions about who was married to whom, and for how long, and how that was all working out), would have me position Mom before she began working.

You know the end is coming, but you don't know exactly when. When pressed, the hospice nurses would shrug, then guess, and then shrug again. They've seen it all. Some people cling to life with all their waning strength; some slip away faster than anyone expects.

You don't know when the last things have happened, until it turns out they have. The bathing attendant was going to come back on Friday, but Wednesday was the last bath. We refilled a prescription that we never opened.

I didn't know that last porta-toilet trip was my last dance with Mom.

❀ ❀ ❀

STEPDAD HAD THE BRILLIANT idea of setting up a FaceTime call aimed at her bed, when she was in her last sleep. We sat out on the deck after the hot summer day became the warm summer evening, and drank our beers, and watched Mom on the phone. Told her we loved her.

We think she heard us. We have to believe that.

❀ ❀ ❀

SIX MONTHS. NOT NEARLY long enough to absorb this.

I miss you, Mom.

I'm So Glad You All Are Enjoying Pot So Much

Recreational marijuana is currently legal in eleven states—including the one I live in—plus Washington, D.C., and Guam. This is *great*. I hope it spreads to all the rest of the states. I think it was dumb and pointless, expensive and futile, a complete waste of public resources to have ever criminalized pot in the first place.

Yes, I know it's not utterly harmless. But neither are lots of other legal things, like sugar and cars and alcohol and oh yeah what about guns.

Our laws would look very different if we banned things on a strictly rational basis, ranked from most harmful to least harmful. That isn't how we do things, of course. So I'm glad that we at least seem to be coming to our senses about marijuana.

Even so, it's not for me.

❋ ❋ ❋

I grew up with the fragrant, familiar aroma of pot all around me. My parents were counterculture back-to-the-land hippies. They smoked pot even before we moved to the Land; they grew it once it felt safe enough to hide a plot on our remote property, even in the days of scary helicopters that would fly over the Mendocino County backwoods looking for pot gardens to burn and hippies to bust.

My dad kept his home stash in a frisbee on the shelf by the cassette tape deck (run by a car battery, as we had no electricity). Stems and seeds and leaves all together, plus rolling papers and matches. I'm sure the adults didn't just sit around rolling and smoking joints all day long, but I do remember plenty of that. I loved the smell then, and I love it now. I loved how mellow everyone got, and how giggly. How cheerful.

By high school, I had tried pot a few times myself. It didn't have the lure of the forbidden, the unknown; but I was a teenager and eager to do whatever my friends were doing. Smoking it was all right, though it didn't seem to do a whole lot for me.

Eating it was terrible. I had a couple of seemingly endless, deeply uncomfortable, almost hallucinatory experiences after pot brownies (which I ate on purpose) and pot-laced spaghetti sauce (which someone had thought was a funny joke to spring on unsuspecting victims).

By the time I got to college, pot had gotten so strong, one hit off a joint or bong was enough to send me close to that *I'm way too stoned* place. My skin would get oversensitive, almost sore; I'd become cranky, and starving, and exhausted.

"I only smoke pot grown by women," one friend told me. "Such better energy."

"Hash is mellower," other friends would say. "Try hash."

"Try hash laced with opium!"

"You all go ahead," I would say. "I'll just drink this-here wine."

❈ ❈ ❈

I HAD A BOUT of cervical radiculopathy earlier this year. It was indeed ridiculous; and very painful and debilitating. My shoulders felt tight as rocks, at first. Then I had awful pain and numbness radiating down my left arm—which grew weak as a kitten's. Nothing would ease it—I was taking so much ibuprofen, my stomach was rebelling, and it wasn't helping.

Try pot, try pot, try pot, everyone urged.

So I went to our little dispensary here on the island and bought a tincture to take with water, and a gel to rub on the sore spots. I did those things, following the instructions carefully.

It got *worse.*

I still had all the pain, but now I had paranoia and anxious tension on top of it. I'm told that's not possible, given the formulations I was taking; but, there it was. I *hated* it. I couldn't sleep for the pain, and finally ended up in Urgent Care, where I was given steroids and opioids.

I'm no fan of opioids (though I wish we could all take steroids forever, alas); but that did the trick. Finally I could function again, and I could sleep at night, and eventually, eventually, the inflammation died down, I didn't have to have surgery, and now I feel pretty much normal once more.

I gave away the pot-stuff.

❊ ❊ ❊

I MUST HAVE INHERITED this from my mom. She did smoke on the Land, but I don't remember it ever being a big thing for her. When she stopped being a hippie, she gave up pot without a backwards glance (and loved her wine).

Last year, when she was in hospice the weeks before she died, uncomfortable and anxious and barely able to eat, everyone encouraged her to *try pot, try pot.* The local medical dispensary was visited; tinctures and gummy bears and potions were brought home.

She *hated* them. They made her feel worse—paranoid, more anxious.

I get it.

❊ ❊ ❊

I'M THRILLED THAT IT's legal (in the states that it is). I have family members and dear friends who regularly enjoy pot to this day. I like smelling it on them—it smells sweet and cozy, like home—and I'm glad they don't have to buy it illegally or give even a thought to getting into any kind of trouble over it. I think pot plants are beautiful (they smell amazing too).

But I'll just be sitting back here, enjoying my glass of wine.

My Name Is Shannon, and I Have a Shrub Problem

I love making shrub—flavor-infused vinegar syrup. It's all the rage at farmers' markets and in trendy bars and restaurants. Mix it with sparkling water and it's a delicious non-alcoholic beverage; mix it into any number of cocktails and it's, well, an even better cocktail.

You can also add it to salad dressings, cook it into chutneys, pour it over ice cream (no, really, try it, it's AMAZING).

It's expensive to buy—we were paying fifteen bucks and up, for small bottles—but, as it turns out, so easy to make! Vinegar and sugar, plus whatever flavoring strikes your fancy. Put it all together in a mason jar in the fridge, shake a few times a day for a few days...and voila! A little flavor explosion, ready to decant into fun bottles and make pretty labels for.

So...a hobby was born.

In the last year alone, my husband and I have made: strawberry, strawberry-balsamic-black pepper, basil, mint, basil-mint, ruby grapefruit, Meyer lemon (both with and without zest), lavender, peach, nectarine, blueberry, blackberry, lemon lavender, honeymoon melon, blueberry-basil, and I know I'm forgetting at least half a dozen.

It all started when we moved away from Portland, Oregon, to an island an hour's ferry-ride from big-box stores and affordable farmers' markets and, well, much of the rest of civilization. It's expensive and time-consuming to go to the mainland. *Hey*, we decided, *let's figure out how to make stuff!*

So I bought a book on making shrubs. I ordered adorable bottles by the dozen. And then the labels! Fortunately, my husband is an artist, so I didn't have to pay a designer for excellent labels…printed on label stock on his fine art printer…

Were we saving money? Um, *maybe…*

But hey, great news—I got invited to buy a table at a community flea market/craft fair. Perfect! I had to ramp up my inventory, of course; I made a dozen bottles of my four most popular flavors. They sold very well! To this day I run into people in town who call me The Shrub Lady.

Ooh, I thought, *I should do this as a business! Sell at the farmers' market on the island! Tourists will love it! Locals too!* I ordered several more cases of bottles. We bought another color printer, and labels, and toner. We experimented with more flavors—it was summer by now, and all the stone fruits and berries were coming along, bursting with flavor and juice.

And then I researched the legal requirements in our state for getting a "cottage kitchen" certification…*that* took the wind out of my sails. *Okay,* I thought. *We'll just make them for our own private use, and to give to friends.* (Plus that one lady who bought some lavender shrub at the flea market last spring, got my contact info, and orders a bottle or two every few months. We meet at the post office in town and exchange goods for cash, like good little bootleggers.)

The fridge is FULL, we realized: *we will stop making any more until we finish what we've got on hand.*

But then…whoops, here's some fruit that's overripe and we don't want to throw that away, do we? And ooh, these peaches are *amazing,* must buy more and preserve them somehow. And we could use a little more basil shrub, I used the last of what we had in that herbal cocktail…

So, um, yeah. My name is Shannon, and we now own a second full-size refrigerator in the garage.

I have a shrub problem.

The Absolutely Liberating Delight of Being a Woman Over Fifty

I'm fifty-two years old and I weigh more than I ever have in my life and my hair is going grey and I work at home wearing yoga pants and REI fleece and sports bras that have lost their elastic, and I'm freaking *gorgeous*.

Admittedly, my eyesight is getting that soft blur, so everything looks prettier than it really does. When I look in the mirror, I just don't see the detail I used to. "No spinach in the teeth—belly isn't poking out from under my shirt—good to go!"

In all seriousness, though, the truth runs a lot deeper than just blurry vision. It's not that I don't *care* how I look, but…well, okay, I actually kinda don't. At some deep, inner level, "how I look" has lost its meaning for me.

I was recently reminded of this as I read an earnest article (I won't provide identifying details—I know she's only trying to help) about the tyranny of waxing and shaving all those tender intimate areas…not to mention, um, *sparkles*? Seriously, don't google this if you're faint of heart.

Oh, am I glad to be over fifty.

❋ ❋ ❋

I USED THE KEYWORD "beauty" in my search for an illustration when I first published this article online. Up came a bunch of pictures of lovely young women, of course, and SO MANY pictures of makeup.

Makeup! Heh. I haven't worn it at all in over a decade; I only did so occasionally for at least a decade before that. Mascara was the last thing to go. I have always had the thinnest, nothing-est eyelashes; I painted on eyeliner and brushed on mascara for much of my teenage and young-adult years. Of course half the time I would promptly forget five minutes later and would rub my eyes, smearing it, and then have to apply it all over again. Not to mention the hassle of removing it before bed every night.

I've never been able to wear lipstick. I love how lipstick looks, and I have all the envy for those of you who can keep it where it belongs, not chew it off or leave it on everything you eat and drink and kiss. It's Chapstick for me, always has been.

I haven't even gotten my hair cut in, hmm, I can't remember how long. I wash it every other day, then shove it behind my ears while it dries, or give it a messy braid; later, I find a scrunchie when it starts to bother me. The other evening, I took out the scrunchie in front of newish friends (the wife and I were comparing our grey); the husband expressed astonishment that my hair falls nearly to my waist. "I've never seen your hair down! Wow!"

There was a time in my life when I would have sought that male attention. Just as a matter of course—not from having any designs on that, or any, particular man. In my younger years, it was as though I did not exist until a man noticed me; and I was desperate to exist. Now it was like, *Oh, huh, yep,* and I scrunchied my hair back up again.

❀ ❀ ❀

EARLY IN MY TEENAGE years—thirteen? fourteen?—I noticed a little tiny broken blood vessel on the bridge of my nose. It was red and ugly. I covered it with a concealer stick and brushed powder over that. Powder I was convinced I needed anyway, because of the oiliness of the rest of my nose.

(Oily noses! Oh save us all from the deadly scourge of oily noses!)

I was a victim of that awful headspace, being so convinced that EVERYONE NOTICES. And that IT MATTERS. That everyone is a) paying such close attention to you and b) judging you for any imperfection. That's a real thing, that conviction; I don't mean to minimize it. Even though, everywhere else *except* in that self-conscious mind, it's basically bullshit. Nobody ever noticed that broken blood vessel—and even if they had, they wouldn't have cared. Yet I carefully covered it with makeup for *years.* Convinced that it shone like Rudolph's headlight-nose.

Guess what? IT'S STILL THERE. (Though I had to put on my reading glasses and turn the light on bright and really lean into the mirror to see it, just now.)

I worried about so much more than that broken blood vessel. I blow-dried and curled my hair just so, and fretted when the weather messed it up; I not only worried about my clothes, whether my outfit was perfectly coordinated and whether it accentuated or concealed all the body parts that should be noticed or obscured, but I also felt compelled to pay attention to when I had worn this particular outfit last. God forbid I should repeat it too soon… (Lest the world end?) And of course I kept SUCH careful control of my weight when I was younger, to the point where I overtipped the balance for a while and was weirdly underweight (though a diligent program of ice cream and wine eventually rectified that).

I just…I just can't find it in me to care about all that anymore.

✳ ✳ ✳

IT GOES FURTHER THAN just no longer being obsessed about how I look, how much I weigh. I believe I really *do* look good, because I'm an awesome human being who is happy and smart and creative, and who has something to say, something to contribute. I *belong* here; I believe that, now, in ways I never did before. Frankly, taking up more space—literally and metaphorically—doesn't seem like the end of the world to me. It's kind of cool, in fact. No: it's *entirely* cool. It's a tangible declaration of my right to be here.

I not only tried to be so *pretty* when I was younger, I tried to be so *small*. I strove to be a tiny decorative ornament. A very quiet one.

Ugh! I want to go back to my younger self and give her a huge hug and a tumbler of blood-red wine and a giant slice of German chocolate cake.

And then tell her that she's okay no matter what she decides to do with the wine and the cake.

(Though she should consume those good things, take them into her hungry little body. Come on.)

✳ ✳ ✳

AS I MENTIONED, I learned so early in life to seek, to *crave,* male attention and approval. Like, before I was ten. Was it because of my parents' divorce and the subsequent absence of my beloved father? Was it because I'm a Scorpio and destined to be sexual, to dance that dance of the body and its lures? Was it because of our shitty culture and its terrible messages about girls and women and our bodies and our worth? (Was it all of the above, and more?) Who knows? But it was there, and it was mighty. Pervasive. I worked hard to be desirable, in the ways that made sense to me, according to the rules I was taught. I tried.

It felt so *important*. Vital. I don't even think I really thought about it, certainly not like this. It was like the need for food and water and air: just there. The rule that I had to be a well-put-together object of desire.

I'm so not feeling that now. I'm fifty-two. I'm happily married, which undoubtedly has *something* to do with this degree of freedom I feel from the need for male approval; but I've been married twice before, and—though those marriages ended—they were both happy for a while, at least. Yet even in those good times, I never stopped primping and fussing and worrying.

It was as though I could only see myself reflected back in the male gaze.

If a man wanted me, then I had value. I was worthy. I lit up when I could see the light in their eyes. I felt warm when I could sense the heat of their attraction.

In fact, for the longest time, I didn't even understand my own sexuality, the desires of my own body, the lusts in my own heart. I was so reactive, I thought the hottest thing was a man who found me hot.

I've learned a thing or two about myself in the last decade or so. For example, I learned about the male body. That I could want it, could reach out and touch it. Sex is about so much more than *his* hands on *me*.

It's heartbreaking that I could have gotten into my forties without understanding all of this. Better late than never, I suppose.

❃ ❃ ❃

IF I AM BEING perfectly honest here (and I do try to do that), I must admit to an ambivalence, one that is less about my appearance in general and more about the weight gain specifically. I actually do want to be healthy. I'm *not* 100 percent thrilled to be heavier than I've ever been. (Most of my favorite clothes don't fit, for one thing.) I gained about thirty pounds over the last year, as I saw my mother through cancer surgeries and treatments, and hospice, and the eventual end of her life. There were so many reasons for that weight gain…emotional eating, comfort eating. Being too busy and too stressed to focus on healthy living.

In a women's magazine decades ago, I read the best metaphor for keeping to a diet and exercise plan: it's like holding a beach ball underwater. It's not *hard*, in and of itself, particularly once you get the hang of it; but you can't ever let go of the focus on it, or the beach ball pops right up out of the water.

I am normally a person who exercises regularly—even if I'm eating whatever I want (and letting that beach ball pop up and bounce away down the sand)—but for about a month now, I've been sidelined by a severe pinched nerve in my neck that has sent me to the emergency room twice and has kept me either in awful pain or on strong drugs. I've managed a walk most days, but that's about it—no swimming, no weights, no racquetball.

I would much rather be in good health—no matter what I weigh or what I look like—than be suffering through this. And I have no idea how much the accumulated stress, and grief, and general out-of-shape-ness has contributed to the pinched nerve. But I do know that everything works better when I'm in better shape.

※ ※ ※

Even so. I don't dread getting older. Yes, I'm dealing with the aches and pains and pinched nerves and diminished abilities, not to mention some weighty, profound losses; but each decade, on balance I've gotten, well, better. Happier, more solid, more comfortable in my own skin.

I took up yoga when I turned thirty, and though my thirties were fraught in many ways, that's also when I picked my writing back up, after abandoning it in college. I grew so much in my thirties.

Not long after I turned forty, my life got *really* fraught for a while, when I blew up my marriage and career and everything and started down a different path altogether. And my forties were *great*. That's when I began taking my writing truly seriously. When I first got published. And when I really began to figure out who I was, who I wanted to be, and who I wanted to spend my life with.

After I turned fifty, my husband and I made another big change, moving out of a city to a lovely, sparsely populated island at the edge of everything. And—despite the challenges—my fifties are already giving me some of the greatest gifts I've ever received.

Including this proud, comfortable, satisfied delight in who I am, and in this body that contains me. A delight which sits right alongside the strong desire to keep learning, keep growing, keep challenging myself—body and mind. To keep an open heart. I've been wrong so many times before; I've changed so many directions that I'd once been quite certain about. I'm entirely prepared—even eager—to do so again.

I look forward to getting smarter, and more grounded, and (who knows?) maybe even wiser as the years go on. I am excited to grow older—to read all the books that haven't been written yet; to meet new young people with new ideas that challenge and startle me (*and* to be free to reject them for myself, especially if they involve sparkles anywhere inside my underwear). I can't wait to taste foods I've never heard of, to travel to places I wouldn't have dared to as a young woman, to hear music crafted by minds as yet unborn.

And to gaze into the mirror at a radiant—if blurry—crone smiling back at me.

No, Really, I Want to Be in the Kitchen Today

WAIT WAIT—BEFORE YOU TAKE away my Feminist card—hear me out.

I think it's great that everybody is offering to help me prepare, and clean up after, this huge Christmas feast—my husband first and foremost (which is only fitting, as he is the one responsible for all the meal planning, shopping, and cooking around here, usually).

But today? For a big holiday meal, with guests, and many hours of hanging around and playing games and snacking and visiting and sipping wine and talking and visiting and more talking…today I really, really want to be in the kitchen.

You know this about me, beloved ones; if you just think about it, you'll understand what I mean. You gave me a pair of "Go away, I'm introverting" socks just this morning, after all. Everyone laughed, knowingly; I did too, gratefully.

I'm wearing them now. They're very cozy, and validating.

❋ ❋ ❋

BEING AN INTROVERT IN a group of extroverts is—well, I like it a whole lot better than I used to, before I learned these words, and learned which one of them I am. In my childhood, up through my twenties and even into my early thirties, I just thought I was weird, or fussy, or shy, or some other way of feeling wrong. Broken.

Learning this language was just the start, though. There was another whole process of learning what it all meant, and learning what my needs are, and *then* figuring out how to communicate those needs to people.

(Whew!)

It's complicated. I actually like people, I like being around people. I like entertaining. I have so looked forward to having you all here for this holiday. I got real excited planning the meal and shopping for it, and thinking about what parts had to be done when, and thinking about how much you all would enjoy it. It was great when you all arrived, and we visited for a bit.

Now it's great that I can come into the kitchen and work on it, while you all stay out there and play a game together.

I like hearing your conversation and laughter, from the next room. I like wandering in from time to time, with my glass of wine, and standing on the edge of the game circle, watching you play for a few minutes before going back to my cooking.

And I appreciate every time you come in and ask if there's anything you can do, but really, you can stop. I'm good. I'm *so* good.

❀ ❀ ❀

I'm GOOD LATER, TOO, when we're stuffed to the gills and everyone's in the living room by the fire, still chatting, talking about games, talking about people we know, talking about people we don't know, talking about (shudder) politics… I'm good here in the kitchen, washing dishes. I actually love washing dishes. I love making order out of chaos. (It's also why I love proofreading, and vacuuming, and weeding: finding all the small imperfections and smoothing, straightening them.) It's nice when my husband dries the dishes and puts them away, especially with a big pile like this; but honestly, I could do that too, if it meant he was keeping the rest of you, my beloveds, out of my hair. Letting me stay in here with my Resting Introvert Face.

❀ ❀ ❀

MY POOR MOTHER. SHE was not an introvert like me, but she did all the planning, shopping, cooking and cleaning up for the holiday feasts. (All the other domestic stuff too, pretty much, always.) She would be stuck in the kitchen for hours, listening to the rest of us in the other room having fun without her, wishing she was part of the party. She would accept a tiny bit of help, but mostly she wanted to do it all herself. It was her early training, her lifelong habit, her way of keeping control of things; I don't even know what all it was. In later years, she would allow me into the kitchen more and more (which this introvert really appreciated—one-on-one interactions are the BEST!), but she was definitely the boss.

I miss her. I would have let her into my kitchen today, happily. Maybe let her make the gravy. Or her famous pressed cookies. She was there in my heart, anyway. This is my first Christmas without Mom, and it was about as hard as they tell you it'll be.

※ ※ ※

As for the rest of you, I'm so happy you're here…over there in the other room. I'll be in to hang out soon. Maybe I'll even join in for one last round of cards before bed.

Notes from the End of Our Third Full Day of Being Snowed In

Everything is fine. Fine, I say!

Sunday evening, we had an early dinner at the house of some friends just down the road. When we got there, the world outside was green and muddy—typical Pacific Northwest winter.

Two hours later, several inches of snow were on the ground and more was falling, fast.

We hurried home and tucked ourselves in, grateful that we'd stocked up on groceries, and gotten the propane tank filled.

Snow is so pretty!

❊ ❊ ❊

MONDAY MORNING THE WORLD was blanketed in white. That's great! So pretty! We took lots of photos through the windows, posted them on social media, and got to work.

Good thing we work at home! In this nice big house! With plenty of supplies!

❊ ❊ ❊

MONDAY AFTERNOON WE GOT tired of trading out the hummingbird feeders every hour or two. Bringing the frozen one in to thaw by the fire; taking the thawed one out. Wiping our feet carefully but still managing to track snow all over the house.

I hadn't seen a hummingbird since early in the morning, anyway. Maybe they've gone somewhere warm to hunker down.

Sure, that's it, that's what they've done.

Boy, is it cold! Even with the fire burning all day, and all the little space heaters cranked up full blast. I used the oven to make dinner, even though it was a packaged thing from Trader Joe's that I could have done in the microwave. Because oven! That heated up that part of the house for a little while.

Why do we have such a big house anyway?

❀ ❀ ❀

MORE SNOW TUESDAY MORNING! So pretty.

Yeah, yeah.

❀ ❀ ❀

TUESDAY AFTERNOON, MY HUSBAND took a two-and-a-half-hour nap. I drank some tap water and got a brain freeze. So I switched to wine.

Thank goodness we have plenty of wine!

Too bad "cellar temperature" is nearly freezing. I should move a few wine bottles to the mantel by the hummingbird feeder.

My racquetball friend texted to cancel our game because the roof at the gym had leaked and ruined the court floor. That's okay, I told her, I'm snowed in anyway.

That evening, my husband and I watched TV under a blanket together. Very cozy. At least the TV is upstairs, and heat rises.

❀ ❀ ❀

YOU'LL NEVER BELIEVE IT, but this morning (Wednesday) there was *even more snow* on the ground.

The ferry system sent me eight emails explaining that they were in Super Emergency Winter Weather Schedule Mode and that all the boats were delayed and all the parking lots and approach lanes were covered in snow.

I took a hot bath. I kept adding more hot water. Add, stir. Add, stir. Am I soup yet?

I haven't been outside in days. I wonder if the mail is getting delivered? It's a half-mile walk to the mailbox—a walk that is usually a highlight of my day. Not today, snowman!

I was supposed to get an Amazon package yesterday, but I called the delivery folks and told them that my recipe book insert pages and hand lotion were not urgent, and that they should please not attempt our road or our driveway—or even the main road—till this melts. They were happy to oblige.

❉ ❉ ❉

I'M GETTING A LITTLE restless. This house feels both too big and too small. I'll be busy working and then suddenly find myself standing before the fridge. Or staring out a window. I haven't exercised in days.

Why am I not getting more work done? I'm stuck inside, and everything is canceled.

Oh look, wine!

In Praise of Social Media

THAT ARTICLE WITH THE phones removed from people's hands is going around again—on social media, where else?—making the point, I guess, that we're all such zombies staring blankly at our phones that we don't pay attention to the people actually in the room with us, and that's making the world so sad and lonely and tragic, it's the end of civilization as we know it, blah blah whatever.

I have some friends, more clever than me (well, that's most of them, but I digress), who have been pointing out other absurd lengths you could go with this idea—"Remove forks from the photos, there's a bunch of people sitting around with their mouths open!" "Remove cars, how hilarious would traffic look!"

Take away *any* key element from *any* picture, leaving the rest unchanged, and see what you get.

❋ ❋ ❋

YESTERDAY EVENING, MY HUSBAND cooked a delicious dinner, and we enjoyed it together, with a glass of wine. Then we finished up a jigsaw puzzle that his mom had started when she last visited; after that, we watched two episodes of a cool new TV show we're into. Then he sat down at his computer to check his email while I brushed my teeth and got into bed.

Once there, I picked up my phone and logged into That Social Media Site With The Blue Letter Logo, and the first thing I saw was a post from a dear friend of ours. She lives in the city we moved away from two years ago, so we don't see her nearly as often as we'd like to.

This post was *magical*. It was a lengthy story, with a bunch of astonishing photos. It was heartfelt and uplifting; it spoke of love and loss and redemption, memory and identity and agency, beauty and the meaning of life, and in such glorious, specific detail, that it was as if our friend had suddenly stepped into the room with me and was talking to me personally. I could hear her voice; I could see her smile.

"Hey," I called out to my husband. "Did you see this post from Esmerelda[1]?"

He quickly found it, and was just as moved as I was. We both left comments; she answered them and we each had a little exchange; and then he came to bed and we talked about Esmerelda, and how meaningful that post was, and what a remarkable person she is.

We're hundreds of miles away from her, we see her maybe twice a year if we're lucky, these days but there she was, reaching out and touching us in our hearts, here on our remote island.

Just because I pulled my phone out and looked at it. Even though there was another person right here in the house with me.

       ❀ ❀ ❀

I'M NOT AN IDIOT, or all that naive. I know the online world is a toxic dumpster fire, and that the ratio of Amazing Esmerelda Posts to anger and trolls and hate and garbage is…unfavorable, shall we say…but also: that was a potent reminder that *we are not alone here.* That this is what social media is *for.* It sucks that it's for other things too, but I just absolutely love that I am still in touch with so many people in my life, who are so important to me, yet so far removed in time and distance.

I have elementary school friends in my virtual world. Friends of my parents, who knew me when I was a child, and who now read my books. People I hired as young college students, decades ago—I love seeing photos of their children, who will be in college themselves any minute now (no, that cannot be true, can it?).

And I have a whole crowd of "industry" friends—fellow writers, many of whom I have not met in person, yet who somehow are still my tribe. They post their memes, and their photos of their pets and that new thing they cooked, and their political opinions, and their triumphs and traumas (in both publishing and 'real life'), and it all makes me feel even less alone.

---

1   *Not her real name.*

I spend all day on this computer, writing and editing and working. I take frequent breaks, pop over to social media—to rest my brain, to stay in touch, to listen to the ongoing conversation.

My husband, whose brain operates differently than mine (he's momentum-based; flitting about from project to break to other project to other break, like I do, would shatter him), relies on me to let him know what our "tribe" is talking about. Just yesterday, in fact, I gave him a list of feminist men to follow, and told him what sealioning means.

I wouldn't know any of that without social media.

❀ ❀ ❀

WHEN I WAS TWENTY-TWO and fresh out of college, I moved back to my hometown—foolishly, it turned out, because nobody I'd gone to high school with was still there. I worked alone, at home; I'd always wanted the luxury of working at home.

I *hated* it. I've never been so lonely in my life, before or since. I was married, but my then-husband worked outside the home, in a job that left him stressed and exhausted. He got home every evening ready to zone out and relax. I, on the other hand, was SO EXCITED to see another human being…I dumped all my pent-up thoughts and feelings and chatter on him the moment he walked in the door.

This didn't go well.

Other than my husband's return, the highlight of my day was the mail delivery. I exchanged letters with a dear friend I'd left behind in the big city—yes, letters, written on paper, mailed via the United States Postal Service, in envelopes, with stamps on them.

I would count the minimum number of days possible until I could legitimately expect a letter from my friend. *I mailed my letter to her on Thursday…she would have gotten it on Friday at the earliest but probably Saturday…then it's the weekend…maybe she wrote me back on Sunday and mailed it Monday…maybe I'll get a letter Tuesday! Or Wednesday.*

Let me tell you. If I didn't get a letter back on Wednesday…or Thursday…then by Friday, I was a wreck. I might have been willing to spring for a long-distance phone call—which, of course, was expensive.

It was 1989. Imagine if there had been even *email*, much less social media.

❀ ❀ ❀

I LOVE THAT THERE'S a whole community of friends right here on this computer, and in my phone. I love that people want to see my photographs of frogs, and sunsets, and mushrooms, and our new deck; that if I think of something funny and post it, people all over the world laugh with me.

Though I live off beyond the edge of the universe (or, at least, the continent), you're all right here with me.

And I'm right there with you. Hi! I see you! Your cat is adorable. And your dinner looks yummy. Can I have a bite?

The Beauty of Fewer Options

This afternoon I drove past our island's one movie theater on my way to our island's one gym. I checked the marquee, like I always do, to see what movie will be playing this weekend. That's right: one movie. And only two showings, one on Friday evening and one on Saturday evening. If you don't like the movie, that's okay, you do still have a choice. You can stay home, saving the fourteen bucks (or twenty-eight, if you'd wanted to bring a friend).

I was excited to see that this week is *A Beautiful Day in the Neighborhood*! Because our one theater is of course not a *first-run* theater. Mister Rogers got here pretty fast, though; that movie hasn't even been out for a month. We had to wait forty-three days after its release to see *Avengers: Endgame*. Somehow, I managed to avoid all spoilers for that whole time.

Go, me!

Before we moved here two years ago, my husband and I lived in Portland, Oregon, a city with many, many movie theaters—first-run, second-run, art-house, IMAX, fancy venues where you can order food and drinks brought to your seat, funky-wonderful old places with couches and beer and pizza—you name it, Portland has it. Any time of day or night, you can choose between dozens, even hundreds of movies. 3-D or regular; at the mall or downtown or in a trendy shopping district; matinee or evening or late night…

We love movies, but we go out to the theater a lot more often here than we ever did in Portland. There were just *too many options* there. We were as busy then as we are now; it was always possible to put off going to see something we wanted to see. Why not? It would be there tomorrow, or next week…and if not, ten more movies we were interested in would be there.

Which we would also fail to go see.

We're not at the theater every single week now—next week is *Frozen 2*, no thank you—but we go two or three times a month, I'd say. The decision is so much easier: Yes or No? If yes: Friday or Saturday?

That's it.

❊ ❊ ❊

I THINK THAT'S WHY I like writing prompts. "Write a story containing an armadillo, a candy cane, and the planet Mars." That narrows down the universe of possibilities so much! Heck, the story practically writes itself.

But, since creativity is so widespread, so unique, and so personal, my writes-itself armadillo-candy cane-Mars story isn't going to look anything like yours. A few years ago, I edited an anthology called *Witches, Stitches & Bitches*. Each story had to contain (you guessed it) a witch, a stitch, and a bitch. What the authors did with those elements varied widely, and hugely entertainingly. No two stories were even sort of alike—in content, tone, style, or details.

And it's why I hate restaurants with huge, multi-page menus. We have a longstanding family joke where the punchline is "pork sandwich!", because that's what my stepmom ordered in bewildered despair after flipping back and forth through the tome of a menu in one of those absurd places, letting the rest of us order while she tried to decide between shrimp tacos and fettuccini Alfredo. "Tacos…pasta…tacos…pasta… pork sandwich!"

We all stared at her. "Pork sandwich? That's even on the menu?"

"Yes! Page seventeen, after the chapter on burgers!"

❊ ❊ ❊

MY HUSBAND IS AN illustrator. Back in the 1990s, he worked in the video game industry, which was in its, if not infancy, then definitely its toddlerhood at the time. Computers were simpler creatures with far less storage capacity and operating speed, and artists were given just a handful of colors and clunky tools to work with.

Even with those limitations, he (and many of his fellow-illustrators) created a lot of beautiful work.

As he said in a recent interview:

"...an extremely limited environment of artistic options and choices made it both possible and necessary for me to take every possible approach as far as it could go—which ultimately meant very thorough exploration of each possibility, which led to lots of 'mastery' of tools, inventive uses and approaches, and perhaps most important, COMPLETION of experiments and goals undertaken. Now, in the age of virtually infinite options and choices, relentlessly evolving and expanding tools, NO option, choice or possibility is ever fully explored, or taken anywhere near 'as far as it can go' toward completion or mastery. ... Limitations are GOOD for CREATIVITY! Having to create the Eiffel Tower with three wooden matches and two foil gum wrappers will require all the exercise your creativity is capable of. Having to create it with whatever you wish to choose from any and every art-supply catalog in the world will just numb your creativity into unconsciousness from overwhelm."

Simpler can be better. More options don't necessarily make things easier.

❉ ❉ ❉

I DO WANT CHOICES; I'm not saying *Make all my decisions for me please, I don't want to think.* Even if the choices are binary—movie or not?—I still want to be able to choose.

And then, of course, to extend our movie example, even though we likely won't go see *Frozen 2* next week, that doesn't mean a movie is off the table entirely: we can stay home and watch one on TV (where there are of course hundreds, thousands, *millions* of options).

Tellingly, however, we've probably watched four or five movies at home all year, as compared with thirty or forty in the theater.

It's *just too hard* to choose a movie to stream.

So I sing the praises of the limited option-set. Give me the short menu with five amazing things on it, not a twenty-page booklet covering eight different cuisines. Give me only one font for these essays (with *Italics* and **bold** in case I need to be fancy!). Give me four colors on a new car—especially if three of them are boring.

Don't make me have to figure out the whole universe every time there's a decision to be made. I might end up ordering a pork sandwich.

My Procedure, Told Entirely in Euphemisms

I had a medical screening procedure today, one of those that they want you to get after you pass your mid-century mark.

It was my first time having this procedure, as I am only a couple of years past said mid-century mark, so this was new territory for me. I thought you all might like to hear how it went, but also, you know, *not*.

So, I will speak of it entirely indirectly.

You're welcome.

❊ ❊ ❊

THIS PARTICULAR PROCEDURE, AS you are probably aware, requires some advance preparation. The day before, one is to cease consumption of solid sustenance, and of liquid sustenance of specific bright colors. The color of the ichor that flows within our veins, most particularly.

Other colors are fine, as long as you can see through them. For that is the other thing: liquids that, for example, are derived from members of the bovine family (and related and/or substitute fluids that resemble same) are off-limits, even if they are so pale as to be color-free.

That part wasn't so bad, although I do prefer to take my morning per-colated caffeinated roasted-bean beverage with a healthy dose of thick bovine juice. So I had tea instead.

I did sort of miss solid sustenance, though not as much as I'd expected to. I greatly enjoyed the extracts of pale fruits I drank, and an essence of brewed bovine bone and connective tissue.

❋ ❋ ❋

THE REAL JOY STARTED in the evening, when various purgatives were employed to render the area to be examined free of its naturally occurring contents.

I likely need go into no detail here—euphemistically or otherwise. Suffice it to say, I enjoyed this part not so much.

❋ ❋ ❋

THIS MORNING BROUGHT A second helping of purgatives, almost as fun as last night's. All was worth it later, though, as the physician's post-procedure notes include the phrase "Prep was excellent."

But we get ahead of our story.

I presented at the institution of medicine, checked in, and, after handing all my valuables to my husband, was taken back to the preparation area, where I was asked to disrobe completely (socks and all) (*why??*) and was shown to a bed. There, the procedure was explained in exhaustive detail, I consented to it one final time, and a thin hollow steel device was inserted into a vein in my hand, so that fluids of both inert and active properties could be introduced into my circulatory system.

My bed was wheeled into the procedure area, anesthetizing fluids were put into my body via the steel device, and the procedure began.

Sadly, I apparently have an anatomical abnormality[2]. The physician needed to take several different approaches to achieve his examination, and I experienced some discomfort, despite the anesthetizing fluids. Happily, once these issues were resolved, he was able to view the entire area under question, and found it to be free of any inclusions or other worrisome matter.

The investigating device and the fluid-delivery device were removed, I was returned to the preparation area, and set free. I spent a good deal of the rest of the day recovering from the muzzying effects of the anesthesia, enjoying a bit of solid sustenance, and returning home. I am experiencing no residual pain or discomfort.

I do not have to have another such procedure for ten more years. You can be certain that I am grateful for that outcome.

---

2   "Sigmoid diverticulosis with significant tortuosity," to be specific. I also get to improve my diet considerably if I don't want big trouble down the road. Whee!

We Are All in This Together

id you know Miata drivers wave at each other when we pass on the road? It's true, we do. I was driving home from a sweaty game of racquetball down at the gym this evening and passed a little white ragtop Miata, and, as I was in my copper-red hardtop Miata, I waved at the woman driving it. She gave a big smile and waved back.

I don't know her; even though this is a small island, I may never see her again. (Maybe she doesn't even live here—who knows? We've been known to have a tourist or two around these parts.) But for that moment, we were kin. Members of the Great Concatenation of Mazda Miata Drivers.

It made me feel good, and it made me reflect on the things that link us together. Big deep fundamental things—family, love, politics. External things—where we work, where our interests and passions are.

And random frivolous things, like driving the absolute bestest car ever made.

❋ ❋ ❋

I FANCY MYSELF AN introvert, and I do indeed enjoy the company of me, myself, and I. Big groups exhaust me; being asked a bunch of personal questions exhausts me; people who like to make a lot of eye contact exhaust me. (And public speaking pretty near PANICS me.)

And yet—my husband and I leave the day after tomorrow for a writing retreat with a double handful of old friends plus a few people we don't know at all, and I am *so excited*. I'm so looking forward to this. Yes, the writing part will be fun, but I can (and do) write at home.

It's the social part I'm looking forward to.

This last summer, we had so many houseguests it made me want to weep; but now? I'm really stoked to spend three nights in a big crazy old barracks house with a bunch of cool folks, cooking together and drinking too much and singing along (very badly) to a guitar.

Also, I'm the one who waved at that Miata-drivin' woman on the road.

So, this whole introvert thing: it's complicated, I guess is what I'm saying.

❊ ❊ ❊

WE ARE ALL PART of the human family. We are all in this together. I love other people, generally and specifically. I love finding things in common, finding a connection. "Oh, you write? Me too!", or "Yes, red wine is the best!", or "I **love** cats!" And of course, "If it's not a stick-shift, it ain't driving."

The other day I posted on social media about having had an ocular migraine that day—only my second one ever. (I knew it as a "visual migraine," that's how rare they are for me.) *So many people* commented: "Me too! I get those!" One friend even posted a picture of what it looks like, and he was exactly right.

It was very cool to feel even just that much less alone.

❊ ❊ ❊

WE ARE ALL IN this together. The human race is an aggregate of individuals who need one another. We cannot live in isolation (I think a clever fellow even wrote a poem about this once upon a time). Even those of us who love to be alone want, need, maybe sometimes even *enjoy* other people.

We cannot survive alone. Solitary confinement is a terrible punishment; shunning can make us crazy.

We search for connection. We need teammates, partners, friends, folks who have our back.

And yet we *are* all individuals, with our own life experiences and history and psychology and weirdnesses. In addition, we can belong to many little tribes, subsets of the great human community, some of which overlap, some of which conflict. My Miata Drivers Cohort no doubt includes people who feel very differently than I do about (oh, say) who might be best to lead our country. Even one of my dearest friends, with whom I have a *lot* in common, thinks that single-payer universal health care would be more expensive than the terrible not-system we have now.

But we are all in this together.

We have to be.

We're a social species. We comfort one another, we take care of our weaker members, we will sink or swim together.

We need each other.

I love being a part of the human community.

I love you guys—all of you; the ones I know and the ones I'll never meet; even the ones who disagree with me or think I'm dumb.

I love racquetball players, I love introverted writers, and I even love people who are indifferent to cats, dislike red wine, and won't even consider learning how to drive a stick-shift. (I *must* love them. After all, I married one.)

The Quiet Radicalism of Asking for What You Want

I feel like I spent the first half—or more—of my life cycling between a) imagining my loved ones could read my mind and know what I wanted; b) feeling hurt and disappointed because they had failed to read my mind and weren't giving me what I wanted; and—sometimes—c) making a *huge and daring effort* to murmur vague, indirect hints about what I wanted.

In bed, at work, with friends—it was just *so damn hard* for me to express what I wanted, never mind what I needed. Not that that stopped me from wanting or needing things. Yet I somehow, very early on, got the message that it was not okay to ask.

As you can imagine, this didn't work out so well for me. And honestly, not for anyone else either. It's one thing to negotiate and compromise when different agendas are in conflict; it's quite another when one person's desires never even get expressed. I'm quite sure that all those friends and lovers and husbands and bosses had no idea that I was silently nursing my wounded dismay about so many unfulfilled wants.

How would they have known? I could barely breathe a word about it.

I haven't read Amanda Palmer's book *The Art of Asking*, but I did watch her TED talk on the subject, and yes, I am talking about much the same thing here as she does. Except I'm not a rock star with a huge following eager to shower me with love and help and money, and my middle name isn't Fucking, and I've never married Neil Gaiman. Other than that, Amanda and me—we're, like, *twinsies*.

Or at least, she's an inspiration to me, a bold and fearless model of knowing what she wants and straight up asking for it.

❁ ❁ ❁

I'VE MENTIONED BEFORE THAT when I got my first job after college, they offered me a disappointingly low salary, but I accepted it without asking for more. A few months later, they gave me a small raise. That was nice. Only much later did I learn that they'd just hired a new secretary below me, and she'd asked for a salary that was higher than what I made. They agreed, and then raised mine to match it, in case we ever compared numbers.

I had probably known that you could negotiate salary, but I hadn't dared to ask.

I know this is gendered. So many of us women were taught not to ask, not to demand, not to make trouble, not to take up any extra space or resources. I have the envy *so hard* for women who somehow escaped this twisted lesson. It's an uphill battle to unlearn it—but I'm working on it.

❁ ❁ ❁

THE FUNNY THING ABOUT asking is, it often works. Right now I'm working on an article for a client where I'm being paid by the word. They gave me a pretty small word-count limit, but as I've gotten into it, I've realized that the story would be much better told at twice that length.

So I asked if we could up the limit.

"Sure," they said.

I almost didn't ask. This is a brand-new client, and I didn't want to look like a bother, a greedy, demanding trouble maker right out the gate. I could have made the article work at the smaller word count. But I'm going to be a lot happier with the piece at the length it needs to be, and—I hope—so will they.

Because that's the other thing about asking: it has to be okay to hear "no." The shorter article would have been fine; if they just didn't have the budget or the space, I would have done the best I could.

My husband and I do this all the time. I can't feel comfortable asking for a backrub if I can't trust that he'll say no if he's exhausted, or his hands hurt, or if he just doesn't feel like giving me one—for whatever reason. Sure, I want that backrub. (I basically *always* want that backrub.) But I don't want him to resent having to give me one, or to bend over backwards taking care of me if he doesn't have the reserves he needs for himself.

I can *try* to read his mind, to guess about his mental and emotional state, his energy. Just like I used to twist myself in knots reading the tea leaves with my ex, trying to figure out if he was angry at me, or just tired from work, or frowning because he'd stubbed his toe, or because the moon was in Gemini, or there was a bad smell in the basement. But it's easier—and so much more honest and straightforward—to just ask.

It's crazy and wild and radical…and I get what I want, and need, a lot more often now.

I Joined a Bean Club and Didn't Tell My Husband

I t all started when I had my first-ever colonoscopy earlier this year and they told me that I was healthy and all, pretty much, but that I should get more fiber in my diet—including more beans.

No, that's not actually true, not about where it started. That's just where it started *this* time.

I actually love beans. My hippie parents were vegetarians during my formative years, and beans were a *very* important part of our diet.

(Plus tofu, of course, and cheese, and way too much broccoli—but this story is about beans.)

❀ ❀ ❀

I DIDN'T MEAN TO not tell my husband. I believe in honesty in a marriage, especially considering that I haven't always perfectly managed the truthfulness-thing in prior marriages. Marriages which ended, for lots of reasons which aren't really part of this story about beans, but the failure of the truthfulness-thing was definitely part of the equation.

Anyway the point is, I feel pretty strongly about telling the truth now, not just in marriage but everywhere. Particularly as it relates to figuring out who I am, and what I want, and what I need—in a relationship, in a friendship, in a diet. Giant things and "frivolous" things, which often, as it turns out, are really not all that frivolous at all.

(Small digression: I really like sausage too, and mushrooms. I still, so many years later, fondly remember a time when my then-husband was out of town, and I got to cook my own dinner, just for myself. I sliced up a sausage and I sliced up some mushrooms and I cooked them together in a pan and I ate that for dinner, and I loved it *so much*. My then-husband would have found that an entirely unacceptable dinner. He would have found the dish unacceptable as even a part of a dinner.

(There are many reasons why I am not still married to that man, and the sausage-and-mushrooms thing is only one of them.)

❁ ❁ ❁

So I joined the bean club last week. It was very spur-of-the-moment. It only has openings every now and then, and I got the word from my friend Chaz that The Time Was Now, and I just…signed up.

I got the welcome letter a few minutes later, and the shipping confirmation a few minutes after that.

Beans were coming! I had actually done this thing. It was happening, it was real.

And yet I still didn't say anything to my husband.

Until this afternoon…I checked the mailbox on my way home from town, and there was that little slip from the post office, "Item too big for your box, come pick it up."

I walked into the house, and my husband was in the kitchen, preparing to head to town himself for shopping and errands. He spotted the slip in my hand and said, "Oh, a package—do you know what it is?"

"Beans!" I cried.

He looked puzzled. As well he might.

❁ ❁ ❁

I explained everything, a little amused, a little apologetic, a little self-deprecating. Yes, we're going to have a box of beans delivered every three months. No, we won't know what they are till they get here. Yes, it was all Chaz's fault…except also *not*.

An important part of how I'm trying to live my life these days—these days, and all the rest of the days I get, if I can manage it—is what I was getting at up above there, a few paragraphs ago. One: I need to figure out what I want, what I need, as specifically as possible. And two: I need to ask for that thing, or demand that thing, or manifest that thing, or whatever—I need to *make it happen*.

This is harder than it sounds, for me. Both parts of that: the getting-really-clear-on-what-I-want part, and the getting-that-information-out-there part.

Maybe this stuff isn't as hard for you. If so, that's marvelous! Celebrate that, appreciate that.

It's been a lifelong challenge for me.

❈ ❈ ❈

MY HUSBAND ISN'T REALLY a bean person. I mean, he likes them okay, but he performs a different ratio-of-calories-to-delight calculus than I do.

(You know that calculus: "I like wine, wine is a very important part of my life, so I'll spend calories on it even if I'm trying to cut down; I'll skip dessert if I must, before I'll go without my wine." Just as an *entirely random* and *completely hypothetical* example.)

So when I mentioned, after my colonoscopy earlier this year, that I ought to be eating more beans, he said, "Okay," and then continued shopping for and cooking our meals just as he had been.

I've been doing more solo-bean eating, like, stocking up on cans of chili at the supermarket that I can heat for lunch, that sort of thing. Opening a can of garbanzos and having a little bowl of them, tossed with salt and olive oil. And if we're out at a restaurant, odds are that whatever I order, it'll have some beans in it somewhere.

But now...I want beans with dinner. At home.

Tonight.

❈ ❈ ❈

DESPITE MY LIFELONG LOVE of beans, I really don't know how to cook them. Not from dried, not for real; I have been way too reliant on canned beans. Which are great, in their way, but...it's...a lack. Something missing in my life.

I need to know how to do this.

Once, I'd have been nervous to try. But since everything in my life changed over the past decade—since leaving that last marriage and moving to a different state and changing careers and then ultimately marrying this husband and then moving to this island—I've gotten a lot less scared of *trying* new things.

What's the worst that could happen? It fails? Okay.

It's all right to fail. I mean, if I've asked for two divorces, surely I can risk cooking a bag of beans wrong.

❈ ❈ ❈

I'VE BEEN COOKING A pot of my new beans for several hours now. Nearly three hours, actually. They've more than doubled in size, and they smell marvelous.

They're still *not quite done*, though. They've been *not quite done* for nearly an hour. Just a little *al dente*; a little too chewy, not quite the creamy that was promised.

I started with the prescribed amount of water, but it simmers away (into the beans, mostly). I keep adding more water, bringing to a boil, reducing to simmer. Again. Again. Again.

Persistence.

I think we're going to have something else for dinner, while the beans are finishing up.

They'll still be amazing tomorrow.

It's important to do what's actually happening, not what you wish were happening. I wish these beans were ready now.

What's actually happening is my husband is heating up frozen enchiladas.

❀ ❀ ❀

SOMETIMES, WHEN I GET unexpected bad news, I have to sit with it for a while before I can even know it. If that makes sense. It's like, I take it in, but only partway; I go along with my life for a while, not really knowing it, not speaking of it or thinking about it; eventually, it filters down further, and I can begin to actually know it.

A friend died recently. Not a close friend, but somebody we both liked an awful lot, who had done small, generous, unusually thoughtful things for each of us in the past. We didn't even know he was ill—we later learned that he'd told very few people—so it was shocking, and very dismaying.

I heard the news, and then I sort of…shoved it aside for a few hours, and did other things, before I even went upstairs to tell my husband about it. Before I was ready to process it, even between the two of us.

I'm not saying that signing up for a bean club without telling my husband is anything like waiting a few hours to tell him about the loss of our friend. It's just…it takes me a while to get to the heart of things, especially hard things, even when I'm trying to.

And apparently somehow, somewhere, I've internalized the lesson that

I need external permission to do even small things that I want to do. Like, to eat more beans, fancy beans, beans that will cost forty dollars every three months. Something in me believes that that's a hard thing, an unallowed thing, a frivolous thing, a thing I don't get to decide to do.

❋ ❋ ❋

IT IS NOW SEVERAL hours after I began writing this article. We ate the enchiladas, while the beans cooked on; after dinner, I checked them again.

They're pretty damn good, though not perfect. Some of them are thoroughly cooked, and creamy, and amazingly delicious. Some of them are…still a little *not quite.*

They'd been cooking for nearly four hours by then. I put them in a container for the fridge and we'll see what we can do with them tomorrow.

They need a little more, what would I call it, external flavor, I think. The beans themselves are yummy, but—well, they're beans, you know. I have a few pieces of peppered bacon in the fridge, left over from a weekend breakfast. I bet those would help.

And perhaps a little more cooking time.

❋ ❋ ❋

MAYBE I WILL GET this all the way down, someday. Maybe I will finally, truly learn that it's okay for me to want things, and to manifest them—ask for them, insist upon them, go get them without "permission."

We've been married five years, and together five years before that. In all that time, my husband has not only never told me I couldn't want things, he has in fact encouraged me to speak up, to ask, to make my desires and preferences clear. Not that he lets me trample all over him—he's good at getting his own needs met too, even while he respects mine.

This is older stuff I'm struggling with. Childhood-old. First-relationships-old.

I have the box of beans (minus the package I took out to cook) in my office here. Just looking at it makes me smile.

I wanted beans. I bought beans. I joined a bean *club*, dammit.

Go, me!

This Will Be My First Mother's Day Without Mom

My mom died last summer. Last July, to be precise: in the wee hours of the morning of Friday the 13th.

After the bewildering chaos and fresh grief in the aftermath of her death, after we all went back to our lives as best we could, back to "normal", after the memorial service; that's when the little ambushes started.

I missed her on my birthday, in October, when she didn't call, or send a card.

I missed her at Thanksgiving, and I couldn't call her on her birthday in early December. I really missed her at Christmas: she *loved* Christmas. She was a Santa-worshipper, filling her and my stepdad's house with Santa pictures, Santa dolls, Santa figurines, and setting the Christmas table with Santa candles—which have never been lit, so they stay intact year after year to bring their *ho-ho-ho* spirit to the table.

I miss her every Saturday morning at eleven, when we would always have our weekly phone calls.

❄ ❄ ❄

AND NOW HERE COMES Mother's Day. One of my Facebook friends, who has lost both her parents, posted a heartfelt plaint that began "Dear internet marketers…" Basically asking them to please remember that not everyone is a target for mom-centric shopping appeals this time of year… and warning them that she will make a similar post next month.

It's been a year of milestones for me, but this is my first time going through this particular one with so much company. Birthdays come throughout the year; holidays are about so many more things than moms. But Mother's Day: well, it's right there on the label, isn't it?

I posted a reply on my friend's page: "This is my first year in this club."

"I'm so sorry," she wrote. "It's a terrible club."

✻ ✻ ✻

THE MILESTONES ARE HARD, but at least you can see them coming. It's the grief-ambush moments that really get me. Where I'm thinking about something I want to tell her and—. Oops, nope, no can do.

She wasn't a big reader, but she loved my writing, and she was so proud of me. She would have really enjoyed my personal essays, I think. She told everyone she knew that her daughter was a *published writer*, and she even read several of my novels, though novel-reading was really not her thing.

But I didn't even start writing these pieces until she was gone.

My stepdad is enjoying them, though. And that makes me feel good.

✻ ✻ ✻

I REALLY AM LUCKY, actually. I do know that, and I'm careful to remember to appreciate it. I had a loving mom until I was past fifty years of age; I have friends who lost parents so much younger. And I am not lacking for mom-figures in my life, either. My stepmom, for example: the loving, kind, creative woman who has been in my life since I was a pre-teen, who helped raise me. A beloved auntie, Mom's older sister, in Italy. A marvelous mother-in-law, who will be visiting us this weekend so we can celebrate Mother's Day together. So many other women who have nurtured and guided me.

And that's just moms. I have a couple of amazing dads, too, both of whom walked me down the aisle when I got married five years ago.

But I still miss Mom.

✻ ✻ ✻

I WILL THINK ABOUT her this Sunday, as I am thinking about her now. As I think about her often. She never even got to see this house my husband and I moved to nearly two years ago, on this lovely island. Blue irises— her favorite flower—grow in the front yard. She would have found it so peaceful here, though she would have missed her television (we did not get a TV till fairly recently). Watching the tropical fish tank just isn't the same, as she was always sure to point out—with a smile—whenever she and my stepdad visited our last home.

I will think about her Sunday, and I will hug my mother-in-law, and I will call my stepmom, and maybe even FaceTime with my auntie in Italy.

And we can all miss Mom together, and take joy in one another.

My Husband and I Discuss Getting a Cat

SCENE: Our house and surrounding five-acre property on a rural island in the Pacific Northwest.

MY HUSBAND: Rats!

ME: What's wrong?

HUSBAND: Rats are what's wrong! The basement and crawl space are full of rats. They're tearing out the insulation and peeing and pooping everywhere. I'll set up traps.

ME: Better you than me, o manly man.

❁ ❁ ❁

[WAVY LINES INDICATING THE passage of time]

HUSBAND: I've killed and disposed of dozens of rats, and now the traps aren't working anymore. Rats are pretty smart. They've already figured out all the different kinds of traps. They trip them, get the bait, and leave unharmed, thumbing their little pink ratty noses at me. I don't want to put up all new insulation a *third* time. Plus it's really gross down there.

ME: We should get a cat! I love cats. [consults the Internet Of Friends]

ENTIRE INTERNET: You should get a cat!!!

HUSBAND: Remember that I'm allergic to cats.

INTERNET: Hypo-allergenic cats!!!

HUSBAND: And that I really don't like cats or dogs or anything more complicated than fish, and you agreed that we would never have such a pet.

ME: I do remember that, I remember it very well, it was our deal from day one. What about an outdoor cat?

HUSBAND: [gazing sadly at the rat-infested basement] Well maybe.

❧ ❧ ❧

[MORE PASSAGE OF TIME. I do some research.]

NICE LADY AT THE SHELTER: Well the first thing you need to do is get rid of your three bird feeders that your husband keeps topped up with birdseed that spills all over the ground in great quantities and attracts the rats.

ME: Haha, not a tiny chance, but I'll pass that along to him.

HUSBAND: [when I tell him] Not a tiny chance!

ME: What about that outdoor cat idea?

HUSBAND: What about rat poison?

ME: But the eagles and the owls and the hawks!

HUSBAND and ME, together: *Sigh.*

❧ ❧ ❧

[MORE RESEARCH]

ME: Barn cats! Barn cats are a thing!

HUSBAND: We don't have a barn.

ME: Well that's true.

ENTIRE INTERNET: Outdoor cats will eat all the birds! Outdoor cats don't live as long! Outdoor cats will run away! Outdoor cats will get eaten by the eagles and the owls and the hawks—and the raccoons and the otters and the chupacabras! Cats need a warm and sheltered and safe place! Like your bed. Just get an "outdoor cat" and it will charm its way inside and then it will be sleeping in your bed and you will win.

ME: Well yes, that's what *I* want, but I've already got someone sleeping in my bed who really really really *doesn't* want that, and that was kind of our deal that I signed up for, from day one, so.

HUSBAND: Maybe the rats aren't so bad.

❧ ❧ ❧

[THIS MORNING]

FRIEND, IN TEXT: Hey I'm at a farm that's giving away barn kittens, want one?

ME: I do, but…

HUSBAND: …we're not equipped for a cat, and certainly not for a kitten.

ME: *Sigh.*

FRIEND: I'll bring them all to my house and my cat will train them to hunt and then you can take one later!

ME: Yes!

HUSBAND: Well maybe.

On the First Anniversary of
Losing My Mom

It's been a year now.

I just reread "Anniversary," the essay I wrote six months in—I hadn't read it again since I wrote it.

What can I add now? It's all still true. But more time has passed; the raw edges are a bit less raw. I don't keep getting startled by her absence, the "missing step" of wanting to tell her something and forgetting I can't. I haven't had a dream about her in quite a while.

Yesterday was weirder than today, I think; the anticipation of "anniversary syndrome" was worse than the reality. Today, I talked to my brother, and to my stepdad.

We're all doing fine.

We all still miss her.

❖ ❖ ❖

I WISH SHE COULD have visited this house. We moved here before she died, but it's a long ways to come—a flight and a drive and a ferry and more driving—and she was already sick, although we didn't know the cancer was going to be terminal. We were all still living in the universe where there was going to be chemo, and surgery, and some complicated and annoying recovery from those things; but she *was* going to recover, and she and Stepdad were going to resume their lives, with all their travel and adventures, including coming to see our new home.

That's not what happened.

She would have liked this house, I think, and the lovely clawfoot tub in the guest bathroom (she was a bath person, not a shower person). She would have thought the grounds were pretty, if a bit rural. She would not have liked—she *did* not like—how far away this is from where she lived. We talked on the phone every Saturday morning at eleven. She didn't mention the distance *every* time.

❀ ❀ ❀

I DO SOMETIMES GET mad at people who still have moms. I mean, not at them specifically; I get mad at the fact of them having moms, moms who are older than mine was and yet are still here. That just seems pretty unfair, doesn't it?

Okay, so I have not yet achieved perfect grace.

(And I have dear friends who lost parents—one or both—far younger than I did. I acknowledge that none of this is logical. It's why they call them emotions, I guess.)

❀ ❀ ❀

I'M THINKING TODAY ABOUT Friday the 13th, three hundred and sixty-five days ago. What an odd, out-of-reality day that was. The neighbor who read my stepdad's middle-of-the-night Facebook post and went to his kitchen and whipped up a quiche and brought it by, so we would have breakfast. The friends and relatives who came by, so many people, I don't even remember who all was there. The sober, suited men from the mortuary (it was such a hot day, weren't they boiling in those suits?). I drifted from room to room, wanting to talk to people and wanting them all to go away. There was nothing really for me to do anymore. Mom didn't need any more help getting up and down, didn't need any ice cream or pudding or water or Kleenex brought to her, didn't need us keeping track of her meds.

It had been such an intimate time. Helping someone who is dying is a powerful experience. I can't describe it. I'm sure it's different for everyone, but it's also...there must be some commonalities there. Whole books have been written about it, after all. I even read a few.

Books are nothing like actually being there.

Anyway. I think what I'm trying to say is that, suddenly the house was full of people, and none of them were my mom, even though her body was still there.

Does that make sense?

❋ ❋ ❋

I AM MY MOTHER's daughter. I'm a planner, and I handle the finances, and I have systems and lists and spreadsheets and procedures.

As if being organized can keep the boogeyman away.

As if all her records and checklists and notes kept cancer away.

❋ ❋ ❋

I MISS YOU, MOM.

How We Stay Kind to Each Other When Things Are Hard

It's been hard lately—everything, all of it. Is that true for you too? Things are challenging out there in the world, and they're hard at home.

My sweet crazy uncle died a few weeks ago, victim of his demons, his lifelong grief, and his more recent grief at losing his sister—my mother—last summer. I'm getting uncomfortably good at writing family obituaries: item number one on the list of "skills you never wanted."

My husband and I flew to Los Angeles for my uncle's funeral last weekend, and to deal with the absolute mess he left behind. It was truly awful, and heartbreaking.

Things had been stressful already around here. The dishwasher broke, then my husband's computer died; and that was before we got our horrifying tax bill. My shoulder was already bothering me before the trip—I'd tried to see a doctor for it, but all the providers in our little rural clinic were out sick with the awful flu that's been going around.

So I ended up in Urgent Care in LA the morning of the funeral, in tears from the pain, begging for any kind of relief. I was given opioids and steroids, and that got me through the weekend, more or less. We took the ferry out to the emergency room on the mainland the day after we got home, and added muscle relaxants and lidocaine patches to my pile of drugs.

The diagnosis? "Radiculopathy." Pronounced "ridiculopathy," and that perfectly describes it. It's a pinched nerve in my neck, radiating pain down through my shoulder and arm, making half my hand numb.

Every provider I saw asked, "Did you fall? Have a car accident, some other injury? Twist it wrong? Anything?" No, no, no, and no.

"Have you been under any stress lately?"

Hahahaha.

❋ ❋ ❋

MY HUSBAND HAS BEEN a saint through this. He rubs my sore muscles for hours on end and puts on the lidocaine patches where I can't reach; he's been driving me everywhere because the meds make me loopy; he's patiently enduring my freak-outs about the money, about my numb fingers, about the drama around my uncle.

But human beings are not saints, and he's not getting his own work done, as a result of all of this. He's also navigating his own set of cascading crises, demands from others, and things falling apart (well above and beyond the dead computer).

It became a perfect storm of *too much*.

The other night, when he'd struggled all day to make just a tiny bit of progress on something that should have been easy but was proving impossible, he came downstairs in a foul mood. Stomping around and banging dishes and muttering angrily.

I'm no good with anger. If I'm forced to face it, I cry. I'd much rather run away. So I went upstairs and shut myself in the bedroom. Which made him feel like a monster, and like he wasn't even allowed to have feelings, much less express them.

We weren't upset or mad at *each other*. We're in this together, after all—us against the world, it can sometimes feel like. Yet we were the only ones here, the only ones to see and hear each other. I'm the only audience for his anger; he's my only audience for my pain and panic and anxiety.

We're both so frustrated, so exhausted, so overwhelmed.

❋ ❋ ❋

WE GOT THROUGH THAT evening; had dinner and went to sleep early. And the next morning, we sat in front of the fire with our mugs of coffee and talked about it.

And listened to each other.

Until he met me, ten years ago, my husband had lived largely alone. When he got angry, he could stomp and swear and bang around his apartment until the steam had all been released, and nobody was any the wiser. And once the emotional storm had passed through, he felt better. Bottling it up would only make the eventual eruption worse, so he would let it out when it needed to be released.

When we were first dating, of course it was all delight and bliss at the outset, but then there came a time when he got angry. He raised his voice. I cringed, and cried. He got alarmed, and felt awful, but also confused; he wasn't mad *at me*, he was mad at that other driver (who was, it is true, a complete asswipe); why was I so upset?

It took us some time, and a few more episodes, to work this through. To learn what was going on in each of us, and how each of our reactions—my fear, his anger—were normal. Not deal-breakers, not game-enders. We figured out that he had learned early in life to stuff his emotions, and that he had suppressed them so hard as a child that he actually had to learn—in his twenties and thirties—to *feel* the anger, and then how to express it.

And that I, early in life, had also learned that my feelings were not okay, not allowed. But I took a different path. I learned to display vulnerability, to cry and hide and go silent. *Don't hurt me*, my crying says. *I'm sorry. I'll be good.*

If I have anger, it's buried so deep, I may never find it.

❊ ❊ ❊

EMOTIONS ARE MESSY AND uncomfortable. Anger clearly doesn't feel good; my husband does not enjoy getting pushed to that place where he cannot help but stomp and swear. I hate the stymied, frustrated place that gets me crying; I feel helpless and fraudulent, like a child pretending to be an intelligent, accomplished woman, suddenly fooling nobody.

But the thing is: it's all *okay.*

It's okay to get mad and bang dishes around. It's okay to cry and run away to the bedroom. It's sometimes necessary, in fact.

In my previous marriage, the trophy wife marriage, none of this was okay. My ex and I had built this perfect, gorgeous, flawless-looking life, and anything messy or uncomfortable *just couldn't happen.* We could never speak of his depression, or my insecurities, or his financial anxiety, or my frustrated ambition. Yet they were all there. When he was unhappy—about anything, whether it had to do with me or not—he could not say a word about it. "I'm fine." "It's nothing." I was left feeling attacked and blamed, skulking around the edges of his simmering silent misery, even though I know he did not mean to do that.

It was this awful, soul-crushing code of silence. That marriage ended for a lot of reasons, but I think they all boiled down to one thing: we couldn't truly *talk* to one another. We just didn't know how.

Here, in front of the fire the other morning, my husband and I did. We talked. We talked about all the stressors going on—in the world, with our loved ones, and in our lives here—and how overwhelmed we both feel. We told each other how much we love each other.

But the most important thing we said to each other is that it's okay to have those emotions—*and* that it's okay to react to them, in turn, with our own emotions. He feels bad that his anger sends me fleeing. Well, yep, I don't like it much either; but it would be even worse if I felt I had to stay and face it, or pretend like it's not happening. (And I know from sad experience that I would feel just as awful if *he* tried to pretend it wasn't happening.) I am never going to smile and shrug, or just not notice when he's angry; but that doesn't mean he's breaking something when it happens.

It's weather. It's a storm, blowing through. It will pass, and we will dry off, and pick ourselves up and move forward again.

❀ ❀ ❀

So how do we stay kind to each other—in a marriage, in our lives?

We keep talking.

We allow the sad and the hard and the messy to exist. We don't have to love them, or welcome them; but we make room for them when they show up.

Because they will. Times will be hard. The dishwasher will break and the computer will die and the asswipe will cut you off and take the last parking spot and scream at you in the bargain. And there will be nothing you can do but let your emotions out—where they will get all over those closest to you. Your nearest and dearest.

A marriage is made up of the glorious and the joyful and the fun, *and* the hard and the scary and the ugly. It's right there in the vows: "For better or for worse, in sickness and in health…" We're all flawed human beings, doing the best we can with what we've got. Making mistakes. Falling over and picking ourselves back up again; lending each other a hand up. Rubbing each other's shoulders. (Okay, that one pretty much goes only one way…I'm a lucky woman.)

We don't just love each other; we *like* each other. We are interested in each other, in what makes us tick. In why we are who we are. Even ten years into our acquaintance, I feel like I learn new things about him every time we have one of those conversations like the one before the fire the other morning.

As long as we can keep talking to one another, and keep *listening* to one another, I know we're going to be all right.

When a Widowed Parent Starts Dating Again

I have four parents.

My birth parents split up when I was pretty young. I remember them being married, but there's a part of me that can't quite believe it. They…aren't a natural couple, shall we say.

Fortunately for everyone, they found much, much better matches after they divorced. Equally fortunately, everyone stayed cooperative and cordial during the split-up, joint child-rearing, and beyond. This cordiality grew into actual friendship and then deep affection over the decades. My stepdad and my stepmom raised me as much as my mom and dad did. When my now-husband and I were dating, and things became serious enough for me to introduce him to my parents, he remained a bit confused for a while about which parent was "real" and which was "step". Because they're all real, all four of them.

❄ ❄ ❄

WELL, I *HAD* FOUR parents. But my mom died last summer. Now I have three parents. Three living parents.

It's really hard to think of Mom in the past tense.

She and my stepdad were like swans: mated for life. They did everything together. They shared an email address and a Facebook account, and a lovely house with only one bathroom. They traveled the world together and took thousands of photos. They agreed on everything (except the garbage disposal; don't bring up the garbage disposal). My mom's how-to-make-a-holiday-meal instructions to me literally say "Hand the prepped turkey to your man…three hours later, your man hands back the cooked turkey and then you…"

❊ ❊ ❊

I ALWAYS USED TO joke that, when their time came, they had better go together (maybe on one of their fabulous trips), because there was no way either of them was going to survive without the other one.

But that's not what happened.

When Mom got her cancer diagnosis, it was scary, but there was reason for hope. My stepdad, however, just had a *feeling* that things weren't going to go well. He began facing the fact of losing her long before any of the rest of us.

I don't mean to suggest that he didn't do everything he could to love and support her in every way, and to try everything the medical system was willing and able to do to cure her. Not at all. He couldn't bear the thought of losing her…but somehow, somewhere deep inside, he knew he was going to have to.

❊ ❊ ❊

THE SECOND NIGHT THEY ever spent apart (the first being an overnight business trip she took in the 1980s), in thirty-four years of marriage, was when she was in the hospital recovering from the first surgery.

They would go on to spend more nights apart, as she had additional surgical procedures, and then, sadly, as she went home for the last time, under hospice care, and a hospital bed was brought in. Even then, she preferred their bed; we would help her in and out of it when she became too weak to navigate the climb herself. At this point she was sleeping more, so we gave her a whistle to call for our help if she woke up and no one was in the room.

Then, confused and ill and on so many medications, she'd forget to whistle for us, and would try to get up on her own. After she fell several times, we urged her more strongly into the hospital bed, which of course she hated. Even more than the symbolism of the thing, it was just an awful bed: thin, hard mattress, and so narrow; horrible metal rails on both sides. And of course their good sheets didn't fit on it, so we had to use some old half-polyester ones dredged up from the back of the linen closet. I don't know anyone who would have been comfortable sleeping there.

❊ ❊ ❊

It occurs to me that maybe I'm focusing on beds because focusing on the details of one's mother dying of cancer is just too hard.

❊ ❊ ❊

The day she died is a weird sad blur to me. I know that *so many people* came through the house—the house that had been so quiet in the days leading up to her death, when she was, at last, mostly just sleeping.

My stepdad cried and cried and cried, and dried his eyes and cried some more. My brother and I were more hollowed-out; teary at times, but more empty, disbelieving. Mom was only seventy-three. Far too young to die.

❊ ❊ ❊

Over the next months, my stepdad grieved. He lost weight; he lost hair. We all mourned, of course, but his was the primary loss: fresh and immediate. He had lived with her every day, for so many years, and now he was alone in the house. My brother and I phoned him; our dad and stepmom, who live nearby, stopped by to see him frequently. His twin brother whisked him off to Hawaii for a week.

My stepdad knew he needed to get out and do things, to meet people, to keep busy. Not to deny the loss; but to remember that he's still living.

At a mere sixty-three when she died—ten years younger than my mom—he was far too young to be a widower.

"Don't do anything drastic for a year," we all told him. "Have fun, date, whatever you like; just don't make any commitments till at least a year has gone by."

They had been so happily married. I know that men who have had good marriages are quicker to remarry after the loss of a spouse. But they had had *such* a good marriage, such a *unique* marriage, I wasn't sure if he was ever going to find anyone who would measure up to Mom. I could as easily see him remaining solo forever as pairing up again.

❊ ❊ ❊

Then, not long after the new year, we were talking on the phone and he said, "I've signed up for some online dating sites. Just to see how they work, what's out there."

Oh my god, I thought. *Is he serious? Isn't it **too soon**?* But out loud, I said, "That's great! What are you finding there?"

"I'm not actually going to contact anyone," he said. "No one lives close enough anyway."

"Well, let me know how it goes!" I said.

The next time we talked, he'd actually sent a message to a woman. She hadn't replied.

But the time after that…he'd struck up a correspondence with a woman in a nearby town, and they'd agreed to meet for coffee.

❀ ❀ ❀

"My stepdad is dating again!" I told a few friends.

"Oh my goodness!" they said, and "Good for him," and "That's what men do."

I'm not privy to all the details—and I wouldn't share them here even if I were; it's his story, not mine—but there soon came a point where the word "girlfriend" was used. As in, "My girlfriend…" this, that, or the other. It came up a lot in conversation, that word.

He was *very* happy. It was so nice to see. And so weird.

There is no longer a girlfriend. Again, not my story to tell. He's a little sad, but he's all right. He's eager to move forward again. He's happy to have had the learning experience.

❀ ❀ ❀

Why is this so weird for me? It's not like I want him to sit home and mourn Mom for the rest of his days. Or even a minute longer than he needs to (however one figures such a thing). He's young, he's a great guy, he has decades of experience being an excellent husband; and, perhaps most important, he's lonely. He was in his twenties when he and Mom got together, and he's a twin: he's really never been solo.

I actually do want him to be happy. I want him not to be alone. And yet…every piece of this process feels like another step toward us all putting Mom…in the past. First there were her clothes and other belongings to sort through. Because why does Stepdad need to keep her clothes? He doesn't. But this feels weird too. My auntie and my sister-in-law and I took the things we wanted, and could use; the rest…can go away.

Why does getting rid of *things* feel like another little death? Mom is not her things. She's with us all, in our hearts. And we've kept plenty of tangible mementos.

I'm terrified of what happens when her husband, her most cherished possession, belongs to someone else. What happens when another woman occupies Mom's house with him—or if he sells the house and moves away?

I think that's what "too soon" means, in my initial reaction to his entering the dating pool. It's not *too soon* for *him*; it's too soon for *me*. It seems that I'm not ready to face letting Mom go further than she's already gone.

Well, I had better get ready. Because he's *not* her possession, no matter how much she cherished him (and she did). He's his own person, and he gets to be the boss of his own life. He grieved, honestly and thoroughly; and he'll miss Mom for the rest of his days; but he's now ready to open his heart to someone else now—or at least, he's ready to give it a try.

I hope for the best for him. I really do. And, as I think about it more deeply, it occurs to me that there's another angle to look at this all from: the amazing man who is my stepdad is not going to fall in love with an unremarkable woman.

This doesn't have to be a loss. He's not going to leave us; he'll be bringing a new person into our family. She won't be my mom—but no one could be.

I already have plenty of room in my heart for four parents.

I'll bet I can find a place in there for a fifth.

On Sleep

I woke up at four thirty this morning, when it got light. This happens frequently this time of year; morning comes early at our latitude. But I almost always fall back asleep again.

Today, I made the mistake of starting to think about all the things on my to-do list… Finally, I gave up and decided to see what you lark-people are always going on about.

I even got up before the *coffee* had started brewing. I had to bypass the timer and actually push the button!

❀ ❀ ❀

SLEEP AND I HAVE a complicated relationship.

I can go for long periods getting pretty good sleep, night after night. Not perfect, not eight uninterrupted hours; but truly quite adequate. I'll wake up feeling rested, and (after coffee *of course*) ready to face the day.

Then, sometimes, sleep is just the most elusive thing ever. My fabulous perfect bed is now lumpy, my feather pillow is a rock, my down comforter is too hot, no too cold, no too hot…

It's emotional, of course; if I'm stressed out, sleep scatters. I almost added something along the lines of "like every other human being," but then I thought about my husband, who's just the opposite. When he's upset or depressed, sleep grabs him in its sticky arms and pulls him down, down, down into its inky depths, holding him close for ten hours a night, plus lengthy naps. He'll fall over into sleep like someone has hit him with a stick.

❀ ❀ ❀

I WASN'T A BAD sleeper as a child, though it did always take me a while to fall asleep—at least ten or fifteen minutes, maybe more. That's still true. Something about the letting-go process can send my system into red alert, if things aren't right.

My worst instance of *I can't fall asleep* was when my then-husband and I rushed across the country, trying to get to his mother's bedside before she died. We didn't quite make it; she passed just before our plane landed. That night, I lay in an unfamiliar bed, startling back awake every time I drew within shouting distance of sleep, trembling all over. It felt like my body was afraid of following my mother-in-law across the veil. I couldn't let go. *I forgot how to fall asleep.*

Years later, during our divorce, sleep was also a stranger. The new life I dove headfirst into was exciting and joyful, but not without its own challenges, as I left everything behind—career, my friends and family—to move to a different state and start over. My new boyfriend, a devotee of polyamory, was a lightning rod for chaos and interpersonal drama. (Yes, I know now that's not how polyamory is supposed to work, but I was new at the whole thing then.)

A noteworthy *I cannot sleep* night came when, for reasons I can't even remember now, I was sharing a bed with one of his other girlfriends. Not sexually (though it had been made clear that she'd be willing, if I were), just sleeping.

Supposedly, anyway.

She fell asleep and began sort of micro-twitching every few seconds, pushing me further and further from sleep with every tiny movement. I lay there far too long; by the time I gave up and snuck off to the nasty cot in my boyfriend's home office, all I could do was spend the night staring at the ceiling, trying make some sense of my new life, to put words to the painful crazy chaos that was swirling around my head.

Gaslighting, that was the biggest word, I later figured out. Again, something I didn't know at the time.

❋ ❋ ❋

I'M NOT SURE WHY sleep eluded me this morning. Yes, I'm crazy-busy, but with good things—work I like, writing I'm happily engaged with, far too many excellent friends and beloved family members visiting this summer.

It's probably just a fluke. But if it's not—if I start to toss and turn again on the regular—I know I need to pay attention to that. Sleep is my canary in the coal mine. When it flees, that's my brain telling me something.

I won't ignore the memo.

I Like Wine

It's kind of impossible to talk about drinking, isn't it?

Not literally, of course; quite the opposite. It's talked about everywhere, all the time. There's the *It's not a party unless we're all drinking* narrative, neatly countered by the *I was a slave to alcohol and it almost ruined my life but I got over it and here's how* narrative. There's happy hours and wine pairings and tiny adorable bottles of booze on airplanes and celebratory champagne-cork-popping and fraternity hazings and fancy bespoke cocktails, beautifully photographed.

But it's kind of impossible to talk about one's own drinking, about how one likes to drink, without…saying so much more than that.

If you know what I mean.

I just read an article about the author Jack London's drinking, about how strenuously he denied having a drinking problem. He just liked to drink! It was no problem, he was totally in control of it.

I don't know about you, but I can't even read such denials without my eyes rolling so hard back into my head…and yet, well, *I* like to drink.

I *like* wine.

❀ ❀ ❀

So many truisms, clichés. "If you have to ask whether you have a drinking problem, you probably do." Okay, so I won't examine it, I'll just drink. "Denial!"

In my early twenties, I traveled through Italy with a friend of a friend. We got along well enough, though we hadn't known each other before the trip; we just both happened to want to go to Italy, and didn't want to do so alone.

I enjoyed trying the local wine in every new region we visited. My traveling companion? Not so much. By about the fourth or fifth new city we explored, she said to me at dinnertime, "Why do you have to drink every night?"

I felt weird, and defensive, and offended, and maybe even a little ashamed (though not enough to stop). I didn't *have* to drink. I *wanted* to drink. I was in Italy, for crying out loud. The wines were notably different as we made our way through the country, and they were almost as cheap as the bottled water. They were delicious, and they complemented the local food amazingly well. And, well, come *on*. Who goes to Italy and doesn't drink?

I *like* wine.

❀ ❀ ❀

WRITERS LIKE WINE—AND EVERY other kind of alcohol. Not just Jack London. So, so many writers.

As Dorothy Parker probably did not say (but I wish she had):
I like to have a martini,
Two at the very most;
After three I'm under the table;
After four, I'm under my host.

There seems to be a clear connection between creativity and alcohol. But which is the chicken and which is the egg? Are creative people inherently a little…off kilter? Prone to crutches, comforts, diversions?

Or more willing to push boundaries, to search for the edges—and fly past them?

Is it that writing is scary, and a drink (or three) loosens the inhibitions? Maybe. I write while drinking wine, in the evenings.

But I also write in the mornings, while drinking coffee. Or mid-day, with nothing. I don't actually notice a lot of difference in my writing, wine versus coffee versus water.

"Write drunk, edit sober," as Ernest Hemingway apparently didn't say. (What is it with all these apocryphal statements? Maybe conventional wisdom is drunk.) It's true that one's judgment is better when one isn't tipsy, so I guess this one makes a certain amount of sense.

Though over-editing—second-guessing yourself, worrying about all possible reactions from all possible audiences, whittling off all the sharp corners—can suck all the life out of a piece of writing. Some of my most powerful pieces were dashed off in the heat of a moment (both with and without alcohol), and tinkering with them would only have made them worse. Would have taken all the spark of "genius" out of them (if I may be so presumptuous). Other pieces that I felt *super great* about in the moment of creation looked…rather less inspired, in the cold sober light of morning.

How do you know the difference?

You don't. That's the problem.

Sometimes you just have to trust your gut.

❊ ❊ ❊

My uncle died from drinking, just a little over a month ago. He was only sixty-six. My brother and my stepdad and I went to his apartment after the funeral, to see if there was anything we wanted, before the junk haulers came.

It was awful. I took photos. You don't want to see them.

All my life, my uncle was a messed-up, cheerful, spookily smart, charming, creative, broken, loving, gentle and damaged man. And yet he somehow always managed to hold it together…until, at last, he didn't. To see where he had spent his last few years was…well, I want to say "sobering," except it actually made us all want to just go and drink.

We drank to celebrate his life. We drank to soften the pain of seeing how he'd lived, how he died. We drank as a sacrament of family togetherness, those of us who remained.

My mother died nine months ago, though not from drinking. She also liked wine, but it was cancer that took her.

We drink to remember. We drink to forget.

❊ ❊ ❊

I like wine. I sometimes stop drinking for a time—for diet reasons, for health reasons, to keep proving to myself that I can do it.

I miss it, during those times. But I can do it. I'm always glad when those times come to their predetermined end, and I can drink wine again. I don't cheat. I drink sparkling water in a wine glass, to satisfy the ritual. It works.

I could stop drinking if I had to.

"I can stop anytime…I just don't want to."

It's true. And yet even just saying this feels...revealing. Like old Jack London, insisting ever more strenuously that he didn't have a drinking problem. *Sure, dude. You just keep on saying that.*

I like wine.

But it sure is impossible to talk about it...without feeling like I'm saying so much more.

I'm On Your Side

Is it too soon to be dating again after your divorce? Or after being widowed? I don't know. What do you think? Do you want to? Go for it! You'll know, and if you don't know now, you'll know eventually. Do what you want to do. And stop when it doesn't feel good.

And tell me everything, or some things, or nothing. There's no wrong answer. You can change your mind. I'm on your side.

Are you sad when it gets dark? Is winter just too gloomy, too cold and wet, too quiet, too...dark?

I know. It happens to a lot of us. We can turn on a light, we can build a fire, and still feel dark. It sucks, and it's okay.

I'm on your side.

Do you want to write your story your way? Even if it's not grammatical or the plot doesn't work or it's a cliché? That's okay with me. Clichés are clichés because they're true. If it's your story, go ahead and tell it. I'm on your side.

Do you want to eat the brownies, or the broccoli, or do you want to not have anything to do with spiced cider? Or should you open another bottle of wine? Or do you wish people would stop offering you wine? Do you want to not drink at all?

Those are all valid choices, and you just need to tell me what you want, because I'm on your side.

And if you don't know now, you can tell me later.

Do you want to look at the box lid while we're doing the puzzle? Do you think it's cheating to look at the box lid? Look, you do you. I'm good either way.

Do you want to get up early? I'll have coffee ready (I know how to make the machine do it automatically). Do you want to sleep late? I know how to keep the coffee warm. We'll have breakfast when we're all ready.

Oh, there's tea, too.

I'm on your side.

Did you like the movie better than the book? Look, sometimes it happens. Books are complex creatures. Sometimes a movie distills the essence in a way the book just didn't. Sometimes a book just rubs a person the wrong way.

Even if I disagree with you, I want you to be you.

It's all okay. You do what you need to do, and I'll tell you what I need. I'm on your side.

How to Subvert the Narrative and Also Grill Steaks

One of our jokes in this marriage is that I'm actually "the man" of the family—I'm the more reliable wage earner; I mow the lawns and drive the stick-shift car; I'm the sports fan; and I'm the one who barbecues. My husband, on the other hand, loves flowers, talks about his feelings, and owns more dresses than I do.

As with any story, this is…both true, and nowhere near the whole picture. I can't really claim to be a sports fan these days, for example, as I now live two states away from the last team I followed with any regularity and can't tell you how they're doing this season; and my husband doesn't actually *wear* all those dresses (he's an illustrator, they're part of his costume collection).

But I do love to barbecue.

❋ ❋ ❋

GRILLED MEAT WASN'T PART of my early upbringing, because meat itself wasn't: we were vegetarian back-to-the-land hippies. Mom cooked our beans and tofu and veggies and brown rice on a wood stove—that was as close to fire as our food got.

By the time I got to high school, though, we'd left our hippie ways behind. We'd moved into "town," where we had electricity and TV and central heating…and the men were now in charge of making fire.

I had to learn about barbecuing from my stepdad and my dad. They both grill to this day, though they have both left the mess of charcoal behind for gas grills. (Not me. I use charcoal. I love me some hot glowing coals.)

I mean, who makes these rules anyway? The ones forbidding women from cooking over flames, out of doors? Who decided that helpless females cannot be expected to use a clutch? Or that big manly men can't enjoy creating and tending a gorgeous garden?

I don't know who, but they're not the boss of me.

❊ ❊ ❊

I GRILLED STEAKS LAST night. Here's how:

• Pull them out of the fridge mid-afternoon and coat them with the seasoning of your choice. I like Montreal Steak Seasoning—a blend of spices that are yummy on meat (and many other things), and salt. The salt is the important part. All hail salt!

• Cover them and leave them out on the counter for a few hours. You want them to get to be something around room temperature (unless your room is, like, 90 degrees).

• Forty-five minutes to an hour before dinner, start the fire. I poured a glass of rosé and went outside to my funky old Weber grill. The important part of *this* step is the grill chimney. No lighter fluid! Just a big tower of briquets (not the fluid-soaked ones either) and crumpled newspaper underneath. Light the paper. Watch it catch. Sit down and drink the rosé as the flames and smoke rise in their chimney, keeping an eye on the whole situation.

• When the flames come licking out of the chimney and even the top briquets are starting to whiten around the edges, then you dump them out, and set the chimney somewhere safe. Like the gravel path. Be careful, it's VERY hot.

• Set the grill rack back over the hot coals, cover the grill, and wait another ten or fifteen minutes. You can still sit outside and enjoy your wine during this part, especially if the house is very crowded and busy and there's any danger of being recruited for some other cooking task, but you can also leave it unsupervised now.

• Then it's time to put the steaks on. We had very thick steaks last night so I went with more indirect heat—not right over the hottest part of the coals. I covered it again, but only for a few minutes, just to let the meat all warm up. Then I removed the cover, and this is when you really want to stick close. The meat will start to drip its delicious juices onto the coals, and those juices will flame up, and while a moment of that is great, a little char on a steak goes a long way.

- Turn the steaks over after about five minutes (less if they're not so thick). Observe how good they look and smell.

- Repeat. Most steaks should be done (medium-rare to medium) by this time. Our big monsters took about five minutes longer. They're done when you poke at them with your tongs and they wiggle a little, but aren't floppy like they were when they were raw.

- Put them on a plate and bring them into the house. Let them rest a few minutes. Last night ours rested almost twenty minutes, and they were *perfect*.

- In my opinion, it's better to take them off a bit early than a bit late. The coals will stay hot for a good long time; any meat that's under-done can be put back on and cooked more. But it's really hard to cook something *less*.

❀ ❀ ❀

BOTH MY DAD AND my stepdad make killer chicken thighs, which I *love*, so I knew that was something I wanted to learn too. I got instructions from both of them, but it wasn't quite working for me.

Then I found a recipe online, in an article titled "How To Barbecue Chicken Thighs: A Guide For People Who Aren't Assholes." I've been using it for years. It's loaded up permanently on my phone, and then I eventually printed it out too, to be on the safe side. It's a hugely entertaining read…and yet it's written by a man, directly addresses men, and makes gentle fun of insufficiently manly men who aren't man enough to man up and make by-god manly grilled meat cooked over charcoal like a *man*.

Guess what? This woman can sip her rosé and make killer chicken thighs too. (While her husband is in the kitchen, making a pear, mint, candied-pecan and chive-flower salad.)

❀ ❀ ❀

I KNOW THESE AREN'T really *rules*. I know the Society for the Preservation of General Masculinity and Manly Barbecuing Ways police aren't going to show up and confiscate my tongs and my giant hot-mitt and send me back inside to the stove (in our case, a Viking Professional that runs on propane and is frankly scarier than a pile of burning coals). I even know, in theory, that there must be other women out there who love to grill as much as I do.

But it's funny how pervasive the gender divisions are. I don't know if I've ever seen another woman, with my own eyes, actually barbecuing.

So I say, *Try it!* Subvert the narrative. Indulge your inner cavewoman. Get your hands a little dirty. Make some smoke.

Barbecuing is fun, and hugely satisfying. There's something primal and intense about the sound and the smell of grilling meat. And on these warm summer days, it's awesome to be outside…drinkin' wine and makin' fire.

Yes I Do Want More Socks

With all the scandals, failing economies, impeachments, once-beloved authors showing us their dark ugly sides, and other crises facing us today, I wanted to come out and make a strong statement...

...about socks.

I want more socks. Yeah I have a lot of socks. But I want more. I want socks that are thick and cozy and great for the wintertime here in the chilly Pacific Northwest. I want socks that are thin and sheer and fit inside my boots that are a little too tight. I want socks that are bright and colorful and cheerful. I want socks that say things about me.

Also I *need* more socks. I have badly behaved toenails: they grow and they poke holes in my socks, and everyone knows that socks with holes in them are just the *worst*.

(I even got a darning kit recently, but I haven't learned how to use it yet. I am totally going to, though. I have too many wonderful socks that I'm not ready to retire yet, just because the big toes are all blown out.)

My mother-in-law bought me a pair of "go away I'm introverting" socks last Christmas. I love them, love them SO MUCH. Another friend bought me socks that have a message on the soles. One says, "If you can read this," and the other says, "Bring me a glass of wine." I have to be careful to get them on the correct feet—although I guess the message works either way.

(They don't work, though; the socks, I mean, even if the message does. No one has followed the instructions. Ever! People just laugh when they see them. Like it's a joke or something!)

My husband is learning, about the sock thing. He couldn't believe it when I told him I want more socks for Christmas. "Really? I bought you socks last year."

Last year?!

But I assured him I meant it, and he seemed to hear me. I think. Ask me again after Christmas.

❋ ❋ ❋

HEY, IT COULD BE worse. I could have a thing for shoes…er, um, never-mind.

I am pleased to be able to inform you that I totally have the shoe thing under control now. (Redirection is a form of control. Totally.)

Besides, socks are way cheaper than shoes, and take up far less space in the closet. So they are a *much* better obsession.

❋ ❋ ❋

I WAS A TEENAGER when the movie *Flashdance* came out. The exact prime age for the leg-warmer fetish. I had many pairs of leg warmers. My favorite were a pale pink pair, much more tightly woven than the usual slouchy-loose ones.

They were *sweet*. They were more like thick socks, and *of course* I wore them over the tightly pegged bottoms of my tight jeans.

It was the 1980s. There were *laws*. We had to dress that way.

❋ ❋ ❋

LEGGINGS ARE LIKE SOCKS for your whole legs. I love leggings too; I am less excited about tights, because I have not yet found a pair where the crotch fits comfortably. They're either too tight, or too baggy; they pull down or they twist or ride up or whatever. I'm not sure why that is.

Maybe it's so I can wear a pair of fun leggings *and* a pair of cool socks at the same time.

Because socks!

❋ ❋ ❋

OKAY, BACK TO WORK, everyone, and to the serious business of surviving these trying times.

But first, pull on a pair of cozy socks. It won't solve any big problems, but your feet will be happy.

We've got to start somewhere.

Live a Life of Saying Yes Today

Aweek ago, I got one of those phone calls. One that's completely unexpected, and yet somehow you know even as you pick up that it's going to be terrible news. Life-changing news. My stepfather had died.

I am not sure if I can fully convey the shock that this brought me—brought us all. Because, of course, parents die, that's the natural order of things. Especially when you get to be my age. It is, as we used to say in the oral history field, when we were trying to time our interviews, the "actuarial imperative."

But Keith wasn't old, or ill, or anything like that. He was a very youthful and active sixty-five.

It was an aneurysm, a little ticking time bomb in his brain that went off. No warning.

❀ ❀ ❀

WE LOST MY MOTHER—KEITH'S wife—a year and a half ago. We all miss her so much, but Keith grieved her deeply. They were just the world's most perfect couple, inseparable—they did **everything** together. Well, they didn't work together, but they *drove home for lunch together every single day*.

I think there was one time in their whole nearly forty years together that they spent a night apart—at least until my mom started having to spend nights in hospitals, and even then, he almost always stayed there with her, if he could.

❀ ❀ ❀

I KNOW IT'S A thing that longtime spouses tend to die within a year or two of one another. And honestly, at first, we wondered. *What is he going to do without her?*

Well, first, he mourned. Honestly, and thoroughly and deeply. For about six months, every time anyone saw him, he would talk about Mom, about losing her; he would end up in tears (and he usually wasn't the only one). He did not shy away from his grief. He told everyone about how he was doing, how much he missed her, how strange it was to be alone. How hard those last months, weeks, days of her illness had been.

He said yes to his grief. He let it happen.

And then? Just about at the turn of last year, he made a pivot. He was still bereft, he was still a widower who missed his wife profoundly, but the clouds cleared a bit, and he got up and decided it was time to go out and live his life. The pain of his loss had faded just enough to not be a raw, terrible wound anymore; he discovered some hope for the future.

He went back to the health club and joined a Pickleball league, and went to stretch classes—the same classes he and Mom had gone to together.

He joined a meet-up group to do hiking and trail maintenance, and another meet-up group to host and attend movie nights around the neighborhood, and he went to see live music on Friday nights at a local winery—alone if he couldn't find someone to go with him.

He deepened his friendship with a neighbor; he went camping with old college friends; he went on a weekend retreat with other old friends; he went to Hawaii with his brother and family; he came to visit us.

He joined a ukulele group and started learning to play.

He signed up with a few online dating sites.

❄ ❄ ❄

DATING! THAT WAS AN adjustment for us, his children, our mother's children. I mean, Mom was gone, and we wanted Keith to be happy, we really, honestly did, but I think you can understand that it was also a little weird. Nevertheless, we supported this move, but since our family does honesty, I also told him this was great but weird. (And of course I wrote an essay about it, because apparently that's how I process things.)

He fell hard for the first woman he went on a second date with.

After a few weeks, she broke up with him—by text.

He licked his wounds, straightened his spine, girded his loins, and every other cliché you can think of, and dove back into dating.

I know he had some fun. Even a lot of fun. I don't know a whole lot of details. We were still figuring out how to talk to each other about his dating experiences. (Heck, we were still learning how to talk to each other without Mom there, in the room, on the phone line, in the mix.) After one particularly poignant conversation about another complicated romantic situation, he laughed a little self-consciously and said, "I probably shouldn't be telling you all this!"

"Tell me anything you want, or nothing at all," I assured him. "It's all good, whatever you need to do. I'm on your side."

❅ ❅ ❅

THE POINT IS, KEITH said yes. He said yes to dating and lunch invitations from friends and trips to Hawaii and trying new things.

How was he ever going to know how he wanted to live the rest of his life if he didn't try things?

There was a fearlessness in him that I'm only really appreciating now. A woman who he was dating but a little unsure about called to ask him to go to the coast with her and six other friends for the weekend. They were leaving in half an hour: did he want to come? "Sure," he said, thinking, *This will make us or break us. Then at least I'll know.*

Just a few weeks before he died, the family was all up visiting my husband and me for the holidays. My brother and Keith and I went out to a local sports bar to see an Important Football Game that the rest of the house wasn't interested in.

Of course, when we got there, all the tables were filled with fans. But one guy was sitting alone at a booth. "Should we ask if we can sit with him?" Keith asked.

My brother and I, good introverts that we are, cringed and shrugged and shrank, all "Oh, gosh, I don't know, hmm." I was already casting my mind around for other places the game might be showing, or wondering if we should just go back to the house and let everyone deal with it—when Keith marched across the room, introduced himself to the guy, and then waved us over with a big smile. He bought a pitcher of IPA for the table, getting a glass for our new host, and then proceeded to tell the guy his whole life story. We were all fast friends by the end of the first quarter (and the end of the second pitcher of IPA).

Keith said yes to life, to experiences, to friends, old and new. To beer and sports and travel and family, and more friends.

It's inspiring.

❀ ❀ ❀

NOBODY THOUGHT HIS LAST year would be…his last year. Everyone, including Keith, thought he was embarking on the rest of his life. Figuring out who he was—and wanted to be—without my mother. Figuring out what that life would look like.

The aneurysm took him quickly, we think; he was alone in the house, but he didn't call 911, didn't call his friend across the street. Just slipped away.

If there's anything after this life, he's with Mom now. I wouldn't put it past her to have called him to her, though she *said* she was all in favor of his remarrying and enjoying a long, happy second act.

We're devastated that he's gone, but we're also all so happy that he had such a great life, both with Mom and after she was gone. He didn't wait around; he did what there was to do when it needed doing. He said yes to loving my mom, and then he said yes to grieving her, and then he said yes to stepping fully into his new life.

I'm sad that he only had a year of it. But I'm so grateful for the forty years that that excellent, loving man was my parent. He taught me a lot: the arcane rules of baseball; appreciation for (hmm how to put it) underappreciated music; how to be honest, genuine, and direct; what to do with *salmiakki* (dissolve it in vodka, drink after dinner).

He's still teaching me.

I miss you, Keith. We all do.

Give Mom a hug for me, will you?

How We're Maintaining Marital Happiness During Quarantine

My husband and I were already pretty well-equipped to handle our governor's order to shelter in place, when it finally came on March 23. (It's April 2, 2020, as I write this.) First off, we both work at home, freelancing for distant clients; we have separate offices on separate floors of the house, and a long-established (and mostly effective) daily routine for getting our work done.

Secondly, since we live on an island far from big-box stores, Trader Joe's, and other niceties of civilization, we make a practice of shopping as if for an apocalypse: spending hundreds and hundreds of dollars filling our Subaru with staples and coolers of perishables once every month or two. We do supplement with trips to the local grocery store, but our basics are in good supply. (We have plenty of toilet paper. PLENTY.)

Thirdly, though we both like people and—in normal times—enjoy an active social life, we're both happy and comfortable being alone. I'm more of an introvert than he is, but he can easily get wrapped up in a creative project and work till late in the night, forgetting to eat meal after meal. (I know. Who *does* that?)

So when the order to stay at home came down—well, we were pretty much already doing it. I'd played racquetball with a friend on March 10; my husband had gone to the grocery store a few days after that. By then, the news had become dire enough that we saw where this was going, and just hunkered down. The last thing we did "out in the world" was fetch his mom from her retirement community just off-island, after they had their first COVID-19 case. She's been quarantined upstairs in our house since then; once fourteen days have passed and we're all still symptom-free, we'll integrate our household and shelter in place together.

❊ ❊ ❊

As we've been basically going about our normal lives (plus carrying meals upstairs on a tray for the "Madwoman in the Attic"), it's been hard not to notice what a difficult time so many other couples are having, as they suddenly find themselves at home, together, All. Day. Long. Trying to be productive. Trying to stay sane.

Trying not to scream at each other.

I see all the memes, the threads, the jokes, the complaints. "I'm married to the 'let's circle back' guy." "I dressed up my pets!" "What day of the week is it?" All the hobbies being taken up—the knitting, the baking. The gardening. Repapering the pantry shelves.

Mostly, though, I see people trying to figure out how to tolerate spending all day, every day, cooped up with the person they love enough to have combined households with. Even, sometimes, the person they swore—in front of witnesses—to spend the rest of their lives with.

❊ ❊ ❊

Clearly, love isn't the problem here. So many people frustrated with their partners still obviously love them, they just…don't like them?

And that, I think, is the difference. Love, I would argue, is easy. Love is jump-started by hormones, that giddy rush of infatuation and lust that initiates so many long-term relationships. You can love someone even when they annoy you so badly, you just want them to *go away*. I've been divorced twice; I never stopped loving those men. I just couldn't abide being married to them any longer.

This marriage, however, is fundamentally different. Our big secret for staying comfortably connected while quarantined together? **We don't just love each other, we *like* each other.**

❊ ❊ ❊

This was clear the day we met. Yes, there was the hormonal rush of attraction; but I also just wanted him to *keep talking to me*. Keep telling me his story, his opinions, his thoughts. And he wanted the same from me. I've never had a relationship where I've felt as heard, listened to, known as this one.

We're ten-plus years into our acquaintance, and this aspect is not slow-ing down at all. We have to be disciplined: when we finish our morning coffee and breakfast, it's easy to just go on talking about whatever topic we're wrangling that day. "You're good company," my husband often tells me.

So is he.

Good company, liking one another: I think that's the key. Everything else unfolds from there—maintaining good communication; being respectful of one another; thanking each other for the big things *and* the little things—it all starts with genuine positive feelings for your partner. Enjoying them, looking forward to connecting with them.

We all know couples who clearly don't like each other. The little resentments, the sniping, the eye-rolling. When a relationship becomes a contest, a battle, when being able to leave the house to go to work is the only escape—I feel for those couples. It's hard enough to be forced to stay inside, to forgo restaurant meals, gym routines, travel, the company of other people. But to be locked in with someone you don't like…that's bound to be tremendously difficult.

I feel so fortunate to already have *I like him* as my baseline feeling about my husband. If you don't have that with your partner, can you find it? Can you reach back into the mists of time to when you first met, and remember what you liked about them? Not just the happy sexy crush-romance feelings, but the other stuff? Books and movies you had in common; opinions, hobbies, interests. Long talks about your childhoods, who you used to be, who you want to be. Hopes and dreams.

Can you use this quarantine to rekindle your most important friendship?

I hope so. The world is hard enough already—so much grief and fear and uncertainty and loss, so much financial uncertainty, so much isolation. I hope those who are partnered can find comfort from their mates… can remember that they are on the same team.

Be kind to each other. We'll get through this.

※ ※ ※

It is now August 8, 2020, and I am editing this essay for inclusion in this book you're reading. Some marriages won't survive this time; I already know, anecdotally, of a handful of divorces and separations in process.

I still think my words stand, though, for the marriages (and other relationships) that *are* meant to hold together.

And for those relationships that do end: I don't think that's a tragedy. Very painful, yes, and deeply disappointing; but as a woman who's been divorced twice, I can say with great confidence that it is better to end a fundamentally flawed relationship than to "tough it out."

Life is too short to stay with the wrong partner.

I'm so grateful I finally found the right one.

I'm the Worst Yogini in the Room

I've never been very flexible, or very athletic. In elementary school, I was usually the last kid picked for any team sport (unless the "sport" was a spelling bee). I was a scrawny child, slow of reflex, weak of arm; a girl who would much rather be sitting under a tree, reading a book.

I'm still a bookworm, but I did discover the joys of exercise once I grew a little older. I jogged for years; I lifted weights; I love to swim.

But, being so not-flexible, yoga scared me. What if I was terrible at it? What if I looked stupid? What if I injured myself? Would they even let me try—whoever "they" are, the mysterious gatekeepers of yoga?

Well, long story short, I finally did try it when I was about thirty. And it was AMAZING. After my very first class, I felt…magical, almost. Like channels had opened up inside me, that I had never known were there. I called my brother (who had been practicing for a few years) and said, "Why didn't you *tell* me?"

"I did," he said. I could hear him smiling even over the phone.

That very first class was hard, too: I was the least flexible person in the room, and totally weak, and I knew I looked like a fool. But it FELT so good! I was hooked.

❀ ❀ ❀

FAST-FORWARD A COUPLE OF years, and I was looking for something more than the three-mornings-a-week beginner class offered at work. There was a yoga studio near my home which offered something called "Mysore" in the early mornings; I decided to give it a try.

"Mysore" turned out to be short for Mysore Style Ashtanga, and Ashtanga is one of the two "hot yogas" that were all the rage in the late nineties. (Bikram is the other one, which I have never tried.)

Mysore classes are self-paced; an instructor is in the room, but the students arrive and just start practicing, doing the poses in order. The teacher walks around and gives adjustments and pointers.

Unless, of course, you don't *know* the poses yet. Then the teacher stands with you and teaches them to you, one at a time, while you try not to look at all the crazy-flexible strong thin people practicing all around you.

Also, it's *hard*. Like, out-of-breath-and-sweating hard (and not just from the 80-degree room).

I made it through my first day, having been taught maybe 10 percent of the practice. My arms were trembling and aching; my face was beet red; my hips and calves were screaming. *This is way beyond me*, I thought, *but maybe I can do it once a week or so, and build up my strength...*

"Okay, see you tomorrow," said the teacher.

I gulped. "Tomorrow?"

"Yes, we practice every day except Saturdays and Moon Days." (Full moons and new moons, that is, when the energy is either too high or too low, and you can hurt yourself.)

❋ ❋ ❋

SOMEHOW...I SHOWED UP THE next day. And the next day. And before you knew it, I was a totally devoted Ashtangini. I practiced every day, except Saturdays and Moon Days. I took a travel mat with me whenever I left town and made sure my accommodations included a span of hardwood floor. I gained strength and flexibility.

And I was always the worst yogini in the room.

It took me about a year to even get my fingertips to the floor in a standing forward bend—much less my palms. My twists were not very twisty; my balances wobbled. And I never managed a smooth vinyasa—the jump-back-Upward-Dog-Downward-Dog-jump-through sequence between every Ashtanga pose that gives the practice its energy and flow.

But it didn't matter. My body grew stronger and healthier, and nobody was judging.

That, in fact, was the greatest thing: yoga was not a competitive sport. At least, not in the community I found myself in. We all had different bodies, different levels of experience, different old injuries, different potential. I never felt judged in that room—or in the next room, after my first teacher quit a few years later; or in the room after that, when the new studio closed and we all had to find another. We were a great community, helping each other with poses when the teacher was busy, and gathering for potlucks every few months, where we'd joke about how different everyone looked with their clothes on.

I figured I'd do this practice forever.

❀ ❀ ❀

THEN I MOVED AWAY, to a different city in a different state. I'd done my research, finding the city's one Mysore Style Ashtanga room. I showed up once I got settled, introduced myself to the young teacher, and began practicing there, looking forward to getting to know my new community.

These people seemed a little less friendly, though; even among each other, I didn't see the little greetings and mutual assistance my old crowd did. And if I'd find myself in the outer room at the same time as another student, they never introduced themselves, never even said hi.

After I'd been practicing there a few months, the studio's floors were refinished, polished to a high gloss. They were very beautiful, and clearly the young teacher was very proud of them. He began to criticize my vinyasas, telling me to not knock my heels on the floor during my jump-throughs.

I said, "Yes, I have always struggled with this. Can you help me learn how to keep my feet up?"

He said, "Just don't let them hit the floor."

I tried. Reader, I tried.

We had basically that same exchange a few more times. Then he pointed out how I was marring the finish on the beautiful new floor, with my nasty, disobedient heels.

I stopped practicing there.

❀ ❀ ❀

BUT SEE, THE BEAUTY of Ashtanga is that you can do it completely alone, at home. On your own hardwood floor, to your own schedule.

It's nice to have a community, and it's very helpful to have a teacher—but once you know the poses, you don't *need* those things.

So I practiced at home, for several years.

Until the practice sort of started to…fall away from me. I got busy. I joined a gym and started doing other exercise; and who has time for an hour-plus of yoga in the mornings, if you're also going for a swim later? My home practice shrunk to a fifteen- or twenty-minute routine of basically rolling around on the floor and waking my muscles up, then reaching for a big cup of coffee.

By the time the pandemic hit, it had been probably eight or nine years since I'd done Ashtanga. I'm older now. Heavier. Even less limber. All our hardwood floors are covered in rugs.

But now, two months into shelter-in-place, there's no gym to go to, no pool, and my daily walks out to the mailbox just aren't cutting it. So… after mulling it over, I pulled out the old cheat sheet and dove in.

Oooooh those sun salutations were hard. And…so were the rest of the poses. On the first day, I managed maybe twenty minutes, maybe a quarter of the practice. After two days, my arms were so sore, I worried I'd pulled something.

But it's gotten a little easier every day. I've gotten a little stronger, a little more flexible.

I will probably never make it back to the practice that I used to do. I am, however, doing something resembling all the Primary Series poses now—at least, someone familiar with the practice would probably recognize what I am doing as a rough attempt at them. If they squinted.

I am now three weeks in. Tomorrow is Saturday: Ashtanga holiday. I forgot about Moon Days until I started writing this essay, so I practiced yesterday, though it was a full moon. I am looking forward to tomorrow's day of rest. My body needs it.

❊ ❊ ❊

YOGA HAS TAUGHT ME so much about my body, over the decades. About its limits, and its capabilities. I've learned how to tell the difference between a move or position that is uncomfortable but will be good for me if I push through it, and one that is injurious.

Even more deeply, I think, yoga has taught me a great deal about self-acceptance. Once I got past my initial fear, shame, and embarrassment about being so inflexible and weak, I began to delight in what I *could* actually do, and in seeing that ability grow with time and effort.

I can stand on my head! (That took about five years to learn.) I can put my palms on the floor in forward bend! (Four years.) I can…well, okay, I can't yet manage the vinyasas between every pose anymore (even banging my heels on the floor), but I have faith that I will get that back too.

And if I don't? That's okay too. Just doing the practice that I'm doing now has already made me feel so much better—physically and mentally.

Right now, I am the *very* best yogini in the room.

Maintaining a Practice in Challenging Times

I thought I was going to write four books this year.

(I'll wait, so you can finish laughing hysterically, while also crying.) (Or is that just me?)

I had a plan and everything, a system, a schedule. I made a big cheerful public commitment about it, and recruited a team of folks to write with me. We would check in with each other, cheer each other on, share our word counts and triumphs and challenges.

Ha.

❀ ❀ ❀

I WAS ALSO EXERCISING regularly, when 2020 started. I belonged to a gym. Remember gyms? I swam three times a week, and played racquetball with a friend twice a week. Racquetball! An hour running around and sweating inside an airtight box with another sweaty person.

Good times.

Our local gym has closed down for good now, and the owners have put the business up for sale. Though I can't imagine anyone investing in a health club right now.

❀ ❀ ❀

WHEN THE PANDEMIC HIT, things were of course hard and scary and confusing, but I, along with so many others, took all this positive productive energy and redirected it. We baked bread, ordered dried beans, read all the news about how to stay safe. Stocked up on toilet paper, hand sanitizer, latex gloves. Came up with hand-washing songs. Learned how to use Zoom. Experimented with different kinds of face masks. I made a whole bunch of ice cream, and also limoncello.

What I didn't do was write. The book I was working on in February...I haven't opened that file since, well, February. I used to write essays regularly—that fell by the wayside as well.

Now it's looking like we need to stay hunkered down for the longer haul. Things are still hard and scary and confusing, and all that "novelty energy" is long spent.

It's time to get reacquainted with practice.

❊ ❊ ❊

As a longtime yoga fan, I love the concept of practice. I am never going to achieve some ultimate end point—in yoga, in writing, in limoncello-making (okay, maybe I do have *that* one down). Practice is making an attempt, showing up, even if the results are disappointing. I roll out my mat in the morning and assume the position (Downward Facing Dog, for starters).

In April, before the first round of novelty energy had abandoned me, I restarted my Ashtanga yoga practice. I'd let it drop, since I was doing all that swimming and racquetball, so it was quite a process to rebuild my strength and flexibility.

I will never look like the people in the videos, or even like the thirty-year-old I was when I first took up the practice, but I am beyond pleased to report that I now do an hour of sweaty yoga every morning.

Well, except for the mornings when I don't, because I'm tired, or a spider bit me and made my eyes swell up, or because the moon is full. But that's the great thing about a *practice*. Every day is a new opportunity to roll that mat out again.

It doesn't matter if it ever "goes" anywhere. The important part is the doing—and the being kind to yourself about it.

Everything is hard. It's going to be hard for some time to come. Do what you can, and try again tomorrow.

And the next day. And the day after that.

❊ ❊ ❊

I am rediscovering my writing practice as well. The book I set aside in February was a memoir; I don't have it in me to work on that right now.

Not this year. I don't know enough about what this world is going to look like, and how I'm going to be in it, to even approach it.

But I do have a novel due to a publisher in a few months. So, after an enormous amount of delaying and avoiding and making more bread (and more limoncello), back to fiction I went.

At first, it was *hard*. I could not find the voice, the story, the characters. Everything they were doing seemed so—well, frivolous, and unrealistic. It feels really strange to write about a world in which people travel, eat in restaurants, meet up in bars. Even join hands to work magic together. Is anyone going to want to read about my witches and warlocks and their love lives and power struggles?

Actually, I bet they are. If we can't escape into fiction now, even just for an hour here and there, then we will never make it through these times.

And once I found the voice again, the words started to flow. So I'm writing a few thousand words a day—most days—on the novel.

❀ ❀ ❀

AND THAT'S WHAT'S BRINGING me back to essay writing too, I think. The practice of writing regularly was healthy for me. Yes, most writers (me included) write with an audience in mind—but the real reward was, and always has been, internal.

For months, I felt like I didn't have anything to contribute, anything to say about the huge global calamity we're living through. My husband and I live in a peaceful, safe place; we already worked at home, and that work is still showing up; why was my voice needed out there?

I've finally realized that *out there* isn't really important for me and my words. I need to do this practice for myself; I want to do it for myself. If others read my words and enjoy them, so much the better—don't get me wrong, I love an audience. If you find comfort or inspiration or even a chuckle about something I wrote, that's great!

But I need to write for me.

Just like I need to do yoga, and go for daily walks, and…make limoncello. (Hey, a girl's gotta have *some* fun.)

Money

Getting Slammed by Taxes:
Life as a Freelancer

My heart is pounding, my mouth is dry, my gut is churning. It's April of 2019 and I'm staring at a huge tax bill—thousands of dollars. Like, more than $5,000. It's all the more astonishing because this is not what I'd been expecting.

My husband and I are both freelancers who work at home for clients all over the world. We love our work, and it's a great lifestyle—except for a few little details. For one, all our income is 1099 income, which means that we are taxed differently here in the U.S. than salaried employees.

This has been true at least as long as we've been freelancing, which is the last ten years for me and nearly all his working life for my husband. We understand 1099 taxation; we know it's part of the payoff for the flexibility and freedom of our work, of being our own bosses. We make quarterly payments to the IRS with the amount estimated based on our prior year's taxes so the hit isn't as bad on tax day itself. We always owe something then, but it's never a big deal.

This year, however, things turned out very differently.

❋ ❋ ❋

At the end of 2017, new tax legislation passed that took effect for the 2018 tax year. I've read several articles about people who are surprised that their refunds are smaller. (Refunds—ha! What an idea.) I understood the shell game our wretched government was playing, giving salaried workers more in their take-home paychecks (paychecks—ha!) while changing the tax code so their actual tax liability is at least as much, if not more, than before.

Fools, I remember thinking. *Pay attention! This isn't real!* I marched along, smug in my knowledge that as a freelancer household, none of that applied to us.

I was entirely oblivious to what was coming.

Here's how it breaks down for us: Our income is not a lot—we made rather less than $50,000 last year between both of us; it was not a super great year for a lot of reasons. Because all of that is 1099 income, it's subject to self-employment taxes. Those taxes are applied to our net income, not our gross income, which means we can deduct legitimate business expenses and are taxed on what's left.

We had some business expenses last year, though fewer than in a typical year. My husband, a commercial illustrator, bought a large-format printer (several thousand dollars) and one initial batch of ink (another cool thousand). I, an editor and writer, bought lots of paper, toner, and red pens.

We didn't go to any conventions in 2018, so we had no travel expenses. (I traveled plenty to be with my mother while she was in hospice before she died, but that, of course, was not business related, and therefore not deductible.) I didn't buy a new computer though I sorely need one. Mine crashes on the regular, but I've worked out ways to keep it limping along—for now.

We both have home offices, so we can claim a percentage of the mortgage and utility costs proportional to the square footage of those spaces. That's nice. But speaking of that mortgage, we moved in the summer of 2017 and bought a house that cost more than the house we sold—a house that had been fully paid for. So, for the first time, we have a mortgage. We paid over $9,500 in mortgage interest in 2018, and I was so looking forward to being able to deduct that. In fact, the only reason I felt we could afford to take on such debt with this house in the first place was because I knew the mortgage interest would be deductible.

But, hey, guess what? Our mortgage interest is not deductible. It's not a business expense; it's just an expense, along with groceries and health care and utilities and firewood and insurance and gas and car repairs and all the umpty-billion things a family spends money on. What the new law cleverly did was raise the standard deduction so a lot of things that used to reduce your tax burden simply no longer do.

What it boils down to is that after self-employment tax is figured on our total income, that very same income is totted up again, the standard deduction is applied, and we're taxed on the remainder.

Last year, our total tax liability amounted to not quite 11 percent of our total gross income, the money that came in the door. This year? Nearly 20 percent.

❊ ❊ ❊

I AM APPALLED, SHOCKED, and freaking out about how to pay this bill. I've already investigated the IRS's payment-plan program, and we're going to do that. We'll have to pay interest and penalties, but they don't seem to be too onerous. I know the changes to what we owe now aren't entirely due to the new tax bill; we deducted some moving expenses in 2017, and we did have more business expenses that year as well. But what I'm seeing all over—from so many other freelancers I know or follow on social media—is that this problem is much more widespread than just my husband and me. Not a day goes by when I don't see a new, unhappy post about taxes.

How are we supposed to make this work? How are we supposed to survive on 80 percent of the small amount we earn—especially when this was so unexpected?

We could try to raise our rates, but that's always risky. I also feel like I'm adequately, even comfortably, paid for what I do. I know what other freelance editors charge. My rates are probably on the lowish end of the scale, but they feel fair to me.

Working more is not the answer. I can barely keep up with the work I've got; my desk is piled high with manuscripts I'm eager to get my red pen on. My husband and I routinely mention to each other how nice it would be to actually have—you know—weekends. Even one-day ones. Maybe even once a month. Maybe?

My husband is actually working to get out of the freelance-illustration-for-hire business. He's hard at work on a new art and writing project that we hope to take directly to an audience. I hope we can afford to give him the time to finish creating and launching that this summer. But this, too, isn't an answer for everyone facing this 1099 tax conundrum.

❊ ❊ ❊

IT'S HARD TO PIN down the exact percentage of the U.S. workforce that is self-employed, though everyone agrees the number is rising. Companies love to hire contract workers: It gives them flexibility to grow or shrink their payrolls at a moment's notice—not to mention saving on benefits, which cost more all the time. Gone are the days when a worker would be hired in an entry-level position right out of school and spend his (and it was usually "his") entire career at that same company, rising through the ranks with experience, receiving periodic salary increases, and retiring with a good pension and health benefits.

Many workers enjoy the freedom and flexibility of self-employment. I definitely chose this path, quitting one of those increasingly rare career jobs that I'd held since college to go out on my own. I earn a lot more per hour than I ever did at the university—depending on how you count the hours, that is. I only manage to spend four or five hours of my day doing actual proofreading, copy editing, or writing. Those are the hours I keep track of on my spreadsheet.

The rest of my far-more-than-eight-hour workday is spent doing all the business of running one's own business: communicating with clients, billing, reconciling, chasing down late payments, taking checks to the bank and packages to the post office. Also, ordering those red pens and boxes of toner and paper. And, of course, keeping up with social media; since my entire business has grown through word of mouth, it's important to stay present and connected.

I've worked so hard to get where we are. It starts to feel…personal, somehow.

I would hate to give up what I've built and the life I enjoy. But I have to confess, when I look at what it costs—particularly as I gaze upon this horrific tax bill—I remember that secure, salaried university job and think, *Should at least one of us try to get a job?* That's assuming we could even get jobs at our age, with our résumés, in our tiny community.

I honestly don't know the answer. Our world is changing, and we're all scurrying about trying to adapt. Everyone I know is feeling squeezed and pinched and facing burnout, financial uncertainty, and distressing politics. It's a big reason why my husband and I moved to a remote, serene island and into a house I sure hope we can continue to afford.

※ ※ ※

DON'T GET ME WRONG: I believe in paying taxes. I am, in fact, happy to do so. I want to live in a society of people who support each other in this way; I like roads and schools and safety regulations. Heck, I would like single-payer health care, too, if that's not too much to ask.

It's just, when I read about how Amazon is going to pay zero taxes on its $11.2 billion profit this year, it's hard to feel like the system is working at all, much less working fairly. (Wow, this may be the first time I've even kinda-sorta agreed with Donald Trump on something!)

I never thought I'd reach middle age and feel so on the edge. I began supporting myself at age eighteen and paid my own way through college. After my trophy-wife years, I've been not only supporting myself, but often my husband as well. Yet, seeing our tax return made me feel like an irresponsible child. Like I'd had my head in the sand. Like I can't take care of us.

I hate this. I've worked so hard to get where we are. It starts to feel... personal, somehow.

I think it's important—crucial—that we talk about this stuff. It's the only way things have any hope of ever changing.

And change they must.

The Money Taboo

Do your friends know how much money you make? How much—or how little—you have to live on?

Do you know how much *they* make? Beyond just a general, ballpark guess based on lifestyle clues?

When you get together to grab drinks and dinner, are there unspoken negotiations around what to order, about "splitting something for the table"? What happens when the bill comes? When you chose where to go, was there any discussion about who could—and couldn't—afford certain places?

❊ ❊ ❊

THERE'S SUCH A TABOO about talking about money. And this hurts us all—not just women, and not just in the workplace, but anyone who feels they cannot speak up about their everyday realities, the challenges we face when we're already juggling the bills, triaging their due dates, finally thinking we can make it all work out…and then the dishwasher breaks.

Maybe we can't talk about it, but we're surely always thinking about it. Paying intense attention to it. Watching how everyone else is doing. Wondering if we're falling short.

Money is definitely a lot on my mind these days. Tax time has something to do with it, of course, but it's bigger than just our whopping tax bill, still here on my desk, waiting till we get as close to April 15 as possible to start that 120-day clock ticking on the IRS's payment plan. (Speaking of triage.) Money is the great scorekeeper in our society—certainly U.S. society, though I imagine it goes far beyond these shores. It's how we measure success, and failure.

A huge serving of shame comes with not having enough money. If it's the benchmark of success, and we're falling short…what does that say about our worth? Our capabilities, our intelligence, our maturity?

But "money can't buy happiness," they say, and that's true, as far as it goes. Unless you're a completely selfish jerk, on the other side comes guilt. Guilt about having so much *more* money than those around us.

I have lived on both sides of that divide, at different times of my life. I've been so poor there wasn't enough to eat for days on end and we had to just hope the car repairs could be held off for another month and that there really were a few gallons of gas still in the tank though who knew because the gauge was broken and oh *crap* that last check bounced *why why why*; I've been so rich that I once bought white-sapphire stud earrings to travel with so that I didn't risk taking my diamond studs to scary dangerous places (like Paris or Rome) and I put the maximum allowable amount into my 401(k) every year without batting an eye.

(Though it's all relative, of course; the divide isn't by any means clean or clear-cut. When I was the wealthiest I've ever been in my life, my then-husband did not feel rich at all. He worked for members of a family so wealthy and so prominent, you have absolutely heard of them; you probably interact with their name several times a day. Yeah, we were middle class compared with them, just getting by.)

I am in neither of those places now. My now-husband and I are somewhere in the great in-between. I mean, I *think* we are. But I don't really know.

Because nobody talks about money.

❉ ❉ ❉

My husband and I live in a gorgeous house on five acres of land (with a freakin' *pond*) on an exquisitely beautiful island in the Pacific Northwest. We moved here from Portland, Oregon, a few years ago, where we owned a paid-for hundred-year-old "Portland foursquare" house in the inner Southeast. I'd bought that house seven years earlier, with divorce money from my trophy wife years; it sold for not quite double what I'd paid for it. I'm a multi-published writer; my husband is an artist and illustrator of some note, in addition to having written a novel which sold well.

So we're sitting pretty, right?

Well…yes and no.

Yes: we have a (lovely) roof over our heads; we have enough to eat, and two paid-off cars plus a hand-me-down beater pickup truck; if I want to buy a book or my husband wants some more plants for the garden, we can afford that. We like to have friends over and cook for them. Our house is filled with nice furniture that matches, and Oriental carpets, and good art on the walls, and high-thread-count percale sheets on our bed.

We have health insurance (THANKS OBAMA)—massively subsidized by tax credits.

We have parents who can bail us out if we get into unexpected trouble. Parents who have already surprised us with generous gifts. *Very* helpful gifts.

We are so much better off than so many people. We know this.

But also: No. We're both self-employed, as I've mentioned. Not only does that mean our taxes are handled differently (i.e. we pay a lot more), but it also means that the work is uneven—while the bills march on, inexorably. It means that any time we're not working, we aren't getting paid. No vacation or sick leave. So if I have to have surgery to repair this disc in my neck…which has already taken me to the emergency room twice and eaten up a lot of my productive time over the last month… well, I just can't really think about that. Because of course we don't have disability insurance—that was prohibitively expensive, when we looked into it. We're already paying for home insurance and auto insurance and life insurance and an umbrella policy (you know, in case someone falls into that pond and sues us), plus our share of that health insurance.

We keep it all together by being as frugal as we can. We go off-island once a month or so to the big box stores for most of our staples. We don't eat out a lot, or buy new clothes (well, my husband recently bought some pants, but only because his other pair fell apart). My ancient computer limps along. I borrow most of the books I read from friends, and from the library. I drink cheap wine. All that furniture and those carpets and percale sheets I told you about—well, I'm a master bargain hunter. And I haven't put any money into my 401(k) in at least a decade.

❈ ❈ ❈

WHO BENEFITS FROM MAKING it rude, or awkward, or downright forbidden, to talk about money?

Well, those who have the most of it, I think. Those who control it. Those who are the most invested in keeping the system as it is.

My first job out of college was executive secretary to the president of a medium-sized engineering and manufacturing company. It was only when human resources called to offer me the job that I learned what the salary would be. I was a little disappointed, but it was enough, so I said yes.

After I'd worked there three or four months, the head of the sales department hired a new secretary for himself; at the same time, I got a little raise. (Fifty more dollars a month.) I was pleased: they liked my work. It's nice to be appreciated.

It wasn't until almost a year after that that I learned that the sales secretary—a woman even younger than me, without a college degree—had had the presence of mind, and the guts, to demand more than she'd been offered. The sales manager agreed to it. Then he and the president realized that if she and I ever compared salaries, I'd know she made more than me. So they matched mine to hers.

I only found this out by accident; if management had had its way, I never would have learned it.

❋ ❋ ❋

IT SEEMS TO ME that we would all be better served by more openness about money. I'm doing what I can, in writing articles like this.

But I think the problem is actually bigger than transparency-or-not about money. It has to do with how we think about money itself: that guilt and shame I talked about above; how money takes on this outsized importance. How it comes to mean more than it should. How it maps onto our identity.

Don't get me wrong: I'm not saying that money *isn't* important—not at all. It's the way we live, in the system we've created. Having enough money doesn't just mean being able to have nice shiny things or fun vacations; it means security, and safety, and the ability to take care of yourself and your loved ones. *Not* having enough money is associated with long-term poor health and shorter lives, in addition to just plain old garden-variety stress.

Money is a tool, a mechanism. A flawed one, sure, but it's the one we've got. It's the way we put value on goods and services, and organize the exchange of those things. It is *not* a benison or an indictment of who we are as human beings. And I think, all too often, we treat it as such.

Though the outer details have certainly changed, and though I think I have perhaps matured a bit over the years, I am, at the core, exactly the same person I was when I was very poor, as well as when I was very rich. It's all still *me* in here.

I am not my bank account. (And neither are you—or that Hollywood star, or that guy living under a bridge who has no bank account.)

Do I dare tell the world how much is in that account?

Do I dare even tell my friends?

What would happen if we all did? What would happen if we decided to defy the taboo and talk about this stuff?

Could we all be a little freer?

Could we start to crack open this system of secrecy that's keeping us all in its stifling grip?

I feel like we can. I feel like so many things are breaking open these days…it's a scary time, but I also feel a lot of hope in the air.

Let's change things. Let's talk about the taboo stuff. (And why does talking about money feel even scarier than talking about, oh, say, polyamory?)

Here's me, starting, just a little. Fingers crossed.

Money and (In)Equality in Relationships

Who makes more, you or your partner? One of you does, almost certainly; the odds of you both earning exactly the same are vanishingly small.

I'm earning about 85 percent of our household income at the moment; last year my contribution was around 65 percent. It'll change. It already has, more than once. Just a few years ago, my husband brought in almost three-quarters of our income.

Before we even lived together, I supported him for a while. That was largely a selfish act on my part, though; he'd been living off his savings while he worked on a novel, always intending to go back to the computer gaming industry when he ran out of money. I knew what hours he'd be working if he did that, though, and I decided I would rather have a boyfriend I ever got to see than watch him go back into that grind. (Luckily, I could afford to be so generous; it wasn't a hardship for me at the time.)

❖ ❖ ❖

In all my relationships until this one, I have consistently been the lower earner, sometimes dramatically so. As a woman who has relationships with men, that is not unusual. Even so, I've always been the one who keeps track of the household finances, pays the bills, and manages the budget. Apparently, this is not unusual either. In my first, brief marriage, my husband and I were fresh out of college, and poor as church mice. He was also, shall we say, financially reckless.

True story: he actually got tossed in jail one night for cracking open a beer in a subway station. Harsh, huh? Well, actually…turns out he'd been given a ticket for smoking a cigarette in that same (open-air, nearly empty) subway station a few months earlier, but he knew we couldn't afford to pay it, so he never told me about it. By the time he popped open that can of beer, there was a warrant out for him.

Guess what? A night in jail plus an unpaid ticket plus a new ticket costs a *lot* more than a single infraction would have. (Not to mention entirely freaking his partner out by *just not coming home* from work that night.)

I was also the budget manager in my second marriage, my trophy wife years, though my "control" over our finances was limited to routine household expenditures—groceries, vet bills, car maintenance, dry cleaners. All the investing was handled by my husband, and any major purchases were discussed and decided on by both of us.

Actually, that isn't entirely accurate. Yes, we did talk about whether and when to buy a new car, to travel to Europe, to remodel the house. But… since my then-husband earned four or five times what I did (and his salary rose to ten times mine just before we separated), his opinions and desires carried far more weight than mine did. If there was something he didn't want us to do, we didn't do it.

I did get to buy new shoes or clothes without his "permission," though he would invariably tease me about *yet another pair of black boots*. If he wanted to buy a techno-gadget, though, he didn't hesitate—nor did I tease him. He made most of the money, after all. Even though we both denied that we saw it this way, it's clear that we both regarded it as *his money*.

❋ ❋ ❋

IT'S BEEN INTERESTING TO at last begin to occupy the other side of that equation—even though, as I mentioned, my husband and I have handed the "biggest earner" baton back and forth. Our plans, however, call for him phasing out the work-for-hire portion of his occupation, in order to devote the bulk of his time to his own art and writing. Perhaps what he produces will result in money in the future; perhaps it will only "pay off" in greater life satisfaction for him (and, therefore, both of us). He is closer to retirement age than I am. We're not actually trying to build that kind of a career for him. And just as I didn't want to see him vanish into the ninety-plus-hour-a-week gaming industry workforce when we were dating, I'd rather not see him spending the ramp-up to his golden years chasing illustration jobs while wishing he could—finally—be doing his own creative work.

Again, though, this is a selfish urge on my part. Yes, I want my husband to be happy and creatively fulfilled...but I also kind of like being the bigger earner. I like feeling that I can not only take care of myself, but that I can provide for another person as well. I enjoy the feeling of competence and—I want to say *authority*, though that isn't quite right, it's more subtle and complex than that—that comes with being the Budget Manager. I like handling the finances, being the one who (kinda) understands and can (sorta) control it all.

It isn't all joyous control and empowerment, of course: there are indeed downsides. I am the one who lies awake at two a.m. worrying about money. And I was certainly the one who felt like a miserable failure when we got our taxes back from the accountant and I saw how badly I'd miscalculated what we would be owing this year.

❖ ❖ ❖

I DON'T WANT TO be a jerk about any of this. I try hard to learn from my past experiences with partners and money. But I know I don't always succeed. I truly believe—particularly in this marriage, where we've switched roles several times—that our money is *our* money, it belongs equally to both of us, and we have equal say in how it's spent. That's a huge part of what a partnership, what marriage, means. Yet...as the budget manager, I frequently find myself in the position of saying no to things my husband wants.

That's part of the budget manager's job, of course; I'm the one who knows what we can and cannot afford at the moment, because I'm the one who's keeping track of it. And given our uneven, ever-changing income, he does have to ask; it's not like he's going to magically know, because the answer changes from month to month—heck, even from day to day, when unhappy surprises like the tax bill from hell pop up.

But I never want to make him feel like I felt, shamed for wanting a new pair of boots (or, in his case, a few more annuals for the garden) that we could so, so easily afford.

It's reflexive, I'm afraid; when I get frightened about the money, I clamp down—on everything. Feeling that we need to stop *every* bit of discretionary spending, and that I need to find *more* work, *more* clients. Never mind that I'm busier than ever and don't even have time to take a day off once a month. At least I'm being fair about the clamping-down...I think. I hope.

But how do I know for sure? I can ask my husband, of course, but he's so happy that I'm taking charge of all this, and grateful that I'm earning the lion's share of our income these days—in fact, that's just what his answer always is: "You're the one earning the money. You get to make the decisions." And he seems entirely comfortable with that.

Perhaps it's the gender-flipped aspect of this, that he hasn't had a lifetime of being the "junior partner" in a relationship and, therefore, he doesn't have the baggage that I have around any of this. He does have feelings about money. He doesn't just shrug and let me worry about it all by myself; he always offers to seek out more work whenever I'm really angsting about the bills. Even though I really don't want him to have to do that. I know he feels proud when he brings in a chunk of money: "There! That's the dentist's bill." Though the work was grueling, he really enjoyed the large paychecks that one long job brought in a few years ago.

And I can't pretend not to appreciate his income—sometimes desperately—even if I do wish it wasn't necessary.

❅ ❅ ❅

I GUESS MY REAL goal is to get to a place where I don't have to think about money quite so much. But is that even possible?

We do have plans to retire someday. Social Security is a part of that plan, though how much will actually be there for us is an open question. I will have a small retirement income from my university job—the one that I quit ten years ago, but I was vested, so that money is "guaranteed" (as much as anything is guaranteed these days). I have a 401(k), which I have invested conservatively...but it is invested, so...fingers crossed.

Maybe when we're living on whatever fixed income(s) we manage to arrive at, we can also come up with a system for each of us to know how much there is and what we're "allowed" to spend. Maybe nobody will have to say no, or to feel like they aren't pulling their weight.

I suppose it could happen. But I'm not holding my breath.

It's far more likely that money will continue to matter much more than I wish it did.

Where Are These "Golden Years" We Were Promised?

When I was in my mid-twenties and working for the University of California, our office got invited to a retirement party for the head of another department.

This man had worked his whole career at UC, and now he was retiring. He had just turned fifty.

Although fifty seemed, like, totally old to me at the time, even then I knew that it was an unusually young age to retire. And in fact, this fellow didn't look a day over...maybe forty? He just didn't fit the image of a *retired person.*

We asked him what he planned to do now. "I don't know," he said. "I'll take a few years off, catch up on my sleep. I might work again someday, if I get bored."

He had plenty of time to decide. His UC pension, plus fully paid health care for both him and his spouse for the rest of his life, allowed him that freedom.

❋ ❋ ❋

I'M FIFTY-TWO NOW, AND my husband is sixty-two. And we're every bit as financially insecure as a couple of kids just getting started in their careers.

It's not because we haven't been working hard: we have been, and we still are. I've written before about being slammed by our taxes this year, completely unexpectedly. Not that it makes me feel much better, but we're clearly not alone here; just a few minutes of research online pointed me to articles about how American taxpayers paid over $90 billion more

283

under the new Trump tax law.

In addition to the taxes, we've also had some whopping medical bills this year—one that we'd anticipated and planned for, and then another one right on top of it, when it was too late to postpone the first one yet again. Surprise! But hey, I've met my deductible now, so now I guess it's time to schedule all those optional medical procedures!

(Just kidding. Those aren't covered.)

We've been talking about how to economize. We canceled my husband's gym membership, because he wasn't using it. We've stopped buying snacks when we go to the movies a few times a month. In fact we almost never eat out at all; and he's probably already bought enough three-dollar annuals for the garden this year. Sure, these little luxuries do add up…but economizing also feels just so futile. Every time we trim one thing, a new expense lands on us. Our fixed-rate mortgage payment is going up over $100 a month (because property taxes increased). The electricity rates went up, the water rates went up, and propane (our fuel for hot water and the stove) fluctuates with gas prices. Which go up.

We don't buy daily lattes or take Ubers or eat avocado toast. What else can we trim? Speaking of which, I haven't even had my hair cut in over a year. I just toss it back in a scrunchie every day. Am I rich now?

❊ ❊ ❊

THIS WASN'T HOW IT was all explained to us, when we were starting out. In our parents' day, you got a job, you worked at that job until retirement, and in the process, you grew more and more financially comfortable. You surpassed your parents' place in the great race; but that was okay, because they were fine too. You were just…more fine. And your children were supposed to be more fine still.

Somewhere, something went wrong. I'm not an economist, but you don't have to be one to notice that the "rising tide lifts all boats" mentality of the 1950s and 1960s has turned into an out-of-control flood, and our boats have all capsized. Wealth inequality is vast, and growing. Generation X is being squeezed; it seems we just can't catch a break. As Mark Solheim in Kiplinger's writes:

Gen Xers' net worth was damaged more than that of other generations during the Great Recession, when their retirement account balances tanked along with their home values. At the start of their careers, the era of the pri-

vate-sector pension was coming to a swift end. *Partly because 401(k)s were new, Gen X got a later start saving for retirement.*

And yet it's hard not to feel somehow…at fault for this. As if we're not working hard enough, or we're frittering our money away recklessly. (All those shaming "personal finance" articles don't help.)

I'm a grown-ass adult who has supported myself since the age of eighteen. Yet, when I look at our bank balance, and this pile of bills on my desk, I feel more and more like an irresponsible child.

❁ ❁ ❁

It's these emotions I want to talk about. I've written before about the taboo about talking about money, and how that hurts us all. Even in that wealthy older generation, it's somehow crass and boorish to actually *talk numbers.* Instead, they have to demonstrate their wealth in the things they can buy, the places they can travel to, the shoes and clothes and watches they wear.

I get anxious about money—our situation now, and our future. It wakes me up at night; I lie there and fret, turning numbers over and over in my head, trying to make it all come out differently. I'm lucky enough to have a 401(k), left over from those UC days. But will it be there when I can tap into it?

Fortunately, I worked at UC long enough to also become vested in the pension plan—the same one that let that long-ago department head retire at age fifty (though sadly, no lifetime health care for me). My payout will be small, but it will be something. In fact, I could have started taking it at age fifty myself, though it will grow each year until I'm sixty, so it behooves me to wait till then.

My husband could similarly take his Social Security now, at a reduced rate, though he should also wait if at all possible.

These facts have become, in a sense, my emotional security blanket. If things got really, really dire, we could start that pension of mine, sign him up for Social Security. Those two things together would at least cover the mortgage, and buy us time to…figure out something else.

I hate having to think this way. I hate that I'm worrying so much about money at this age. Wasn't I supposed to have it all figured out by now?

Wasn't my AARP membership supposed to come with brochures for cruises?

❊ ❊ ❊

IT's NOT A MORAL failing to be sinking further and further behind, when the game is so rigged. When we struggle to take a step forward only to have the government shove us two steps back, I know that's not our fault.

But I wish I could really believe that, in the deep dark hours of the night.

I Thought I Would Feel More
Like an Adult By Now

My parents were high school sweethearts. They went to college together in 1962 and got married in their junior year (because Vietnam), and were already expecting me when they graduated (also because Vietnam). They were twenty-one when I was born, and that was considered fully adult—not just technically, legally, but in the eyes of their world and everyone in it. My dad got a good job at an insurance company; they bought a house in the suburbs, started trying for kid number two, and continued checking off all the boxes on the American Dream Checklist.

Of course, five years later they tossed that checklist aside to become back-to-the-land hippies, but that's another story...

Or is it? There was a set of rules and instructions for Rejecting The American Dream too in those days, one every bit as rigid as the two-kids, picket-fence, stay-at-home-wife model they'd started with. They dutifully followed that new manual for another few years, until they realized that that wasn't making them happy either. Only then did they start working on becoming the people they were really meant to be: divorcing and finding their true life partners, the homes they actually wanted, the careers they kept till retirement.

Yet all through those years, even with their few false starts, there was never a time when they weren't grown-ups. I'm sure having kids had something to do with that; but I think their generation just...expected to be adults, and the world expected it of them.

I'm fifty-three, and I still don't feel like an adult.

❋ ❋ ❋

It's not that I'm not responsible. I totally am—I am a freelancer bringing in the lion's share of our household income, managing a client list in the double dozens and juggling deadlines constantly; keeping up with the taxes and the licenses and the forms and the bills; writing fiction on the side, and articles and essays on the side of the side—but it's a constant scramble. It all feels very uncertain, very ersatz. Very arranged-on-the-fly. It could all fall apart at any moment, for any number of reasons. There's no manual for this.

I think there's no manual for my generation, for the lives we lead, for the world we live in.

Lacking that (even while not realizing it), I did try to follow my parents' manual. I too went to college with my high school sweetheart, though we broke up first semester freshman year. I did get married but didn't have children after graduation; I went the Career Route, choosing a fine job with benefits and growth potential…and then another…and then another… Soon there was the Trophy Wife era; though even then, I worked a job that both was and wasn't A Career, that didn't follow the anticipated path. Eventually I gave up on the whole one-job thing in favor of this freelance, many-jobs thing.

Which I actually love, don't get me wrong; but there is always that uncertainty. That faint, ethereal hope that *next month*, the finances are going to get into better shape, there won't be *yet another* giant unplanned expense. (I'm still paying off the hospital for my MRI back in February; we're about to start payments on phase 2 of my husband's huge dental surgery.) That dream that soon, we'll be able to have a weekend…or even half a weekend.

Where's the manual for this?

❋ ❋ ❋

Even isolated out here on our island, we do have the internet and so therefore we have heard of "Okay Boomer." And, I'm sorry to anyone who feels wounded by this, but oh, we can so, *so* relate.

My husband is technically a Boomer, but in his career and his social circle and his life experience and everything else that matters, he's Gen X like me, or even Xennial or Gen Y or whatever they've decided to call the one after me. He has no retirement plan, no savings, no day job with paid holidays or sick leave or vacation time. He has worked hard all his life, and has even achieved some renown in the computer game art world, plus he published a fantasy novel that did quite well. And yet.

And yet.

He feels at least as unmoored as I do, as alienated from any manual or plan or program or checklist. When we met, he was living in a shabby rental room in Seattle's University District, working (and trying to keep up) with people half his age, and planning to find a sturdy cardboard refrigerator box to set up under a scenic bridge when his resources ran out. (It took me some time to realize that he wasn't actually kidding about this.)

We have both been told, for decades now, that Social Security will be gone by the time we retire, or at least that it will not be enough, or maybe it will be enough but only if we're willing to eat cat food and live in a refrigerator box under a scenic bridge. (Although have you *seen* the price of cat food these days?)

But we can't think about retirement—it's an impossibly remote and, well, impossible concept, even though I am fifty-three and he has just turned sixty-three. I can't think about retirement when I'm busy worrying about whether I can afford the two cords of firewood I ordered to keep our house warm this winter, when both cars need repair work *now*.

❄ ❄ ❄

I DIDN'T INTEND FOR this whole essay to devolve into a discussion of money, in fact I'm sorry to be whining about money, but somehow, I cannot untangle in my mind *being an adult* from *having enough money*.

But what do I mean by "enough"? I can't tell you, or, rather, I can tell you too many answers; it has varied, all my life, but it has almost always meant *something other than where I am right now*.

There was a brief, amazing time when it didn't mean that. Early in my trophy wife years, when I could still thrill at going to the grocery store and putting anything I wanted in the cart, without having to keep a running tally in my head. That was enough.

That was *fine*.

Many other things about that life were not fine, especially as the years went by; but filling up the whole gas tank, taking $100 out of an ATM without checking a balance, not having to tally up my grocery cart—those were little things that were very, very large.

❋ ❋ ❋

THERE'S A LOT OF anxiety that accompanies this uncertain, ersatz existence. Particularly at three in the morning. And along with that anxiety comes the inevitable sense of personal failure. *I'm fifty-three years old. I'm smart, I'm hard-working, and I had a good education. Why is my life not more stable, more secure? Why such a constant scramble?*

Why am I not an adult by now?

I think that's why we find "Okay Boomer" so satisfying, so relieving. It speaks to this no-manual thing we're all fumbling with, this world that seems rigged against us at every turn. It soothes the anxiety (or at least acknowledges it); it validates this feeling; it assures me that it's not my fault, or at least that I'm not alone in this. I have been feeling personally responsible for this failure-to-thrive; but no, actually, it's less and less possible to do the kind of bootstrapping the (white, middle-class) adults of previous generations managed. Even expected.

If my parents, for example, had stayed with that first checklist, my father would have been a highly paid insurance executive his whole career, at the same company, retiring at sixty-five with a gold watch and a comfortable pension; my mother would have stayed at home and raised my brother and me; they might have moved once or twice, buying ever-nicer houses in ever-fancier suburbs…if that whole bargain hadn't made them psychotically miserable, they would have been successful and happy, sitting pretty. Safe. Secure.

It's not that they wouldn't have worked hard. But I work hard too; I always have. And yet.

And yet.

❋ ❋ ❋

I CHOSE NOT TO have children, as I've mentioned. Among the many reasons I made that choice is the simple fact that I've never felt old enough to have kids. Grown-up enough. I cannot quite believe that my twenty-one-year-old parents did, that they lived in a world where that seemed even *possible*, much less like a good idea. (I'm entirely grateful that they did!)

If I can barely take care of myself and my husband, how in the world was I supposed to take care of children?

That's a rhetorical question, by the way: don't answer it. I know that people are still having children, that they are somehow managing to figure it out. I understand that it's so hard, and so rewarding.

I just…have never been able to imagine myself doing it.

I've imagined myself into much more improbable things. I wanted to be a published writer, and I did that. I always wanted to work at home: here I am. I wanted to move to a beautiful island.

I'm adult enough to manifest so many things. So why doesn't it feel like it?

❀ ❀ ❀

MAYBE IT JUST IS what it is. Maybe it's a flavor of imposter syndrome; maybe everyone is just putting on their Big Person Disguise and going out into the world, pretending like they know what they're doing, feeling twelve years old inside.

Maybe we're all working on a new manual, or a million new manuals. Figuring it out as we go.

Okay, Boomer. Be kind to us; try and hear what we're saying behind all the snarky memes and catch phrases. None of this has worked out how we expected it to. None of this makes all that much sense, but here we are. Showing up. Doing the best we can.

I'll try and figure out how to be kinder to myself too, to give myself some credit. I mean, I've been through *menopause*.

Surely I'm an adult by now.

Why I Won't Stop Talking About Money

In just the last twenty-four hours, I've heard from two dear friends—people around my age; intelligent, hard-working, capable folks—about the unhappy financial situations they're in. Big, scary, existentially bad situations.

And that's just in the last day. I actually know of quite a few other people barely scraping by. Hanging on from month to month (or even week to week), triaging the bills, hoping to keep it all together just a little longer, until…until some uncertain future windfall, until a miracle happens, until…?

I'm being very vague in talking about all these other people. Not only are their stories not mine to tell, of course, but there's so much shame attached to *not having enough money*. Especially at our age. I wrote just the other day about thinking I'd have more of this "adulting" stuff worked out by now, and I talked about my husband's and my own precarious financial situation. But we all, in addition to worrying about paying the bills and putting food on the table, struggle with feeling terrible about it. Like we've failed: we made the wrong choices, we're doing it wrong, we're not working hard enough, we're bad or stupid or naive or careless.

As a result, so many of us keep quiet about it. Keep our shame, our failure, to ourselves. Put a good face on things.

Which is, if you'll excuse my language, bullshit.

❀ ❀ ❀

NOT EVERYONE IS KEEPING secrets. One can't log into social media these days without seeing a new funding appeal, a request for help with medical catastrophes, unanticipated job losses, emergencies of every kind. My husband and I do help others, a little. A *very* little, not nearly enough, honestly. I wish we could do more. But we do what we can.

Given the things I know privately, though, those emergency appeals are the tip of the iceberg. There are so many, many more of us living on the edge.

I'm glad to see people starting to talk more openly about financial stress—the few people who do, that is. I hope it leads to more openness. I think having a taboo against talking about money keeps us all isolated, frightened, ashamed—and poor. If you think everyone else is doing just fine and you're the only one awake at three a.m. thinking about the bills…that gets pretty lonely.

Fortunately, my friends and I are not the only ones noticing that there's something really wrong with the way money and the economy is working these days—at least in the U.S. I just read a *Washington Post* article with a chart on "the staggering Millennial wealth deficit," but there was also a line for Gen X (my generation) on their chart as well. We're not doing so great, folks. Less than half as well as Boomers, at any point on the chart. We still haven't caught up, at our age, to where Boomers were at thirty-five. Will we ever?

Who knows? Not at this rate, that's for sure.

But it does give me hope that it's being talked about. And you can be sure that I listen to politicians who notice this sort of thing as well, and that I vote accordingly.

❀ ❀ ❀

THERE ARE LAYERS OF nuance to it all. I so often hear things like "Yes, I'm worried; but I'm also grateful, because I can see so many others who have it so much worse." We're in that situation ourselves: we have a beautiful home in a beautiful place; we can afford little treats every now and then; I have as much work—that I enjoy—as I can handle.

But we're not where we "should" be, we're not where that mythical American Dream Manual For Success indicated we ought to be at this stage in our lives, and it's hard not to feel personally responsible for that. *"If I had just…"* If I had just stayed in that career-job with retirement benefits, or studied something more lucrative in college, or…chosen a different life path altogether…

If I had done those things, what would be different? Would health care have become magically cheaper? My employer was already cutting benefits (and salaries) when I left ten years ago, and it hasn't gotten better since then, I can assure you. Should I have become an accountant, rather than a writer/editor? Maybe?

But doesn't the world need writers and editors too? We can't all be accountants.

Somebody has to tell the stories.

❋ ❋ ❋

So I WILL KEEP telling my story, and part of my story is that things are hard. That we're deeply grateful for what we do have, and a little pissed off about the needlessly difficult stuff (like our over $10,000 of out-of-pocket medical expenses so far this year, *despite* having "good" health insurance). That I know a lot of us are struggling, and that we're not alone, even if the Great American Success Narrative tries to make us feel like failures for not being able to win a rigged game.

And that I believe money talk shouldn't need to be secret.

Money Is Not Shameful

I turned in a commissioned article for a publication this week (for more money-per-word than I've ever been paid before! Yay me!), and something I learned in the process really struck me.

In researching the article, I corresponded with dozens of friends, acquaintances, and strangers about their own financial situations, particularly related to retirement savings. People gave me a *lot* of information—far more than I needed for the relatively short piece I was writing, but I had to gather it all before I could figure out what I really needed to know.

Folks were so generous with their information, which was great. I really appreciated the help. Also, nearly everyone asked for my reassurance that I would not share their personal information publicly. That was no problem—I was looking for averages, trends, a general picture from which I could extrapolate.

These requests for privacy made perfect sense to me, too. I think we are all pretty clear on the fact that it's a bad idea to put your personal financial information on the internet.

What I found surprising—and depressing—was the amount of shame people expressed to me.

Not everyone did; some people shared their info in a straightforward, just-the-facts manner. But a striking number told me they felt bad about their situation—**whether it was because they thought they had too much money or too little money.**

❅ ❅ ❅

THE THING IS, I understand both sides of that shame. I've written before—more than once—about how, at age fifty-three, I feel as though I really ought to be doing better by now, financially. That we should have more savings; that I shouldn't be lying awake at night trying to figure out how to triage the bills, how to earn more money, where we can cut our budget to cover *yet another* unexpected expense.

And I've also been wealthy in my life, sometimes uncomfortably so. During my trophy wife years, there were plenty of times when I knew we had so much more money than most of our friends. (Well, most of *my* friends; my then-husband traveled with an older and better-off crowd.) Perhaps I felt ashamed because it wasn't me earning that big salary—though I know my husband felt awkward about it too.

Our sick culture teaches us so many terrible lessons about money. We're taught that money is a measure of our worth. We're taught that if we don't have enough money, that's somehow our fault, that we're not working hard enough or made wrong decisions in the past or squander what we should be saving on buying lattes or avocado toast or whatever this week's shame-item is.

But we're *also* taught to keep quiet about it all. To not share anything about our financial situations with anyone—our friends, our co-workers, certainly not the larger world.

This secrecy leaves everyone alone with their struggle. Imagining that everyone else is getting it right, somehow. Or imagining that they would hate you if they knew that *you* were getting it right.

❋ ❋ ❋

AND YET SO MUCH of this is out of our hands. Yes, there are objectively both smarter and more foolish ways to handle our money—but larger forces have a lot more power than we do. I got a good education at a top-notch university, and I've always worked very hard at whatever job I had; but my ex, who bounced around from college to college before squeaking out with a degree, entered a profession that turned out to be far more lucrative than mine. By the time we divorced, he was making literally *ten times* what I was.

(Which didn't even count his generous end-of-the-year bonuses.)

Should I have chosen his profession instead? Was I stupid to follow my own skill set, my own desires, my own strengths? Should I be ashamed of this?

Even when I thought I was making intelligent financial decisions, sometimes forces outside my control stepped in and squashed them. For years, I avoided debt like the plague. When I finally decided it would make sense to take on a mortgage, the tax code changed. Now the standard deduction is so high that our mortgage interest is not tax-deductible. But of course, we still have to make that payment every month!

❁ ❁ ❁

NOT ONLY DOES THIS secrecy about our personal financial situations keep us isolated and ashamed—it hurts us in a real-world, tangible way. There's a reason you're not supposed to share your salary information at work. It's in the interests of the bosses and the powers-that-be to keep us divided, uninformed, competing blindly against one another. To keep us from focusing on demanding larger, structural changes—like oh say reworking the tax code so that two freelancers working at home don't pay more income tax than Amazon.

Just as an *entirely random* example!

I believe we need to become far more open about our own financial situations, about how hard we're working and how well or poorly we're doing, about how much or little we can control about those situations. I will not break the confidences of any of the people who shared their information with me—everyone needs to decide their own comfort levels about this—but I will tell you that I learned, in general, that more people are doing better at retirement savings than I'd imagined; that nearly everyone who was in this "better" position felt that they were unusual, an outlier; and that my own savings and preparations—which I'd been feeling pretty good about, even in the face of our current cash shortfalls and anxieties—are actually at the low end of the range.

Now, I'm glad to know that. I find it motivating: what more can I do to prepare for our future? It's helped me think more clearly about the timing of taking Social Security and the small pension I'm anticipating. Yes, it's made me feel a little "behind the curve" compared to some of my acquaintances—but not ashamed.

I think more information is a good thing.

Money is a tool—no more and no less. It is a powerful tool, crazy powerful. Money can buy you many wonderful things—luxury, fun, delight; safety and security (though I well know there are no guarantees); having enough money can buy you time to pursue creative endeavors, to learn more, or just to relax. Not having enough money can make you stressed, sick, can even kill you. Chronic poverty can have lifelong effects.

Money is *not* a measure of your worth as a human being. And it is nothing to be ashamed of—no matter how much or how little you have.

When You and Your Partner are Financially Incompatible

I recently read an article on the marvelous Captain Awkward advice-column website about dramatically different approaches to money within a relationship (he owns two houses and multiple collectible cars and is somehow always broke; she is a frugal thrifter) and it got me thinking. I'm not sure I've ever been in a relationship where my partner and I handled money in exactly the same way. And I'm on my third marriage.

This mismatch shouldn't be surprising—I'm not sure I've ever known any two *people*, in a relationship or otherwise, with precisely the same resources, approach, philosophy, comfort with risk, or even income and expenditures.

But you'd think financial compatibility would be high on the list of traits one would look for in seeking a partner.

I mean, if you'd *never fallen in love before*, that is.

Because let's face it: in the first heady rush of endorphins and sexual-romantic attraction to a new person, money matters are…easily ignored.

To everyone's peril.

❋ ❋ ❋

TAKE MY FIRST HUSBAND, for example. We met in college. I was supporting myself, taking a full load of classes while working a part-time job and living in a co-op that gave a break on room-and-board fees in exchange for weekly workshift duties.

He was also a full-time student supporting himself with a part-time job and living in that same co-op—but in addition, he had a maxed-out credit card.

Fortunately, the credit limit on that card wasn't very high, but during our entire five years together, he never managed to make more than minimum payments on it.

It bugged the crap out of me, I don't mind telling you. I had the kind of credit card in those days that you had to pay off every month. I *still* treat credit cards that way. It's just the way my mom raised me, the way I think about money.

It's just the way I am.

It didn't seem to bother him, though. About once every six months, those minimum payments would inch the balance down to where he maybe had thirty or forty dollars credit on it—and then he'd run right out and spend it back up to its limit!

And not even on anything we really needed, like food or toilet paper. He just, you know, wanted a treat. Life was hard, and we were poor; we almost never got to do or buy anything fun. He didn't understand why I couldn't see that.

❈ ❈ ❈

IT WAS NO ACCIDENT that my second husband was far wealthier than I was. He had a well-paying job, he owned a nice house and a luxurious car, he could afford to travel—everything about him screamed *responsible adult*.

I was smitten. I hadn't truly considered how important a man's attitude toward money was, when I'd fallen in love with my first husband, and money had turned out to be our biggest problem. I knew I wasn't going to make that mistake again.

I didn't. I made a *different* mistake, of course.

(Because that's what happens in life. If we're lucky, we get the opportunity to make new, different mistakes—after having learned from our previous ones. Maybe we eventually grow wiser…maybe?)

My second husband was *so* financially responsible, he wasn't really able to enjoy his wealth. I am quite certain he would disagree with me about this (and our many trips and our expensively remodeled home would also argue against my point)—but I know he never *felt* wealthy. He was always anxious about money: did we have enough, had we saved enough, was I buying too many pairs of boots.

Okay, maybe he had a point about the boots. But still. If we could afford to fly to Paris for two weeks, we could afford for me to buy a dang pair of boots there.

It turned out that we were as financially incompatible as my first husband and I were. It was only the details that differed: I wanted to enjoy some of the luxuries that I had never been able to afford before; he wanted to build as big a wall as possible between himself and some unnamed, amorphous future disaster.

❀ ❀ ❀

MY THIRD AND FINAL husband is probably the most like me, money-wise, even though we're still not really all that similar. He lived simply and had no debt when we met, and he made a decent living at his terrible job. He knew the job was terrible, but he was saving up to take a few years off to write. His plan was, when he ran out of money, he'd go get another terrible job, either for that company or one of the many others in that booming industry.

Part of the reason his job was so terrible was that it demanded impossible hours from him—from every employee. People basically lived at the office, especially during the many, many crunch times. I'm not exaggerating: he would frequently sleep there, shower at the company gym, eat the junk food and candy the bosses would supply in the break room, and then sit back down to work another twenty hours.

I wanted to actually ever see this guy, *awake* even, so I offered to help support him if he would leave that terrible job when he'd saved up enough for his few years off—and then never go back.

After some lengthy discussions, he took me up on that, but insisted we keep track of everything I gave him—just in case I changed my mind later, about the support or the relationship itself.

Well, I did keep track, and I didn't change my mind; I still think it was one of the best decisions I ever made, financial or otherwise.

Even though his approach to money is more "oh, an unexpected windfall; who can we give it to who is more needy than us?" while mine is "oh goody, I can squirrel something away for a rainy day!"

(There's *always* a rainy day. And I think I have enough boots for the moment.)

❀ ❀ ❀

WE'VE HIT ON A marvelous solution to this slight incompatibility: I'm in charge of our finances.

I'm only slightly kidding. I've still mostly been the bigger earner throughout our relationship, and I'm definitely the one who loves spreadsheets and going to the bank and making budgets and all that.

I won't commit to any major financial decisions without at least getting his input—but I'm the decider.

It works great. And I'm so glad I won't be writing in to Captain Awkward asking what to do about a guy with two houses and eight cars who's always, somehow, mysteriously broke.

Why Is It So Hard to Charge What We're Worth?

It just happened again.

A friend referred a potential copy editing client to me. I'm busy—*really* busy; I'm actually officially closed to new clients—but, because a *friend* asked, I said sure, I'd talk to the fellow.

We exchanged email messages; I looked at his book; I gave him a quote, and…he very politely said, in essence, *Wow, that's more than I was hoping to spend.*

That should be no problem, right? I'm busy, so busy. I can barely keep up with the work I have. And I'm this booked up because this actually doesn't happen very often; far more frequently, potential new clients say *Sure, sounds great!*

But what did I do?

I copy edited the first fifteen pages of his book, to show him what I thought it needed and what I could bring to it, and I offered to lower my price.

❈ ❈ ❈

I recently raised my rates to this level, after all; if he'd happened by six months ago, my quote would have been lower.

But does that mean I should lower it now?

Why did I raise my rates, anyway? I raised them because nothing in this world ever gets cheaper. I raised them because my rates were (still are) on the far low end of the range for freelance copy editors/proofreaders. I raised them because my husband is bringing in very little money these days—on purpose, this is all part of our Great Plan—while we're being hit with one huge, unexpected expense after another.

I raised them because I *needed* to.

And I didn't even…entirely raise them. Not across the board; for my longtime, repeat clients, I only inched them up a little bit. After all, their loyalty, their continued business, is why I have this career in the first place. My full new rates are only for new clients—which, as I mentioned, I'm not even looking for at the moment.

Even so, I agonized over the raise. Though I don't believe this with my rational mind, there's still a little voice inside me that says, *What if that's too much? What if this turns away new clients?* And, *But we're all in this together.* So many of my clients are also friends, and I know they're not rich either. I'm good at my work, and I'm fast, and I *like* doing it.

And maybe there's even a tiny voice that says, *Who do you think you are, anyway? You're not worth that much.*

❉ ❉ ❉

I DON'T ACTUALLY BELIEVE that, not out here in the real world, the conscious world where I spend my days. I know I'm not perfect, that mistakes slip past me—but I also know that manuscripts are much, much better after my red pen has had its way with them.

And yet…why is it so hard to value ourselves this way? Because I'm not alone in this. Pretty much every other freelancer I know—and I know a *lot* of them—struggles with this. We can't *all* be insecure and afraid of asking for what we're worth.

It takes a certain amount of self-confidence to set out on a solo career in the first place, after all. A belief in what you can offer to people, and why it's valuable.

"Real" businesses don't have this trouble. I have a hard time imagining that the grocery store or the gas station or the electrical utility or the Washington State Ferry System sits there and agonizes about how they're going to break the news to their customers that their prices have had to go up again. If you're lucky, you get some sort of "due to rising costs…" notice; more often, the prices just go up, and you deal with it.

But my business is a real business too, and my costs have gone up. My "fixed rate" mortgage payment is $171 more per month than it was when we bought this house two years ago. (Because surprise! Property taxes went up.) Gas and groceries and propane and red pens and medical insurance and medical care and, yes, ferry fares all got more expensive over that time too—and you can be sure that's all going to keep getting pricier.

I just want to keep our heads above water.

❄ ❄ ❄

I DON'T NEED THAT potential new client. His book sounds really interesting, and his writing is lovely; I would have enjoyed doing the work. (And I still might get to do it—he hasn't exactly said no yet, he's still thinking about it.)

I think another part of my craziness here is the *What if all the clients vanish and I never get any more work and we starve???* mindset. I'm 100 percent aware of this in myself; my husband teases me about it, whenever I talk about how busy I am: "Remember when you didn't have work for a day or two and thought you'd never get work again?"

It makes me want to hoard all the work, ALL of it. To never turn anyone away. Just in case!

Because, honestly? If we really fell into a huge recession, if everyone stopped having any extra money for anything—we'd be screwed. What would you cut first, if your income dropped suddenly: rent and groceries and medicine, or a copy editor for your novel?

❄ ❄ ❄

I KEEP TRACK OF the hours I spend copy editing, proofreading, editing. I charge clients by the job; I'm only accounting for this for myself, so I can be sure my hourly rate is where I'd like it to be, or at least somewhere in an acceptable range.

But this internal accounting is kind of dishonest—or, at least, it doesn't tell the whole story. I don't keep track of the time I spend corresponding with clients, or invoicing and collecting payment and taking checks to the bank, or doing fifteen pages of someone's book for free to show them what I can do for it, or taking manuscripts to the post office (not all my clients work in electrons), or ordering supplies, or all the umpty-jillion other things that fill my day, up to and including time spent on social media and, um, writing articles like this.

The most time I *ever* spend head-down in a manuscript, during a full workday, is five hours. *Very* occasionally six, if I'm on a tight deadline.

Far more often, it's more like three or four hours that I'm proofreading or copy editing. It's intense work; I do an hour, then take a break to do something else (like noodle at articles, or walk out to the mailbox a half-mile away, or update my website, or click over to the little blue "f"), then come back and do another hour.

So my "hourly rate" looks high, if you only count those three to five hours a day as "work." But that's BS: it all serves the mission. Even goofing around on social media is part of connecting, reaching out, staying visible.

And my two most recent big clients—the ones that helped me realize/decide that I could stop accepting new business—came as a direct result of my having written articles about being a copy editor.

I'm in this office, doing *something*, from right after breakfast till long past 5 p.m. If I really counted all those hours…would I think my rates weren't high *enough*?

❀ ❀ ❀

I HOPE THE POTENTIAL new client decides to hire me; and I also kind of hope he doesn't. I have so much on my plate already, with more coming in all the time.

If I did do his book, I'd be wondering the whole time *Is he getting his money's worth? Is he going to **believe** he's getting his money's worth?* Because it is a pretty clean manuscript. Yet I will still have to read it all the way through, carefully, and consider every word; that takes time, even if I only make a correction or suggestion every page or two or ten.

I do understand this is a good problem to have. *Too much work! Too much paying work!* And I'm not really complaining.

I just wish I had the casual confidence of the power company or the county tax assessor. "Happy new year! Here's your new rates. Good luck paying them!"

Our Finances Have Changed but the Awkwardness Hasn't

I have made it a practice in these personal essays to be open and honest about many aspects of my life—including money. I've written about our unexpectedly huge tax bill last year, and how I think keeping our personal financial situations secret hurts us all, and even about how getting a four-book deal didn't even sort of solve all our money worries. I wrote a one-week spending diary for *Business Insider* magazine, detailing our monthly income and outgo (and the unfortunate mismatch there).

There is so much secrecy around money in our culture. In my own industry, publishing, we periodically see movements like the current #PublishingPaidMe, where authors are going public with their book advances, exposing some pretty jaw-dropping racial disparities; and there are a few individual authors, such as John Scalzi and Jim C. Hines, who have been open about their earnings for some time. These, however, are exceptions.

I have long argued that this secrecy only serves the folks at the top. The bosses and the publishers and the politicians, all the people who decide where the money goes: they benefit by keeping us all fragmented, in the dark, and, frankly, ashamed of how poorly we're doing (or think we're doing)—as if our struggles are our own fault, and not the direct result of a system designed to squeeze as much out of as many people as possible, for as little remuneration as can be (legally or not) gotten away with.

Being this open about money has felt fraught and scary, but also kind of liberating. It's felt like the right thing to do: a reaching-out, a connecting with others. *We're not alone here.*

It was starting to become easier for me, to talk about how scarce money was for us.

I have found it far harder now that it suddenly isn't.

※ ※ ※

ACTUALLY, THERE ARE A number of reasons I haven't been writing much—about anything. 2020 hasn't been kind to any of us. In late January, my stepfather died, utterly unexpectedly. He was sixty-five, active and athletic: in seeming excellent health, and beginning to date again after the loss of my mother a year and a half earlier. Nobody, himself included, knew about the aneurysm that lurked in his brain until it killed him.

Our family was just beginning to absorb this loss when the coronavirus pandemic hit. One week before his scheduled memorial service, we postponed it indefinitely, "until we can safely gather in groups and hug each other again," as I wrote at the time.

I have no idea when that will be.

Meanwhile, my brother and I began clearing our parents' house out so we could put it up for sale…or, well, that was what was *supposed* to happen. Instead, I was able to fly down for one very brief visit, just to assess the situation and to begin identifying what I might want from the house. I intended to help with the rest of the work, and take the stuff I wanted, when my husband and I drove down for the memorial. Then all travel stopped.

My brother basically did all the work alone, including getting the house cleaned out, repaired, listed, and sold. It was one of the last houses in town to sell before everything shut down completely. The dishes, books, pictures, curio cabinet, and memorabilia I want are all in storage, two states away from here.

At least I was able to bring Mom's wedding dress home with me on the airplane.

※ ※ ※

THE OTHER THING MY brother handled was the inheritance. Our parents had a simple estate, and everything was in a trust, so there was no lengthy probate or other complications.

When I flew down for that first (and, so far, only) trip, our stepdad's credit union handed us checks closing out his checking and savings accounts. He had a surprising amount of money in there.

Then we visited the investment firm where he and Mom had their IRAs and a brokerage account. More surprises. Those accounts took a few weeks to transfer over...but they're in our hands now.

And, as I mentioned, the house did sell. That money's in the bank now too.

So, just since January, my husband and I have gone from a state of ongoing financial insecurity to...well, essentially the opposite of that.

A small example, to illustrate: Last year, I had a badly pinched nerve in my neck, leading to two ER visits and an MRI. I have just recently, over a year later, finished paying off the hospital. (Yes, we have "good" health insurance. It paid for almost nothing.)

If this should happen again, I won't have to beg the hospital to set me up on a payment plan. I'll just be able to write a check.

❊ ❊ ❊

THIS NEW FINANCIAL REALITY would have been weird even when the world was normal (haha, whatever that means). It is downright surreal now.

Even discounting the inheritance, my husband and I were largely unaffected by the pandemic and quarantine. We both already work full-time at home, for remote clients. That work has continued pretty much uninterrupted. We also already shopped quarantine-style, since we live on an island without big box stores, an hour from the mainland.

If we could, we'd probably be going to restaurants every now and then, having dinner- and houseguests, and traveling; but our day-to-day lives look basically the same as before: work all day in our home offices, do some gardening, cook and bake, watch TV or read aloud or play games in the evenings. Lather, rinse, repeat.

We feel very lucky. All around us, so many people are suffering, hurting, scared; wondering if they're still going to have jobs when the world re-opens. Learning that they will *not* have those jobs. Applying for unemployment, only to have their benefits halted because of the widespread fraud out there. Or being forced back to work, to risk their lives while making less money than before.

In the community where we live, tourism is the major driver of the economy. Tourism has basically been canceled until now, when it is re-opening in a very limited way. (It's mid-June and the ferry system is still using its "winter" schedule.) A few local stores and restaurants have already shut down for good; more will likely follow them. There are no big chain hotels here with deep corporate pockets. It's all small inns and bed-and-breakfasts, run by people who live here.

So much help is needed. Everywhere.

The federal government sent us stimulus money. I appreciate the gesture, and last year—heck, four or five months ago—we would have been among those who needed it, absolutely.

Now that we are in a much roomier financial position, we've made the decision to pass our stimulus money along. We identified a combination of recipients, including personal friends who are having a hard time and a few local businesses that we hope will stay in business.

We were finalizing our lists and beginning to distribute the money when so many of our friends and colleagues, in Seattle and further afield, took to the streets to protest the murder of George Floyd and our nation's egregious problems with systemic racism.

So we've amended our lists to include various national organizations whose missions we support. And we'll probably end up sending more than just the stimulus money.

❀ ❀ ❀

IT FEELS SO WEIRD to talk about this. It's weird to be sitting here on the sidelines, saying, *Oh, I'll write a check.*

This is proving a hard essay to write.

❀ ❀ ❀

THIS IS NOT THE first time in my life when I have had sufficient money; but it is the first time when I have felt like I had agency about it. When I was a trophy wife, we lived very well and I had everything I needed and quite a bit of what I wanted. But.

But there was always this sense that the money wasn't really mine. That I wasn't an equal partner, equally responsible for the disposition of it. That permission to use and enjoy that money was conditional, and could be revoked. If I wanted a shiny new pair of boots (which, to be clear, I did not *need,* though we could well afford them), I either bought the boots and felt like a naughty, disobedient child; or I did not buy them, and felt like a sulky, deprived child.

Neither outcome made me feel much like a grown woman.

And let me be clear about this too: this wasn't something my rotten awful mean husband was doing to poor sweet innocent me. He and I both built the dynamic between us, and we both worked for years to maintain it. There was much that was enjoyable about it—for both of us.

But ultimately, it stopped working. I wanted to grow. I wanted agency. I wanted to feel in charge of the spending decisions, at *least* equally with my partner.

I got what I wanted. And the spending decisions became simpler, for years, because there was a *lot* less money.

❉ ❉ ❉

I HAVE HAD A hard time writing anything, since my stepdad died. His loss brought back Mom's loss, in sharp, painful immediacy. I didn't fully realize how much she was still alive in him; how good it felt to talk to him, to miss her together.

He had just been up to visit us over the new year, and we'd had a marvelous time. We even tried introducing him to a few local ladies, hoping to tempt him to move closer.

He was supposed to have twenty or thirty more years. Heck, so was Mom.

Going through their house—as little of that work as I did—was so hard. All their *stuff*: pictures and knick-knacks from their trips. Their hundreds of fridge magnets. The homebrew he'd made and hadn't yet drunk. Mom's old budget ledgers dating back to the 1970s, handwritten and balanced to the penny.

Christmas ornaments. Homemade quilts. The fancy holiday china. All his Beatles stuff. All her blue iris stuff.

Everything that was *them*.

I'm still grieving them. I can't believe we can't ask him garden questions. Or that I'm never again going to have our Saturday-morning-at-eleven phone call with Mom.

I can't thank either of them for all this financial help.

❉ ❉ ❉

ONCE THE PANDEMIC HIT, and chaos spread across the land, it got even harder to write my chirpy little essays about personal growth.

So I've worked, and baked, and gardened, and worked some more.

I've read, and spent WAY too much time on the internet, and probably drunk a bit too much wine.

I've wanted to write, but I didn't know what to say. *We're fine here. I miss my parents.*

(With 117,000+ coronavirus deaths in this country at the moment I write this, I imagine quite a few people are missing their parents. And children. And spouses and co-workers and partners and neighbors and friends and other loved ones.)

But I'm a writer. And writers write. Even when it's awkward. And painful. And I don't know what to say.

I really don't know how to write about money now. I still think that keeping our financial situations secret hurts us all. But it feels really weird to tell you even that we're giving away our stimulus money. Like I'm looking for some kind of applause or praise or something. (I am not.) Like I think writing a check is somehow letting me off the hook for…any other kind of help, or involvement.

I have to get used to this new reality.

❋ ❋ ❋

I DON'T KNOW HOW often I'll manage it, but the words are starting to try to find their way out again. So I'll just keep trying to show up and write down those honest words. Awkward as they are.

Thanks for reading. Really. I'll write again soon. Meanwhile, as we say these days: stay safe.

AFTERWORD

The Whole Truth and Nothing
But the Truth...

What do you leave out when telling your own story?

Personal essays and memoirs are hot stuff in publishing these days. And with good reason: they're fascinating. I am clearly not alone in loving to read a first-person true story, what *really* happened, told from their own point of view, in their unique voice.

I'm now writing personal essays myself, as must be rather obvious by now, after a lifetime of being a fiction writer who has published dozens of short stories and a growing pile of novels. I didn't really plan to switch genres, and I'm certainly not giving up fiction...but a year or so back, I started writing articles and sharing them online pretty much on a whim, and I found that I just love it.

In any given essay, I write about whatever moves me in the moment. I tell stories drawn from my life, selecting and framing the details in an effort to "say something"—to make some sort of point. To explain something. Maybe even to help others out.

After a while, I noticed that I began running into some overlaps, as far as the timelines go. I mean, it's inevitable: life doesn't happen in an orderly, linear way. Events happen at the same time as other events, piling on top of each other; sometimes these are connected, sometimes they're just coincidence.

And sometimes they get in each other's way.

My story about leaving therapy covers much of the same time as my essay about being a trophy wife. However, I barely referred, in passing, to therapy in the trophy wife piece—and consigned it to the past, quoting only my first therapist, who I saw before the marriage. I never mentioned my weekly sessions with my second psychotherapist, which were an important, ongoing part of big chunks of my life then. But that wasn't the story I was telling in that essay.

Was I dishonest in not talking about that therapy?

Of course, in a 2,000-word essay, it's impossible to put in everything. Heck, if I wrote down every detail of how I spent my day yesterday, it would take more words than that; some of my essays span decades. So no one expects *the whole story* in a short personal essay.

❊ ❊ ❊

BUT WHAT ABOUT A book-length memoir? Surely, in a piece of writing that long, you can get all the details? Or all the *important* details?

I don't know. Some years ago, my best friend from elementary school published a memoir about her childhood. We were absolute besties from first through sixth grade. We played every day at school, inventing complex games and stories during recess, choosing each other for PE teams and spelling bees. Teachers had to separate us, we had so much fun together in class. I spent the night at her house at least once a week; she came to my place a bit less often, mostly because our one-room cabin wasn't really set up to accommodate a couple of giggling girls. We swam in the river in the summers and watched TV (at her house, as ours of course didn't have one) in the winters.

Her memoir, which covered the same years during which we spent nearly all of our unstructured time together, mentioned me only briefly, in one three-page scene—which focused more on my family's weird backwoods hippie-commune life than on our connection as friends.

I was deeply miffed when I read the book, and I carried that hurt for quite a while afterwards. Was I truly so unimportant to her? She was essentially my only friend for such formative years of my life, and yet to her I was just…comic relief?

I think I understand it better now. She wasn't writing an autobiography—that's not the point of a memoir. She was telling a different story, focusing much more on the dramatic lives her parents led, and what it meant to grow up in a household governed by such unusual people. What kind of a person that turned her into, and the lessons she learned.

Her weird hippie-girl best friend didn't really fit into that story. Just as, later, the character of a best friend at school didn't really fit into my novel *Eel River*, which takes place on…a backwoods hippie commune.

❊ ❊ ❊

WHAT DETAILS ARE IMPORTANT? No matter the size of the piece of writing, a short essay or a lengthy multi-volume memoir, the question remains: What is *the truth, the whole truth, and nothing but the truth*?

Who decides?

I've acknowledged, apropos the trophy wife essay, that if my ex-husband had written the story of our marriage and divorce, it would look very, very different. Not that he wouldn't tell the truth—he would, he's an extremely honest man with tremendous integrity. But I told the truth too: the truth as I understand it, filtered through my own life history, my experiences and interpretations, my emotions…my memory.

I tell the truth in all my essays. And yet I have to think, when I'm writing a new piece covering a different aspect of a time I've already written about, *Am I contradicting anything I said before?* Is someone going to line these pieces up together and say, *Hey, wait a minute, that's not what you told us in that other essay.*

No, it probably isn't; because I was making a different point in that other essay. I was focused on different things.

But I still want to keep all my truths straight.

❊ ❊ ❊

THE TROUBLE—AND THE JOY—IS that as you tell the story, any story, it becomes fractally more complicated. A story becomes shaped in the telling of it—it grows, it changes. We write as a form of communication, to reach out to other people; and, I would argue, particularly with personal writing, we write to understand our own lives more clearly.

I write to put it all down in words, to make sense of things that baffled me when I was younger—or that baffle me now. I write to try to understand how my own mind works, and how that then relates to other people and how *their* minds work. (And maybe I even write to set down some ancient wounded feelings toward my childhood best friend.)

My husband and I were discussing this issue recently. For about six months, he worked on a series of very detailed, self-exploratory blog posts. Week by week, he tried to push the narrative forward—only to turn around and re-examine the time frame he'd already "told" from some different angle. He never imagined that he would be able to somehow tell "the whole story," the whole truth; but it didn't stopping him from trying. Working to get as deep, and as thorough, as he could.

I do feel drawn to write a memoir someday. For now, though, I have these essays.

❀ ❀ ❀

WHAT IS THE STORY I am trying to tell of my life? I had a strange childhood and then some romantic disappointments, but I'm happy now. I've been very, very poor, and very, very rich; I am now in neither of those extremes, but we're more comfortable than we were even last year (which is a relief, and also a grief, because inheritance really is the booby prize). I think about money a lot. I have been dishonest—with myself and others—at some critical junctures of my life, and I am now committed to honesty. I am creative and would like to "lean in" even more to that side of myself, to get recognition and acclaim for my creative work. I am frightened and hate conflict, and would love nothing more than to just hide from the world. I want to be stronger. I'm stronger than I've ever been.

It's a jumble.

I am telling my story. I am trying to leave nothing out, even as I understand that I am leaving the vast majority of it out.

I am just going to keep at it. To keep showing up and being honest, telling true stories. I know no other way to learn, and grow, and connect.

Thank you for reading my words.

SHANNON PAGE WAS BORN on Halloween night and spent her early years on a back-to-the-land commune in northern California. A childhood without television gave her a great love of the written word. At seven, she wrote her first book, an illustrated adventure starring her cat Cleo. Sadly, that story is out of print, but her work has appeared in *Clarkesworld*, *Interzone*, *Fantasy*, *Black Static*, Tor.com, the Proceedings of the 2002 International Oral History Association Congress, and many anthologies, including the Australian Shadows Award-winning *Grants Pass*, and *The Mammoth Book of Dieselpunk*. She also regularly publishes articles and personal essays on Medium.com.

Books include *The Queen and The Tower* and *A Sword in The Sun*, the first two books in The Nightcraft Quartet; *Eel River*; the collection *Eastlick and Other Stories*; *Orcas Intrigue*, *Orcas Intruder*, and *Orcas Investigation*, the first three books in the cozy mystery series The Chameleon

Chronicles, in collaboration with Karen G. Berry under the pen name Laura Gayle; and *Our Lady of the Islands*, co-written with the late Jay Lake. *Our Lady* received starred reviews from *Publishers Weekly* and *Library Journal*, was named one of *Publishers Weekly*'s Best Books of 2014, and was a finalist for the Endeavour Award. Forthcoming books include Nightcraft books three and four; a sequel to *Our Lady*; and more Orcas mysteries. Edited books include the anthology *Witches, Stitches & Bitches* and the essay collection *The Usual Path to Publication*.

Shannon is a longtime yoga practitioner, has no tattoos (but she did recently get a television), and lives on lovely, remote Orcas Island, Washington, with her husband, author and illustrator Mark Ferrari. Visit her at www.shannonpage.net.

Made in the USA
Las Vegas, NV
26 November 2020